THE WORLD

Jean-Jacques

CHALLENGE

Servan-Schreiber

SIMON AND SCHUSTER
NEW YORK

COPYRIGHT © 1980 BY AUCTOR PUBLISHING, B.V., AMSTERDAM
ENGLISH LANGUAGE TRANSLATION COPYRIGHT © 1981 BY SIMON & SCHUSTER,
A DIVISION OF GULF & WESTERN CORPORATION.

ALL RIGHTS RESERVED
INCLUDING THE RIGHT OF REPRODUCTION
IN WHOLE OR IN PART IN ANY FORM
PUBLISHED BY SIMON AND SCHUSTER
A DIVISION OF GULF & WESTERN CORPORATION
SIMON & SCHUSTER BUILDING
ROCKEFELLER CENTER
1230 AVENUE OF THE AMERICAS
NEW YORK, NEW YORK 10020
SIMON AND SCHUSTER AND COLOPHON ARE TRADEMARKS OF SIMON & SCHUSTER
DESIGNED BY EVE METZ
MANUFACTURED IN THE UNITED STATES OF AMERICA

10 9 8 7 6 5 4 3 2 1

LIBRARY OF CONGRESS CATALOGING IN PUBLICATION DATA
SERVAN-SCHREIBER, JEAN-JACQUES.
    THE WORLD CHALLENGE.

    TRANSLATION OF: LE DÉFI MONDIAL.
    INCLUDES INDEX.
    I. WORLD POLITICS—1945– . 2. INTERNATIONAL
ECONOMIC RELATIONS. I. TITLE.
D843.S42813   327'.09047   81-4548
ISBN 0-671-42524-2   AACR2

*The publisher would like to thank the following for their trans-
lation and editorial contributions:*
Martin Sokolinsky   *Elizabeth Bartelme*
Léon King

A CHALLENGE
TO AMERICA

The message of *The World Challenge* has gone around the world, lighting a few fires of hope from one continent to another. Now it returns to its source—America.

As I write these lines, on the new frontier where the human spirit expands, I am facing Asia and the Pacific Ocean. I have just returned from the Arabian Gulf, where I chaired a meeting of the pioneers whose thrust toward the future is the fount of this book.

As the president of their group, or "fraternity" as they call it, and more modestly as the recorder of their work, I bring their hope to the citizens of America.

In this spring of 1981, so heavy with drama, men who should be completely opposed to one another were united by their faith—faith in man's ability to overcome the crises of the present and emerge from prehistory.

Who are these men?

Naohiro Amaya, Minister of the legendary MITI of Tokyo, and his colleagues; President Léopold Senghor, the soul and mind of Black Africa; Professor Seymour Papert, Ambassador James Akins, and lawyer Samuel Pisar, of forward-looking America; Ahmed Zaki Yamani, Ali Khalifa al-Sabah, and Abdulatif al-Hamad, who control so much of the world's investments and are trying to define and channel their responsibility to the Third World; Frenchmen and Germans from a Europe which is at once so vulnerable and so rich in new concepts.

Our three days of renewed fraternal endeavor, directed toward the birth of a new, united world, were devoted to a single subject: "The application of the advances in micro-computers to the development of human resources in the Third World, formation of a common plan for the education and training of each people, within its local culture, to enable them to master the new 'computer culture' for their own needs and growth."

This official invitation, issued from the Arabian Gulf, echoed the words of determination of Jean Riboud, a fellow pioneer on this new frontier: "We are at the dawn of a new era: from the search for oil to the acquisition of information. An extraordinary adventure. I have just spent a month in Japan. I told our Japanese friends that I was sure we would win *because we are more than a nation; we are from the whole world.*"

What, then, is the origin of this appeal? Where did *The World Challenge* spring from?

This birth, this quest, this discovery of the new shores which we are approaching together—this is the odyssey on which we now embark.

JEAN-JACQUES SERVAN-SCHREIBER

Malibu, California
April 1981

PART-I

H IGH IN THE MOUNTAINS of Hejaz in Saudi Arabia, before the land drops sharply to the Red Sea, sits a quiet little village lost to the outside world. With its terraced gardens and trees cooled by the crisp mountain air, this tiny settlement has long welcomed the men of the desert seeking refuge from the blistering heat of the sands.

Just a few miles from the village is an airport, the most modern high-altitude airport in the world. On a summer evening in 1980, a jet approaches, circles over the darkening mountains, and descends. The runway lights appear and a sign, in Arabic letters, flashes: TAIF.

The private jets land near the village in quick succession, and as each oil minister deplanes a limousine pulls up, stops and quickly departs. Two officers, their beige uniforms bearing the crossed green sabers of the kingdom, provide a motorcycle escort for the cars as they move down the highway to the ancient village of Taif.

The motorized column passes two minarets echoing the call to evening prayers. The air-conditioned cars carry the oil ministers toward the village where Ibn Saud, warrior, founder of the nation, king, died nearly thirty years ago. To continue on the highway beyond Taif would lead the men to the holiest of Moslem places, Mecca, then on to Jedda and the Sea of Moses.

Each limousine in the procession slows down before a low stone wall. It is all that remains of the shepherd's cottage where the Prophet Mohammed found shelter for a day thirteen centuries before, when he fled from Mecca, pursued by an unbelieving mob.

It was in Taif that the Prophet gathered the small group of followers who, under his command, changed the face of the world by venturing forth to spread the word of Islam by the sword.

It was from Taif in 1973 that King Faisal secretly planned the historic oil embargo—with the full knowledge of the Americans, the Russians, and even the Israelis.

It was in Taif that the Saudis discovered Henry Kissinger had encouraged the Shah of Iran to raise the price of oil while at the same time he was begging the Saudis to lower it—a "secret" which the Shah himself came to reveal to the Saudi King.

And now it is from quiet, secluded Taif that a revolution in world power is about to be launched—once again led by the Arabs of Islam.

The cars make their way around a vast modern palace. It is luxuriously, deceptively simple in the style of ultramodern buildings, yet it is sand-colored to blend into the bleak terrain of the surrounding mountains. Its designers are two world-famous architects, one American and the other Japanese. Not yet a year old, the palace was built for the Crown Prince. One weekend the King himself came out to admire the beautiful palace—and the Prince, his younger brother, graciously presented it to him as a gift.

The procession of cars reaches the heights of the village where the new Sheraton Hotel is flanked by the tall radar antennae that sweep the Red Sea below. The cars pass a small lane at the end of which, surrounded by gardens, stands "Zaki's villa"—the retreat of Saudi Arabia's Oil Minister Sheikh Ahmed Zaki Yamani, the brilliant strategist behind the oil producers' success against the largest companies of the Western world.

Each chauffeur leaves his passengers in front of the isolated cottages that have been prepared for them. Armored cars have been stationed every twenty yards, and a small army of fifteen hundred men is responsible for the oil ministers' security.

A blanket of quiet and calm covers Taif as the ministers begin their work. It is difficult to believe that only an hour away lies Riyadh, the capital of Saudi Arabia, and a new world.

In the hectic atmosphere of Riyadh, merchants and ministers from the four corners of the earth meet. Those men who just years ago were masters of the earth now come to flatter, beg and promise—and sign contract after contract.

In Riyadh, on the reception desk of the grim-looking Intercontinental Hotel, the city's busiest meeting place, the guest list is unequaled anywhere else in the world. On just one day recently, this hotel housed the leader of the Palestine Liberation Organization and his delegation in fifteen rooms, the special envoy of the American President and his aides in only ten rooms, and the leader of Syria and his escort in twenty rooms. All of these people passed the Chancellor of Austria as he was checking out with his own delegation.

Hardly acknowledging one another, each visitor beat the same path to the princes' palaces, seeking a vacant armchair in one of the main-floor drawing rooms. These rooms were filled with the most powerful men in the world, men who controlled multinational corporations manufacturing aircraft, petrochemicals, computers and arms. But powerful as they were in New York, Paris, London, Frankfurt or Tokyo, here they all had one goal—to meet with a Saudi prince to wheedle a deal and tap the enormous wealth of his country.

The billion-dollar wheeling and dealing that goes on in Riyadh now eclipses Wall Street with its stock market, London with its capital market, Zurich with its secrets, and Hong Kong with its mysteries. Merchant bankers fly to Riyadh to get money for such corporations as American Telephone & Telegraph, Dow Chemical and Kimberly Clark. Central bankers run to Riyadh to beg support for their weak currencies and to pay for their governments' growing deficits. They all come to Riyadh—the new financial center of a world that remains all but unknown except to the mightiest players in the secretive international money markets.

But on this summer evening the Saudi kingdom is showing its other face. In the calm atmosphere of Taif, the oil ministers are unpacking their bags. Each man's briefcase contains a personal copy of a secret report on which they have labored for two years within the Ministerial Committee on Long-Term Strategy. It had been their task to map the future of the most threatening organization in the history of the modern world—the Organization of Petroleum Exporting Countries. During two days of plenary sessions, these men would refine the plan of action, and when they were done the Taif Report would emerge as a blueprint for massive revolution in the global economy and the world balance of power.

As the oil ministers sat down to work, they first picked up a personal letter presenting a draft of the Report from their Saudi host and colleague, Yamani. It was he who in 1978 had the foresight to set up a working committee to create a new long-term strategy for the oil producers for the rest of the twentieth century. It was Yamani who could see years earlier that OPEC would quickly succeed in its first task of wresting control of oil pricing and production from the big Western oil companies and that a very different stage in OPEC's global strategy would be needed by the 1980s. And it is now Yamani who chairs the Committee on Long-Term Strategy, which is about to ratify a document symbolizing OPEC's new power and signifying its intention to change the course of world events.

Americans and Europeans may be tempted to focus only on the report's discussion of strategies relating to oil pricing and production. In the past they have ignored OPEC's warnings about the bigger issues of economic development, redistribution of wealth, and political power. For the West, OPEC simply means oil, and whatever else the Arabs and their fellow oil producers say is dismissed.

The myopia may prove fatal this time. Beyond its few paragraphs on oil, the report outlines a major new social contract for the world. The Taif Report aims for nothing less than a new alliance between the Arabs and the peoples of the Third World against their traditional exploiters, the industrialized West. It is conceived as a warning, a challenge and finally a *demand* for a massive transfer of technology from the United States, Europe and Japan to the poor and needy. It is not just another wishful plea—for it is backed up by the most powerful of all new weapons: oil.

Sheikh Yamani had planned to make the secret document public on the twentieth anniversary of the founding of OPEC, at a major conference of heads of state in Baghdad in November 1980. The war between Iraq and Iran postponed that celebration. Yet the war itself has made Sheikh Yamani, the man behind the Taif Report, even stronger in the empire of oil, as the Persian Gulf showed how it could temporarily move to increase oil production and prevent the world from collapsing into economic chaos.

In the capitals of the West, it has become a habit to look upon the Saudi leader as an ally, as someone who "understands," someone who won't let radical elements destroy industrial society. It is true that Sheikh Yamani does not lightly engage in brinkmanship, because he fears the ravages it might entail for his own people, but no one should be deceived—Yamani is as intransigent on the need for a "new international order" as any of the radical leaders.

Behind Yamani's veneer of Western sophistication, picked up as he passed through the "right" schools in Cairo, New York and Boston, the Sheikh shares the strong Arab faith of his mentor, King Faisal. For it was Faisal, when still a prince, who

— 13

chose the son of a modest Mecca judge—and not a member of the royal family—as a protégé. It was Faisal who sent Yamani abroad, and Faisal who appointed him as Oil Minister when he was only thirty-two.

On this Tuesday evening, while awaiting the arrival of colleagues and friends from the oil capitals—Tripoli, Kuwait, Algiers, Baghdad—Ahmed Zaki Yamani relaxes among family and friends to prepare for the most ambitious battle in almost twenty years with the ever-present, multifaceted, domineering enemy—the West.

Here at Taif he is much different from his public image, from the elegant, Westernized figure facing a battery of cameras and microphones as he moves from a powerful limousine to the entrance of a palace, from the man whose deliberately whispered, almost sibylline words are heard around the world and often make it tremble.

No, this evening he is at home. In a silk robe, his head covered and discreetly gilded slippers on his feet, he is at peace, as though he has returned to his roots. He can talk to his friends with enjoyment; he doesn't have to weigh his words or display the toughness he is known for in negotiations; he can be natural and genuinely amiable. Yamani detests passion and has never known hatred, at any rate, never at Taif, his true home, so near Mecca, the city of his birth, which can be seen from the bottom of the valley, at the end of the highway that winds its way to Jedda.

Circumstances, more than any determination on his part, have made Sheikh Yamani one of the leading political stars on the international scene today. He is also unique. Of the ten oil ministers who will join him and whose planes are circling above Taif's airstrip, not one has held his post for more than a few years, often for only a few months. Not one was a member of OPEC when Yamani arrived in 1962. Not one was present at the time of the 1970 and 1973 crises, when the oil-producing countries assumed control of the price and the production of oil.

In addition to the trump cards that he himself has been able to play, Yamani's power rests on two perfectly visible pillars: Saudi Arabia's unequaled financial resources and the unprecedented length of time that he has held his post.

This evening, the only time he will bestir himself before dinner will be to greet the Venezuelan Minister, Umberto Calderon-Berti, OPEC's incumbent president. Never for a moment do these two forget the extent to which the quarrels, the ideological, nationalistic and religious passions exist in the organization just as they do everywhere. The weight of hegemonies, the permanent conflict between Iraq and Iran, the Libyan game, the Palestinian question influence the future every day.

In the attempt to reach the first objective—the union between the Third World and OPEC—which appeared so remote, so doubtful and so uncertain, the Venezuelan has been the Saudi's convinced and efficient ally.

When Americans and Europeans wake up on the day that the Taif Report is finally made public, they will get this message:

Events have given our organization a totally new dimension and a responsibility. We intend to accept this responsibility in full. With the other developing countries we will shape a common, overall program for a new world order, to be negotiated with the industrialized countries.

All our power must be used to achieve a *real* change in the position of the developing countries, as well as our own, by the transfer of creative capacities from the industrialized world.

Beyond this we have to implement a reform of the economic and monetary system which has hitherto reigned over the old order. *That system is no longer acceptable.*

We are determined to take part in this great transformation and, if necessary, to guide it.

The implementation of the Taif Report will launch the greatest challenge to the Western way of life since the Moslems hammered on the gates of Europe a thousand years ago.

Those leaders in Washington, London or Paris who dismiss it as mere Third World rhetoric should think twice. This revolutionary document is, in fact, a chance to be seized. And with the post–World War II boom grinding to a deadly halt, with the European and American economies racked by unemployment and inflation, with trade wars about to break out that threaten social disruption and calls for dictatorships, the Taif Report can suggest an alternative to chaos for rich and poor countries alike.

NO ONE HAS EXPERIENCED GREATER HUMILIATION at the hands of the West than have the Arabs. One Iraqi technocrat in charge of foreign investments in the Ministry of Petroleum at Baghdad expresses it this way: "The political dimension of oil —existent for a long time, but only recently come to the fore— is closely bound up with the history of colonialism. On account of oil, the OPEC countries, and especially the Arab world, have seen and experienced innumerable occupations, wars, instances of blackmail and theft. Foreign rulers exploited us over a long period, dictated our fate to their advantage, sold our oil resources at giveaway prices to themselves, and destroyed or neglected our oil fields. The competition for Arab oil, and the securing of the oil routes are still the basic causes of 'cold' and 'hot' wars between the superpowers. That is why the nationalization of oil, as carried out in Iraq in 1972, has been the objective of all liberation movements in OPEC countries."

Not only did Westerners pump the oil—the lifeblood—of the Arabs at will, but they did it at a price that is hard to believe. In 1900, the price of oil was $1.20 per barrel. Thirty years later, after the Wall Street crash and the Great Depression, that price was down to $1.19 per barrel. After Pearl Harbor and America's entry into World War II, the price of a barrel fell to $1.14. Following the Allied victory, the creation of the Bretton Woods international monetary system, the launching of the Marshall Plan and the founding of the United Nations, the price was back to $1.20. In the 1950s, during the Cold War, the price edged up to $1.70 per barrel. In 1960, at the birth of OPEC, it was $1.80.

Nothing illustrates better the total domination of the most powerful oil companies and the Western governments that backed them up with arms than this history of oil prices. In the late nineteenth century, the companies discovered oil and took control of it. In exchange for unlimited profits, they exploited the oil for the prodigious economic development of the West. For fifty years, from 1920 to 1970, the West based its factories, transportation systems, cities, universities, laboratories—its industrial civilization and growth—*on cheap oil.* And the companies did this without considering the possibility of increasing payments to the producing countries.

No man represented the arrogance of the West more than Monroe Rathbone, chairman of Exxon (then Esso), when in August 1960, sitting in his air-conditioned boardroom overlooking Rockefeller Center, he actually decided to *cut* the posted price of oil in the Middle East. For the oil-producing countries, this decision had grave consequences, for the royalties paid on the posted price of oil made up the *only* revenue they had for their national budgets and for their imports. Without any consultation with the governments involved and citing general overproduction and massive sales of Russian oil in the world, Exxon flatly announced an immediate reduction of ten cents a barrel on the price it would pay. In a few days the other companies, British Petroleum, Shell, Mobil, all fell in line.

From that day on, there was no turning back. The Western oil companies had indicated their contempt for the Arabs and the other oil producers, their indifference to the people for whom oil was the only source of life. A few men had the foresight to predict the result. An American, Howard Page, the Exxon expert on Middle East questions at the time, told his fellow board members, "If we do that, all hell will break loose. You can't imagine the scope and duration of the consequences."

An Englishman, Harold Snow, a mathematician for British Petroleum, wept openly in front of his colleagues. When Exxon actually cut the oil price he was, in his own words, "horrified."

The oil companies had no intention of reversing their decision. They regarded themselves as the energy masters of the globe, and, after all, the producers had no way to fight back. This was the way it had been since the beginning of the century, and this was the way it would always be.

But times had changed. Juan Pablo Pérez Alfonso, then the Oil Minister of Venezuela, was the first to make that clear. Referring to Exxon's unilateral move, Pérez Alfonso said: "Since that's the way it is, we are going to organize a club, a very closed club, a club that will control ninety percent of the crude oil on the world markets. We will work hand in hand. From now on, we are going to make history." He made his statement one month to the day after Exxon's decision.

Pérez Alfonso was a long-time disciple of Egypt's Gamal Abdel Nasser, the driving force of the Middle East in the 1960s. Nasser, in his book *Philosophy of a Revolutionary,* had written: "Oil, my brothers, is the vital artery of civilization. Without it, civilization would no longer be able to exist."

From Caracas, Pérez Alfonso made contact with his counterpart in Riyadh, Saudi Oil Minister Abdullah Tariki. They decided to organize a secret meeting of five countries—Saudi Arabia, Venezuela, Iraq, Kuwait and Iran. The meeting was to take place in Baghdad, and to set it up Pérez Alfonso relied on the skill of Tariki.

The meeting opened on September 9, 1960. Addressing the delegates, Tariki proposed the foundation of a common instrument: the Organization of Petroleum Exporting Countries. That night four initials were written into twentieth-century history: OPEC.

Its first statement was published: "The members of the organization can no longer remain indifferent to the attitude of the petroleum companies. They demand price stability in the future. They are opposed to all unnecessary fluctuations. They shall endeavor *by all possible means* to restore the prices prevailing before the last reduction.''

Abdullah Tariki, in the name of King Saud, son and successor of the formidable warrior Ibn Saud, had forged the weapon of the new era.

Like most of the gifted sons of Middle Eastern families, Tariki had trained in the United States after the war. He had of course specialized in oil and had traveled throughout Texas with its thousands of drilling wells. He had also attended all of the 1952 Senate hearings in which the Federal Trade Commission revealed the oil companies' monopolistic practices and double accounting systems. Tariki witnessed the impunity of these giants who pumped out this lifeblood of civilization and sold it. He noted that they appeared at the very top of the *Fortune 500* list of largest companies, far ahead of the great automobile, steel and chemical firms. Tariki observed the manner in which they quietly divided the markets among themselves, "subsidizing" local political powers whenever necessary. Certain of his rights, Tariki attacked the oil companies on all fronts.

He was supported without reservation by King Saud, who found himself managing a precariously unified country, which was always short of funds because of lavish spending by his huge family. He was a pale reflection of his famous father, the authoritarian and revered Ibn Saud. His younger brother Faisal, however, was Ibn Saud's favorite son and his spiritual heir. Faisal was a competent man who could act decisively in troubled times. And those troubles were shortly upon Saudi Arabia. The country was faced with a confrontation with the big companies over prices; the sudden creation of OPEC and the violent upheaval that it caused; and immediate financial blackmail by the industrial countries.

When the oil companies cut the price of oil, Saudi Arabia already had heavy deficits in both its domestic budget and its foreign accounts. With no resources other than oil, the country was on the edge of bankruptcy.

Faisal saw anxiety growing among the members of the ruling family in Riyadh, Mecca and Taif, and among their allies in the commercial families gathered around the port of Jedda on the Red Sea. The royal family did not think King Saud could handle the storm and asked Faisal to negotiate with his brother for a transfer of power. There was no doubt about the outcome. Under the modest title of vice-prime minister, Faisal assumed control of the important ministries, including Oil and Finance. He now became head of the government—and soon had himself crowned.

King Faisal had always dreamed of an Arab renaissance, and overnight he saw to it that Saudi society began to observe the teachings of the Koran, his own source of inspiration. In their modern air-conditioned oases, scattered over the immense peninsula of sand, the thousands of American technicians working for Aramco could not believe it when they were informed that no longer would a drop of alcohol be allowed within Saudi Arabia's borders, no longer would movie theaters or gambling halls remain open. Faisal was determined to revive the culture, the identity, of Islam.

The peoples of the Middle East were not the only ones to be held down by the West. All of the Third World was experiencing the same humiliation. And that provided the source of the political union between OPEC and the Third World, an alliance that is at once a threat and a hope.

For the Third World countries, life today means a crushing burden of debt to Chase Manhattan Bank, Deutsche Bank, and all the giant Western commercial banks which hold hundreds of billion dollars' worth of IOUs on them. Every year new trade barriers from the West are raised, establishing higher costs for their imports and lower real prices for their exports. So fragile is their existence that many are close to bankruptcy—an event that could send the Western banking system crashing and the entire world economy grinding to a halt. Turkey has already rescheduled its debt. Bolivia is about to join Zaire and Peru in doing the same thing. Brazil is quickly running out of places to borrow its sorely needed funds.

The common interests of OPEC and the Third World were obvious years ago. One of the most trusted friends of Saudi Arabia and Sheikh Yamani himself is the Venezuelan Oil Minister, Humberto Calderón-Berti, who brought to the Arabian Peninsula the support of Latin America. Yamani rarely confers with many people about his strategy against the Western oil companies and the West in general, but Calderón-Berti is regularly consulted. Both have long envisioned a union between OPEC and the Third World.

Calderón-Berti, in 1979, had only recently taken his job as president of OPEC for the year. A lawyer, he came from a volatile region in the grip of social and political ferment. Throughout Latin America, Cuba, Jamaica, Mexico, Costa Rica, all were growing more radical. Each of these countries was struggling with its own future, torn between the colossal, crushing weight of the United States and the chaotic poverty of the South American continent. In this crucial region, the *nouveaux riches* of the oil industry had become targets for attacks by revolutionaries and young demonstrators. The masses regarded Venezuela's and Mexico's political establishments as accomplices of Washington and of the multinational companies who dominate world oil with the backing of "Yankee" policy. Rooted as he was among his own people, Calderón-Berti was able to gauge the force of this ferment and the impotence of the region's leaders. He turned to OPEC and a union with the Third World as the only hope for the future. In his first news conference as president the Venezuelan outlined the basis of what would emerge as the Taif Report: "OPEC will be the most powerful tool ever placed at the disposal of the Third World countries. From now on, we will work with them in dealing with the West. We will use OPEC all the way."

No one listened at the time.
No one is listening today.

The growing alliance between OPEC and the Third World is belittled by the West, which sees the tie either as a maneuver to complicate discussions on oil prices or as a way of easing the conscience of the oil-rich countries about their poor. Americans and Europeans see everything in the alliance except the simple truth: the oil countries are not just linked to the Third World, *they are part of it.*

What the West does not understand is that these nations remain underdeveloped countries, faced with many of the same social, human and political problems that exist throughout Africa, Asia and Latin America. They are overwhelmed by the effects of the colossal transfer of wealth which comes to them daily from the West, and they have not yet learned how to convert this income into creative development. And time is running out for the OPEC nations. They have only some twenty years before their oil reserves are depleted. Without a tremendous surge in development, the hope of a renaissance will die. The oil-producing nations have to move their huge cash surpluses from Western banks to generate a new cycle of development before it is too late, for them and everyone else.

Thus the OPEC countries are now taking matters into their own hands to transform the world imbalance and their own destinies. The Taif Report and the route it lays out is the first step the countries of OPEC must take to seize the future. They have little room to maneuver.

Those Western nations that refuse to accept the political alliance between OPEC and the Third World should look to the recent history of the North-South conferences, and to the changing nature of that crucial financial institution, the International Monetary Fund. In both North-South conferences, in 1976 and 1977, OPEC supported the Third World's demand for higher commodity prices and a better deal from the West. In 1975, OPEC declared at the first summit of the organization, in Algiers:

> The Sovereigns and Heads of State of OPEC reaffirm the natural solidarity which unites their countries with the other developing countries in their struggle to overcome underdevelopment.
>
> They note that the world economic crisis stems from the profound inequalities in social and economic progress among people, inequalities generated by foreign exploitation which has fostered the drainage of natural resources and impeded the effective transfer of capital resources and technology. This fundamental imbalance is the cause of general inflation, the slowdown of economic growth and disorder in the monetary system.
>
> They therefore reaffirm their willingness to cooperate with all the countries exporting raw materials and other basic commodities in order to obtain equitable and remunerative prices.

This is not empty rhetoric. Consider the action taken by Saudi Arabia and other OPEC countries during the last petrodollar crisis in 1975. The IMF ran out of money to lend those nations facing severe balance-of-payments deficits and went to the oil producers for help. Before the Saudis would agree to lend their billions to the IMF, they insisted that the IMF guarantee to lend the money on soft terms only to the needy developing countries. And so the Witteveen Oil Facility, a $10-billion fund named after the president of the IMF, was set up by OPEC to help the Third World countries balance their trade deficits. Never before in the IMF's history had anyone demanded that its funds be lent *only* to the poor of the world. The same request would be repeated in 1980 and 1981.

The IMF is not the only financial institution to push its begging bowl toward the Gulf. The U.S. Treasury was there earlier. In 1975 an event took place that was strange indeed in its novelty and symbolic of the economic and monetary upheaval to come: the U.S. Secretary of the Treasury suddenly requested an audience with King Faisal.

Faisal asked that Sheikh Yamani be with him in Taif when he received William Simon. He knew that the Treasury Secretary and the U.S. government had recently been placed in an unexpected and formerly unimaginable situation. To pay for its huge oil imports, the United States was transferring hundreds of billions of dollars overseas, and these "petrodollars" plus those of all the other nations floating about in the financial centers of Europe and Asia, now exceeded the total volume of money actually held in the United States. The American government no longer controlled the expansion of its own currency.

For the Saudis, this meant trouble. All oil exports are paid for in dollars, and most of the short-term assets in which the oil-producing nations invest are dollar-denominated. Any weakness in the dollar erodes the value of their capital. And any volatility in the international foreign-exchange markets hurts worldwide trade and development. The dollar had become so weak that it could no longer continue to be the world's major reserve currency without the support of Saudi Arabia.

Simon was on a mission from Washington to ask the King if he might consider investing a substantial part of his country's oil profits—billions of dollars each year—in U.S. Treasury bonds. The American move was designed to win a reprieve for the dollar and prevent a banking collapse. The bonds would be guaranteed on a top-priority basis by the Federal Reserve Bank.

The first part of the interview went off smoothly. The King used words and gestures intended to make Simon forget the humiliating and extraordinary nature of his mission. Actually, the King wanted to prevent America's drift from growing any worse. As long as nothing was done to design another international system capable of taking the burden off the shoulders of the United States, he would keep the dollar afloat. Faisal agreed.

Sheikh Yamani had scheduled an intimate supper with Simon at his nearby villa, where they could relax as they talked about the future. He knew that his first official conversation could lead only to agreements in principle. Going beyond that would involve long, hard negotiations.

With the Treasury Secretary, Yamani walked down to the tree-lined lane before his villa, where he was surrounded by members of the world press corps who were with Simon. He asked them to be seated, then answered their questions. As usual, they all centered on the price of a barrel of oil. Yamani told them that oil had not been a subject of discussion at the Faisal-Simon meeting, disappointing the reporters. What else could interest their readers and their editors? Only oil prices made the front page. Anything else would be buried in the business and financial sections of the newspapers.

Nevertheless, there was another word, magical by then, that caught their attention: OPEC. So Yamani entertained a series of questions on OPEC's attitude toward the coming dialogue with the Western world. And then he added, in a foreshadowing of the Taif Report, "You must admit that oil and time are on our side. So it's up to you, in the West. The time will come when we will not renew contracts for our oil, and even less for our financial reserves, unless we have an agreement on *technology transfer to the whole Third World*. Technology and development will have to be granted without restriction if you want oil. *Technology, in short, is the price of oil.*" Technology, development, energy—can any science unite a shattered planet? A *world challenge* was launched.

But once again everything returned to normal. No new proposal came from the West. This silence was the reason for the first, informal meeting in Taif four years later, in 1978. Now OPEC would act unilaterally, and this time the Arabian Gulf had the leverage. For it was not only the Americans who came to Saudi Arabia seeking funds. In 1980 the German Finance Minister arrived in Riyadh to ask the central bank of Saudi Arabia to buy billions of dollars' worth of German government bonds. One of the world's strongest currencies, the German mark, had to be underwritten by the Saudis. The Swiss came to Riyadh as well, selling their own bonds to get the billions needed to keep the once rock-hard Swiss franc afloat. The French also came, very quietly, to sell their paper to the Saudis and then move on to the Kuwaitis.

And finally even the Japanese arrived in Riyadh. Like the Europeans, they too were running huge balance-of-payments deficits owing to heavy oil imports, and they needed infusions of Gulf capital to keep the yen from collapsing. The Japanese, however, were special supplicants to the Saudis. By the beginning of the 1980s Japan had surpassed the Americans and the Europeans in science and technology. By the first months of 1981, Japanese corporations were forging ahead of multinationals around the globe. Their companies were orchestrating the next postindustrial revolution—the Silicon Revolution of information processing and computers that would, in this decade, change the face of the earth.

E XPERTS DATE THE LOSS of Western control of Middle East oil to the unexpected link forged between Faisal, lord of Saudi Arabia, and Muammar al-Qaddafi, the young rebel who had risen from the ranks of the Libyan Army.

The meeting of the minds, within OPEC, between the king of a fabulous empire, a fiercely anti-Communist ally of the United States, opposed to all violent social movements, and the fiery Libyan revolutionary, who hates the West and its values and is determined to destroy the privileges of its elite, appeared to be ephemeral and superficial. But its roots went deep into Islam and Arabism.

The Frenchman Jacques Benoist-Méchin, the best-known historian of the Saudi dynasty, knew Ibn Saud personally. He often visited the monarch's brother, his sons and the rest of his family. He learned Arabic and lived among the Saudis, where he observed with horror the West's ignorance of and disdain for the people. Benoist-Méchin sensed the future power of this great people at the center of the world, and in his key work on the kingdom he attempted to show the way Ibn Saud's mind worked:

> Twice in the course of history the Bedouins of the Arabian desert have erupted into the western seas. Each time, the energy spent in these expeditions had been diverted from the main goal—the formation of an Arab nation. The Arab people emerged from those adventures weak and impoverished. Ibn Saud refused to commit the same mistake.

For him, Islam was the very essence of the Arab genius: a necessary discipline without which the Bedouins would founder. It was a mystique.

This force stemmed from the vision that he had had in the desert—a vision vital to understanding Ibn Saud's whole life. . . . With the growth of the value of oil the Arabs would soon come to know the great temptations of the West. Ibn Saud was quite willing to accept the benefits of western civilization, but he refused to allow his country to be penetrated by destructive aspects which might corrupt his subjects. To keep these forces at bay, he used the Koran.

Thus, although everything seemed to separate Faisal and Qaddafi, deep down the two men were united in the Islamic faith. Secure in the superiority of its planes and missiles, and blinded by the accumulation of material wealth, a contemptuous West failed to perceive this while there was still time.

Nasser, years before, had predicted the inevitability of this alliance to Nehru, Sukarno, Ben Bella and all the leaders of decolonization. Nasser's closest friend, Mohammad Heikal, the inspired editor of the Cairo daily *Al Ahram* and a man regularly consulted by political leaders from North and South, recently repeated Nasser's predictions. Early in 1981, Heikal published an analysis of why men from the industrial civilization cannot understand anything foreign to their culture. In his report he said:

Today the political minds of the West are tying to explain what they term the "Islamic revival," but "revival" would imply something missing. Actually, there has never been anything missing, for Islam's divinity has never transcended history but has always remained within it. Islam makes no distinction between the temporal and the spiritual, and the hand that dispenses justice is the same one that wields the sword. Thus, in the Muslim ethic, religion and nationalism are distinct. Mossadeq's 1951 revolution in Iran formed part of the great movement of national liberation that seized the Third World just after World War II. The 1950s were marked throughout these regions by nationalistic revolution and decolonization punctuated by movements led in Indonesia by Sukarno, by Gandhi and Nehru in India, Jinnah in Pakistan, Mossadeq in Iran, Nasser in Egypt, Nkrumah in Ghana, Ben Bella and Boumédienne in Algeria—they formed one and the same movement.

Robert McNamara, Secretary of Defense under Kennedy and Johnson, had presided over the World Bank for ten years. In his tireless travels—part of an effort to redeem himself for his role in the Vietnam War—he covered eighty-five countries to observe first hand the true face of poverty.

In 1978 he invited Willy Brandt, Nobel Peace Prize laureate and former Chancellor of Germany, to form a group of some leading world figures who would have two years and $3 million to examine the key aspects of the current world economic anemia. The result was a plan entitled "North-South: A Program for Survival." Published in March 1980 as a technical report, it was read only by a small group of the initiated, despite its many crucial proposals.

In the same year, Yamani invited to Taif a young man whose career he had followed for a long time. Yamani liked his clear thinking and audacity—they reminded him of his own youth. Like Yamani, the young man had also been named oil minister of his country at thirty-two. He was Ali Khalifa al-Sabah of Kuwait. Sheikh Ali was an al-Sabah, a member of the reigning family in the Persian Gulf's second most important country. A precocious child, he had been taught by the best teachers in the region. Once he had acquired a solid Arabic education, he studied modern mathematics and economics.

The period when Sheikh Ali was growing up was one of

change. The ideas of the Keynesian era, which had made the West rich, no longer applied. Moreover, the great temples for the teaching of economics were changing. In the 1930s, 1940s and 1960s—from Roosevelt to Kennedy—nothing could compare to Harvard, Princeton, and the great East Coast universities.

But the end of the 1960s saw the foundation of the Bretton Woods international financial system collapse, with the dollar going off the gold standard, the end of fixed foreign-exchange rates, and the massive proliferation of hundreds of billions of Eurodollars, then petrodollars, that were free from any central bank control whatsoever. The seismic shift in world economics was mirrored in American universities which shifted their economic focus away from Europe toward Japan, Asia, the Pacific.

West Coast universities—Stanford, Cal Tech, Berkeley, UCLA, San Francisco—became the new centers of economics. They provided the brains for the "Silicon Valley," where the remarkable inventions in the new field of microcomputers soon appeared. Quickly, a myriad of small factories set up by students and professors themselves grew up to manufacture these revolutionary inventions.

Kuwait's leaders sent Sheikh Ali to California before he was twenty. He returned home confident, sensing the world's economic future. Ali came back with one dominant concern: to build a new economic system that would replace the old one—and to build it fast, to avert collapse. Sheikh Ali believed that "industries of the future" had to be created as soon as inventions emerged from the laboratories. A new monetary system had to be established before the "dollar pillar" was abandoned by the money managers, and before the International Monetary Fund was overwhelmed by the magnitude of world debt. Finally, all these economic decisions had to be unified in a "new international order" that would not just reflect the narrow interests of the West, but pave the way for the vast human resources of the Third World. This was an urgent political necessity if famine was to be avoided. But just as important, it also represented a new economic constraint: if the Third World did not become creative itself there would be no expanding markets for anyone. And if this happened, all the scientific feats of Japan, America and Europe would be meaningless.

Having grasped this vision of the future, Ali Khalifa al-Sabah returned to Kuwait to begin serving a long apprenticeship in the affairs of state. At twenty-four he was named director of administrative affairs; at twenty-eight, assistant to the Minister of Oil. Using tiny but powerful Kuwait as a base, he showed his ability for finding solutions to the problems of energy, trade and investments.

Four days out of every seven, he worked in his office; Thursdays and Fridays were reserved for reading files and books at his home, away from phones and Telexes. On Fridays, the Sabbath, Sheikh Ali took ritual meditative walks in the vast desert surrounding him. His Sundays were devoted to Cabinet meetings, where he soon sat as Minister of Oil.

So in mid 1978 when Sheikh Yamani organized the group to draw up a plan that might reverse the disastrous course of the world, the young Kuwaiti was ready. The two men complemented each other. A blueprint of the overall task was hammered out between them. They were to ask a committee of OPEC to arrive at conclusions and proposals on each point—in two years. They wanted the following:

1. An outline of the framework of the problem, above all an analysis of OPEC's relations with the other Third World countries.
2. A study of the long-term trend for oil, with a specific examination of "the crisis of 1981" and of the future of oil supplies.
3. A permanent system for readjusting oil prices to avoid crises. Sheikh Yamani was specific: "We should not accept price stability, but, rather, price *predictability*. This would be a great help to the consumers."

4. A way to meet the immediate needs of the Third World countries by absorbing their debts and integrating them into the production cycle.

5. An exploration in depth of the economic interdependence of the industrial regions (America, Europe, Japan) and the rest of the world, with special emphasis on the "strong points" and the "weak points" of that interdependence.

6. The conclusion was to be "in five pages or less," at the request of Sheikh Yamani, and was to, "aim at overall coherence, leaving out methods in order to give self-evident facts the freedom to generate forces of change."

The guidelines of a program of action were thus hammered out. OPEC was to be transformed. Through energy and money, their organization could become the instrument that would insure the creation of a "new international economic order."

"This is our duty," concluded the Saudi, who had no illusions about the gigantic difficulties of this undertaking.

"It is our mission," the Kuwaiti remarked with youthful conviction.

A list of members for the working committee was put forward. A date also had to be selected, and a site for the meeting.

"How many members?"

"No more than six, if possible," said Yamani.

They drew up a preliminary list of six countries. All the various political tendencies were represented. The list included both the biggest oil producers and the most heavily populated countries.

The meeting was set for the earliest possible date in 1978.

The place was to be: Taif.

A small working group was set up to deal with the issues that went far beyond the price of oil. It was to examine OPEC's overall economic policy on all fronts, including industry, currency, investment, markets. A political strategy also had to be developed. A Baghdad technocrat, Awni al-Ami, director of international relations in the Iraqi Ministry of Petroleum, worked with the group.

Oil put Awni al-Ani and his companions into the center of world politics. Dozens of reports, commissioned from the great economic research institutes in Kiel, Tokyo, London and New York, had to be discussed, while at the same time the group had to train a new generation of Arab economists.

OPEC's new headquarters were located in Vienna. Geneva authorities had refused, in the 1960s, to allow an "organization not accredited by any diplomatic authority" to maintain offices in their city, which permitted only "recognized" international organizations. That refusal provided Vienna with a new opportunity. The former capital of the Austrian Empire had been downgraded into a provincial suburb by the Third Reich, and then made into an isolated island by the Yalta Agreements. Situated as it is at the crossroads of East and West, Vienna was the right choice for OPEC's administrative capital and as a result is undergoing an amazing revival.

Awni al-Ami, at OPEC's Vienna headquarters, described the teamwork leading up to the Taif meeting in the following way: "We are going to radically transform all the raw-material markets to put an end to the West's looting that spreads injustice and misery throughout the Third World. We have the power to do this because of the exceptional nature of oil. The industries that stem from oil are the most complex and most fruitful in the world. Oil represents more than half of mankind's overall energy needs—54 percent. Just fifty years ago, it made up only 10 percent."

Modern societies have become so dependent on oil that the degree of prosperity of any economy can be measured in terms of its oil consumption. *For the next ten or fifteen years, nothing will alter the bond between oil and development.*

The importance of oil cannot be compared with that of any other raw material or product, since it has several dimensions—namely, economic, military, social and political. There is almost complete agreement that the four principal problems in the world—war, development, energy and environmental pollution—cannot be divorced from crude oil.

In the *economic* sphere, the oil industry is regarded as the largest, most widely ramified and most complicated industry in the world: it is not without reason that the biggest companies in the world are oil companies.

In the energy sector, too, crude oil supplies more than half of total required energy.

The strategic importance of oil for *military* operations has become so great that it is impossible to envisage wars, conducted with today's weapons, without oil. *Socio-politically,* oil consumption represents a yard-stick of economic prosperity and the quality of life: in other words, the less oil it consumes, the more backward the country; the more oil consumed, the more developed and civilized the image it projects.

Access to oil makes the difference between mere survival and prosperity. Oil has become the lifeblood of all *modern transportation*. Thirty-five percent of all oil is consumed by automobiles, trucks, airplanes and ships. The industrial world's progress, its standard of living, goes hand in hand with oil.

At the time of the First World War two million cars and trucks had been manufactured. By the mid 1950s, the number had reached 100 million. Less than twenty-five years later, there were *350 million cars and trucks on the road*. Of that number, 220 million were in Europe and America alone. How much gasoline did these armadas burn up earlier and how much do they burn today? In 1914, the quantity of fuel consumed by cars was 6 million tons. In 1960, it rose to 300 million tons. In 1975, it exceeded 500 million tons. The figures are still growing.

Professor Barry Commoner summarizes the series of circumstances that transformed and continues to transform fuel oil into a raw material. A group of engineers in a petrochemical firm get together to study a plan for the production of ethylene, a by-product of which is prophylene. A young engineer points out that a new reaction makes it possible to convert prophylene into acrylonitrile, the raw material of acrylic fibers. Eventually a new market is created to sell prophylene at the maximum profit.

Over the past twenty-five years, systematic development has led to an incredible collection of molecules and macromolecules: plastics, synthetic fibers and rubbers, insecticides, fertilizer, paint, medicines, detergents, adhesives, inks. It is now estimated that more than eighty thousand products are derived from oil.

Beyond mass transportation dependent on oil, beyond industries that run on oil or derive their products from it, lie two other sectors of modern life to which it is indispensable: heating and electricity. Moreover, this incomparable natural product is being used by the food industry. At the end of the 1970s the world's farmers had 18 million tractors, a quarter of them in the United States, the world's leading exporter of food products. And petroagriculture doesn't stop with fueling tractors. It is already working steadily in a parallel sphere, i.e., the industrial conversion of certain grades of petroleum into "food proteins" which make cheap, nutritious feed for livestock. Hence, petroagriculture produces meat.

Modern society's transportation industry, heating, electricity and agriculture are literally "made of oil." Jean-Claude Balacéanu, of the Institute of Petroleum in Paris, is one of the West's experts who watch and measure the irresistible rise in the use of petroleum. Here is the portrait he paints:

What is the consumer society, after all, but unlimited oil? Imagine, if you will, a France deprived of hydrocarbons. Nothing would move on the roads. There would not even be roads, for lack of tar and asphalt. There would be no more food distribution. Corner grocery stores, supermarkets, wholesale markets and slaughterhouses would all be forced to close down.

No tractors would be in the fields, no planes in the sky. Every ship would have to stay in port, except for a few ancient steamers that burn coal . . . and, of course, sailboats.

There would be no fuel for heating, so over half of our homes, offices, schools and hospitals would be cold. Industry would be paralyzed. Farming would be set back a century.

Almost all plastics and artificial fibers would disappear. No more nylon, no more ballpoint pens, no more shirts, no more waterproof clothes, no more mothproof woolens, no more records. In modern offices, everything is made of oil—from the carpeting to the dials on telephones, from the wall coverings to the painted metal furniture, from wastebaskets to electric fans.

The short period—a mere 30 years—which saw the rise of oil-based prosperity has been described by Professor Carl Sohlberg. According to Sohlberg, in *Oil Power,* America began to reach the peak of its power when oil replaced coal as the main source of energy. The fluidity, ease of handling, compact energy and extraordinary chemical value of the new substance made its discovery and exploitation the quintessential capitalist undertaking. It was because they could count on oil that Western democracies were able to base their industrialization on free enterprise. It is now obvious that democracy is completely dependent on oil. Cheap oil and the billions of barrels extracted and sold at prices that actually dropped in value between the 1950s and the 1970s completely subsidized the rise of industrial societies in Europe and America.

From 1960 to 1973, the compulsive appetite for oil knew no bounds. For the industrial countries as a whole, energy consumption rose by 100 percent in less than fifteen years—and oil consumption by 160 percent. Imports of oil, essentially Middle

East oil, increased for America, Europe and Japan combined from 38 percent to 53 percent. The dependence of the industrial world on the oil-exporting countries became irreversible.

As recently as 1960, the industrial world needed to import only 65 million tons annually. By 1973, the industrial world had to have 290 million tons of oil. Five years later—in the midst of the so-called "crisis" and at prices labeled "unwarranted"—it imported 410 million tons.

"The probable explanation for the industrial countries' inability to foresee the oil crisis is undoubtedly the extraordinarily short duration of the oil era," explains Dennis Hayes, a research worker for Washington's World Watch Institute and author of *Rays of Hope*.

Children of the petroleum era tend to forget how brief this period has been. Just fifty years ago, 80% of the world's commercial energy came from coal, a mere 16% from oil and gas. As recently as 1950, coal still provided 60% of this total. For the next two decades, oil grew rapidly, exceeding coal use in the 1960s. Today, oil alone represents two thirds of the world's commercial energy budget. But there's hardly enough oil for another thirty years.

The fact is that oil prices can only continue to rise. After spiraling upward in ten years from $2 to over $30 a barrel, the price will double again before 1985, over and above any "gluts" and market forces. And prices will double even sooner should a new "accident" of the Iranian type occur—something which is quite likely.

James R. Schlesinger, former Secretary of Energy, has declared that the only true alternative to oil would be to renew American industrial equipment on entirely different technological and energy bases. But even the most optimistic of futurists does not expect this to become possible before the turn of the century. If then. If at all . . .

ONE OF THE MOST WIDESPREAD MISCONCEPTIONS of the "oil crisis" is that it was first triggered by the embargo during the Arab–Israeli war of October 1973. Most people remember only that oil prices quadrupled after that war. Actually, OPEC's decision to hike oil prices began long before. The 1973 embargo was just a spectacular episode within an irreversible trend. The real break with the old order dates back to the meeting with OPEC requested by the big companies, and their governments, after Qaddafi's Libyan revolution.

In 1971, in the New York offices of John McCloy, the top brass of the big oil companies sat in session to map out the line they would use in their talks with OPEC. Up to then, they had scoffed at or simply ignored it. But the times had changed. McCloy, who had been the High Commissioner for Germany at the end of World War II, was one of the powerful lawyers operating on the interface between government and big business.

Those legendary corporate lawyers include Clark Clifford, who had been a leading adviser to American presidents from Truman to Kennedy and Johnson, and George Ball, a close friend of Jean Monnet, father of European unity. Ball had been the American godfather of the European Economic Community and remained the guardian angel of the U.S. Senate's internationalist wing. Of all, John McCloy was the most powerful.

McCloy didn't beat about the bush. He told the companies to stop playing hide and seek with OPEC. He showed them that they were wasting time and energy trying to "break OPEC." He explained that such an approach was as illusory as that of military intervention, and that the first act of common sense, in order to achieve some lasting results, would be to recognize OPEC. Then gradually they could lay down new ground rules and, in time, even collaborate with it. McCloy suggested that the companies sign a joint letter, simple and courteous, that would be sent to the OPEC president, establishing a wholly new climate.

McCloy's modest proposal touched off a great deal of anger. But the combined strength of the facts and his arguments— backed up by the precise explanations of the State Department expert, James Akins—quickly put an end to this outburst. McCloy dictated the letter in front of the twenty-three executives, representing the world's largest oil companies, who sat around him. The letter expressed their desire to present simple and constructive proposals to OPEC and its members. At the same time they declared that they could not discuss demands by the member countries unless the simultaneous agreement of all the producing states was guaranteed.

This was not only *recognition of OPEC* but the benediction of the consumers' cartel for the producers' cartel, one strengthening the other.

Everything from then on moved rapidly. The meeting at McCloy's offices took place in January 1971. By the end of the year everything was settled. At that time a special envoy, Jack Irwin, the brother-in-law of the board chairman of IBM, was sent by President Nixon to see three of the OPEC-country leaders who were considered America's best allies: the King of Saudi Arabia, the Shah of Iran and the Emir of Kuwait.

"My mission," declared Irwin, "was simply to explain to the main leaders of the Gulf producing countries the very deep concern the United States would feel at the possibility of oil production being cut or even halted, and to make it clear that we were ready to deal with them."

None of these leaders, however, would deal directly with

Irwin or the United States government. They told Irwin that the institution qualified to speak on their behalf would henceforth be OPEC. America bowed to their wishes.

OPEC appointed three men to meet the West's emissaries and negotiate with them: Sheikh Yamani (Saudi Arabia), Dr. Amouzegar (Iran) and Saadoun Hammadi (Iraq). They had all studied at American universities. They had all gone through the years of helplessness and self-effacement. They had all experienced the great redistribution in the balance of power.

At the start of the succession of meetings that took place, one of the American negotiators asked Yamani to meet in private "on a very grave matter," before the conversations began. He confided to the Saudi that information had reached Washington indicating that at the last OPEC meeting, in closed session, a plan had been discussed and hammered out.

According to rumors, the plan called for imposing a "true world embargo on oil" if the need were felt or if events dictated such a move. The plan was designed to give OPEC the upper hand in case of a crisis. It was also rumored, the American diplomat said, that this plan "had even received the approval of the King of Saudi Arabia and the Shah of Iran." The American added that this struck him as very doubtful.

On the contrary, confirmed Yamani, it was quite true. The plan had indeed been approved, and he advised the American to take it quite seriously. Astonished, the American diplomat asked him, "Do you realize what another embargo failure, like the last one in 1967, would mean for OPEC? I mean the loss of prestige and power—and just after the organization has received international consecration?"

Yamani replied in the same calm tone of voice, "I don't think that you realize what OPEC has become. You don't seem to realize that although its members have very different and, at times, conflicting views on political questions, they are in total agreement when it comes to oil. Don't deceive yourself about that. You can no longer afford that luxury."

The model protégé of the United States, the Shah of Iran,

gave a news conference in Teheran to put an end to any ideas of division or pressures directed against OPEC, in which he declared that the attitude of the oil companies exemplified economic imperialism. But he warned that, like colonialism, imperialism had had its day. Conditions in Iran were no longer ripe for exploitation; they had changed dramatically in twenty years. Iranians now had a different outlook and were unwilling to submit to peremptory imperialist demands.

There was one last attempt: the American government convened an extraordinary assembly of the developed countries (OECD) in Paris to find out how its allies felt. The answer came very speedily. Neither Europe nor Japan had the slightest desire, they admitted bluntly, to risk conflict over an oil price increase, one that was considered inevitable. They wanted to negotiate.

Without the shadow of a crisis, Yamani and his team of OPEC negotiators then obtained a general revision of the big companies' contracts during a general meeting in Teheran. This was the historic "Teheran Agreement." Yamani got the oil companies to accept the demands of the oil producing countries to raise the posted price and change the distribution of royalties to generate more revenue for the nations of OPEC.

In a letter to the White House justifying this oil settlement, John McCloy wrote that the companies had got the most they could out of the situation in spite of the extremely high cost. The common stand they had taken should now make it possible to better resist any new, collective threats from OPEC.

This diplomatic language scarcely concealed two very important facts. The signing of the Teheran agreements would cost the big companies—and the consumers—the sum of $45 billion over the three coming years. And it marked, in an irrevocable fashion, the end of an era. Speaking to Yamani as they left the last session, the president of Iraq National Oil, Saadoun Hammadi, said, "Well, now everyone knows that the lords of oil are no longer the companies. . . ."

The price per barrel had increased by only 50 percent—from $1.80 to $2.60—but that was not a true index of the event's significance, for that price would subsequently double, then quadruple, and nothing could be done to push it down again. Effectively, control over these decisions had changed hands. And prices weren't everything. The central question, the "share-out," or division of revenue, was now shifting steadily to favor OPEC.

The share-out worked in the following way. At the beginning of the 1950s, in Mossadeq's time, the companies received 70 percent of the revenue on each barrel of oil pumped, and the producing countries got 30 percent. In 1960, with the creation of OPEC and without any change in prices, the share-out became 50 percent for the companies, 50 percent for the countries. In 1970 and 1971, after the Libyan blitz, OPEC's taking charge of negotiations, and the Teheran Agreement, the distribution changed to 30 percent for the companies and 70 percent for the countries. One year later the process was to reach its end, even before the much-publicized "embargo shocks," for the distribution had by then been set once and for all at 95 percent for the producing countries and 5 percent for the companies. In effect it reduced them to salaried workers—no minor revolution.

It was the revolution that OPEC would seek to extend to the other countries of the Third World for the use of and payment for their raw materials. The objective would be the same: 95 percent to the owning countries and 5 percent to the industrial corporations whenever they were needed to do the work.

What seemed less than ten years ago like the beginning of the end for "the West's prosperity" was only a little foretaste of the wrenching shift of power that lies ahead, a shift that the Taif Report projects for the 1980s.

FOR THE ARABS, and for the West, it all started with an obscure incident in Mayfair.

Four young men, two of them Arabs, arrived at London's Les Ambassadeurs, a celebrated night club that features a luxurious gambling casino on the second floor. After supper the two Arabs, on an infrequent leave from their British Army training course, went upstairs to see the casino.

The younger one, a dark brooding man in his twenties, stood near a gambling table and remarked to his friend about one of the gamblers, "I've seen that man somewhere. Who is he? Whom is he gambling with?"

The man was playing blackjack for very high stakes against a famous Greek shipowner. He lost nearly half a million dollars in the space of an hour. He was the personal adviser of King Idris of Libya.

The soldier was stunned looking at the face in that scene, the trembling hands, the piles of bank notes, the frenzied gambling.

His friend took him by the arm and tried to lead him downstairs into the fresh air. But he refused and replied in a whisper, "Let me watch for a while. So, this is what they do with all the gold they steal from us!" He stayed for another hour as if to imprint the scene on his memory.

The young Arab's name was Captain Muammar al-Qaddafi. A devout man, he had grown up in the Libyan desert with the Senussi tribe, who lived in goatskin tents. Qaddafi decided, then and there in the gambling club, that he would obey unhesitatingly and unswervingly the commands of the Prophet. It was a turning point in his life.

Not long afterward, the Libyan captain returned to Idris's kingdom, where in his tent he read late into the night. Aside from the Koran, which plunged him into meditation, there were three books he read regularly. One, *The Philosophy of Revolution,* had been written by his political mentor, Gamal Abdel Nasser. The others were two complete volumes of speeches on the emancipation of the slaves made by Abraham Lincoln during the American Civil War, and the memoirs of Field Marshal Viscount Montgomery of Alamein. Throughout the decisive months of the desert campaign that saw Montgomery's armored columns drive to victory along the Mediterranean coast from Cairo to Tripoli, from Alexandria Bay to the Gulf of Sirte, the British commander had contemplated, every night, a photo of his legendary rival, Field Marshal Erwin Rommel. The photo, which stood under his night-table lamp, helped him to work out the next day's strategy.

Then, one day in 1969, Qaddafi was designated to command the guard of honor at a ceremony marking the opening of the most modern pipeline in North Africa. That honor guard would parade in review past King Idris's guests and ministers.

The King's guests included Armand Hammer, chairman of Occidental Petroleum, and other directors of the American company, which had recently obtained a highly lucrative concession in Libyan territory. Occidental Petroleum, one of the few independent oil companies not one of the Seven Sisters, was steadily expanding its production in Libya.

The ceremony was magnificent. The guests and officials drove up in Cadillacs and Rolls-Royces. There was a buffet with champagne and Havana cigars. Gifts were exchanged, and beautiful hostesses specially invited from Italy entertained the foreign guests.

Though shocked, Qaddafi did not allow himself to be sidetracked. He watched only King Idris as he bowed to the American businessmen and kissed the hands of their wives. Back at his camp in Bab-Izizia that night, he gathered his closest companions and they made their decision.

Three weeks later, on September 1, 1969, the King and his court were in Turkey on an official visit. Qaddafi, who by then had selected accomplices in other regiments placed at strategic points, gave the order to take over key command posts, ministries, and the power plant in Tripoli. None of the generals resisted. In a few hours it was over.

At dawn he announced that the King had been dethroned and the regime was abolished. A Revolutionary Command Council, presided over by Qaddafi, was set up. He was assisted by his one intimate friend, Major Abdul Salam Jallud, who in no way resembled the twenty-seven-year-old officer who had just seized power. Jallud was an affable, eloquent man with connections in both Libyan and Western ruling circles. He knew everyone who held power—a priceless ally.

After consulting with Jallud, Qaddafi triggered his next big operation. He gave orders to the U.S. military headquarters to evacuate strategic Wheelus Air Force Base, the largest in the Mediterranean, without delay. He also ordered all U.S. service personnel to leave the country. This was Qaddafi's greatest gamble.

No one imagined that America would capitulate. The base was impregnable. The Sixth Fleet headed for the Libyan coast.

This unknown twenty-seven-year-old neophyte in no way resembled Mossadeq, that eloquent and cunning demagogue who had managed to carry off something very similar in Iran a full twenty years earlier. The popularity and charisma of Mossadeq (which would reappear thirty years later in the Ayatollah Khomeini) were powerful weapons. Still, it took the oil companies and the CIA only a few months to bring him down, and to return the young Shah, Mohammed Riza Pahlevi, from exile in Rome and restore him to the throne.

Having just returned from his summer house in Taif to his palace in Riyadh, the King of Saudi Arabia was ill-informed about the Libyan coup. Libya, after all, was far away, and a country of secondary importance. When a special envoy arrived from King Idris, who asked for the advice and support of the most powerful man in the region, Faisal replied, "Tell him not to worry too much. He'll be able to come back soon. By making a frontal assault on the Americans these youngsters have gone too far." For once, Faisal was wrong.

For the first time, experts at the U.S. State Department, led by James Akins, were consulted. Acting on their urgent advice, the Nixon White House gave the order to evacuate the military bases in Libya. Washington hoped to trade the bases for an uninterrupted supply of oil. Two weeks and a few riots later, the British government followed suit. It issued instructions to its army—men whose fathers had fought to victory under Montgomery in the Libyan desert—to evacuate the famous bases of Tobruk and Benghazi. Qaddafi had won.

The Arab world was astonished at this upheaval, but an even greater battle was shaping up—not with military garrisons, but with more formidable adversaries: the big oil companies.

The young Libyan revolutionary did not want to slow the pace of events for a second. He confided to Major Jallud that he intended to proclaim the immediate nationalization of all oil companies operating in Libya.

Jallud sensed the danger and had the courage to warn Qaddafi. He did so at length, repeating what he had learned at receptions and dinners about the formidable nature of modern economic power—far more dangerous than military power. Qaddafi listened. He wanted to understand.

"By nationalizing the companies you run the risk of losing everything," Jallud told him. "You run the risk of a boycott that will paralyze us, since all the companies stick together. They'll close down the wells, stop the pumping equipment and transportation, cut off sales and distribution networks. And we don't have a single technician to do it for us. You're running the risk of bankruptcy. That's just what they're waiting for."

"What do you propose?" Qaddafi asked.

"Don't take over the companies—they won't be any good to you," was Jallud's reply. "You're going to have nothing on your hands but empty buildings and wells that can't be used. What you want is their money. That's where it all started, remember? Without warning they decided to lower the 'posted price' per barrel of oil pumped from Arab soil. The price was low enough before the cut! Your job is to make them bend on that crucial point, to make them go back on their decision. Everything will work out, provided we can win this first round . . ."

"Well, then, let's announce it," Qaddafi said.

"No," replied Jallud, "if you tackle all the companies operating in Libya they'll refuse immediately and unanimously. They can do without Libyan oil for a long time. We can't hold out that long. Go after just *one company* and get that company to sign a new contract that calls for a price increase. For example, fifty cents more on the barrel. That will be enough. It will be victory."

The plan was adopted. Qaddafi, together with Jallud and a few advisers, studied the list of foreign firms operating on Libyan soil. Occidental Petroleum—Armand Hammer's company—had no other oil field in the Middle East. Occidental's representative was given an ultimatum: either he accepted a new contract and an increase of fifty cents on the posted price per barrel or Libya would shut down his company's facilities— without touching those of the other companies.

Armand Hammer, fifty years earlier before going into oil, had charmed Lenin himself with assistance for a beleaguered Russia and was thus able to make his first fortune in the Soviet Union. Now he found himself in the position of an isolated hostage. Nobody would feel sorry for him. He was detested by his peers and especially by the Seven Sisters. Hammer was no fool, and it did not take him long to understand that no one would rescue him. He signed.

Within two weeks the other "independents" in Libya,

stunned by Hammer's capitulation, also signed, and before the end of the month the big oil companies gave in as well. On September 14, 1970, an Arab country for the first time imposed a price increase on the whole oil system of the Western world.

But if Libya's Qaddafi took the first step in wresting control of oil away from the West, it was Saudi Arabia's King Faisal who had the cunning to exploit a larger conflict in the Middle East that would create the conditions for a total victory of OPEC. His strategy was simple—but everything depended on his ability to control events. Faisal decided in 1973 that he would agree to organize a general and unlimited oil embargo and he would do it at the moment when a new, and inevitable, Arab war against Israel would erupt. He designed a three-pronged strategy, focusing on Cairo, Washington, Moscow.

Cairo because from there would come the military clash that would create the circumstances for the embargo—a limited confrontation designed to rally the West around Israel. Saudi Arabia's immediate solidarity with the Arabs would follow and thus make it possible to strike while passions ran high.

Faisal's plan also hinged on Washington. The King did not want to create an irrevocable situation as the Japanese had done at Pearl Harbor when they turned America into an implacable foe. He therefore gave the United States one last but firm warning in the light of their very old friendship. This was remembered only after the embargo.

Finally, there was Moscow. A Middle East conflict, opening with a military confrontation and spreading to the alliances, entailed enormous risks of escalation and of confrontation between the nuclear superpowers. Faisal wanted to avoid this. Thus he warned Moscow beforehand that a showdown was coming—at a time that he would indicate later on. He explained to the Russians that the scope of the conflict would be limited and would in no way affect Soviet interests. He was therefore counting on the USSR's neutrality. In exchange for this, Faisal gave them reason to hope for better relations in the future.

Egypt's President Anwar Sadat came to Riyadh to visit the King and returned satisfied because Saudi Arabia had finally agreed to back him with the weapon of oil. Faisal promised that if Egypt launched a war carefully enough planned to ensure several days of success, an oil embargo would be imposed, thereby forcing the West to stop the fighting and shape a new policy for the Middle East.

But first the Saudis wanted to alert the Americans. Sheikh Yamani left for Washington accompanied by his deputy, King Faisal's son Saudi Faisal. An unpalatable surprise awaited them: Watergate.

In Riyadh they had not imagined that the scandal could have reached proportions capable of paralyzing the White House, thus isolating President Nixon. The entire American political world, government and legislature, was concerned with only one issue: Watergate and the call for impeachment. The whole congressional and judicial system was badly shaken. In a few months the crisis would lead to Nixon's resignation. Yamani was received courteously, but no one listened. King Faisal, in Riyadh, was stupefied by such blindness and indifference.

In despair Yamani gave an interview to two reporters from the *Washington Post,* David Ottaway and Ronald Koven. The interview could not be terribly explicit (on the King's orders), but the word that counted, the tabooed word "embargo," was used—in case, explained Yamani in carefully chosen words, "America failed to revise its overall policies in the light of the objectives of the new Arab power."

In all of Washington, only one government official grasped the message. Again it was James Akins, still at his post at the State Department watching the oil front. He carefully prepared a memo and had it delivered to the White House. In his note he warned the President and Henry Kissinger—his boss—about the "real danger, for the first time, of a durable oil embargo."

It would be imposed by Saudi Arabia itself, Akins said, "if the United States failed to enter into Middle East negotiations in coming months—particularly, on the oil question. These inevitable negotiations had been delayed all too long for the stability of world economy, now deeply threatened."

Nixon never read Akins' memo. Kissinger filed it away. He had his own Mideast strategy.

Faisal could now evaluate the first phase of the action. The Soviets, pleased, said they were not going to make any move. The Americans were preoccupied and indicated that they would have to deal with the problem later. And Anwar Sadat was proceeding with serious preparations for war.

The time had come to launch the operation and achieve the twin objectives: Israel's isolation and an oil embargo. This time there would be no exceptions to the oil embargo as there were in 1967. A permanent committee would be set up within OPEC to direct all phases of the embargo until the West capitulated by accepting the general nationalization of wells and production, renouncing all authority over prices, which from now on would be under the "strict sovereignty" of OPEC, and agreeing to a basic dialogue with the Third World on the "revision of the world economic order."

The course of events would unfold as if in a computerized program. Sadat would attack on Saturday, October 6; OPEC would hold a plenary session in Vienna on Monday, October 8; and a meeting of the OAPEC (exclusively Arab members of OPEC) would be convened in Kuwait on Wednesday, October 10.

Only one man understood and gathered complete information about what was going to happen—Henry Kissinger, the American Secretary of State, who, amid the debacle of Watergate, was now running American foreign policy single-handedly.

But Kissinger did nothing to forestall the war or the embargo. He had his own idea about the way to use the tragic events ahead. Their very seriousness could, he thought, give him the power and the opportunity to act. He would follow his own plan —one quite different from that of the King of Saudi Arabia.

The last message to Moscow was sent directly by President Sadat to Chairman Leonid Brezhnev. According to the scenario discussed by Sadat in Taif, two weeks of preparation were left before the launching of operations. But the Russians had to be kept posted on a regular basis. The slightest misunderstanding could entail risks far beyond the framework and objectives of the embargo. At no time must the Russians be caught off guard.

Neither were the Americans. Nor even the Israelis. Henry Kissinger made the strategic decision in Washington, and he told the Israelis, "Don't move." Kissinger insisted that at all costs "a re-run of '67" had to be avoided; the slightest preemptive action was totally excluded. The "geopolitical" risk (as the Secretary of State liked to put it) taken when Israel struck the Arabs first had been acceptable at that time. This was no longer the case. Kissinger felt that Israel's position on the ground remained solid. He therefore believed that the Jewish state could let the other side strike first and still survive.

The Secretary of State was informed of Faisal's decision to back Egypt in its assault. He had no doubt that the embargo might be imposed, but, to his way of thinking, both the embargo and its consequences could be controlled—provided the Israelis didn't move first. If any Israeli preemptive strike led to an Arab military defeat, the whole Middle East might go up in flames. Saudi Arabia and its OPEC allies might react violently, passionately. In that eventuality, Kissinger would no longer be able to control the situation. He deliberately and firmly ruled out the possibility of such an attack by explicitly forbidding the Israelis to make it.

No one in power at that time who is still alive will admit it, but the timing of the Egyptian assault across the Suez Canal was known in advance, not only in Washington but in Tel Aviv as well. Questioned by the press a few days after the outbreak of hostilities, while Nixon was still in a state of seige over Watergate, Kissinger said blatantly, "Three times during the week preceding the Saturday on which the hostilities broke out, we asked our intelligence people as well as those of the Israelis for their evaluation of the situation. Both intelligence communities agreed that the outbreak of war was so unlikely that they assessed the probability at zero."

At 8 A.M. on Saturday, October 6, Israeli Prime Minister Golda Meir met with her Defense Minister, General Moshe Dayan, and the head of the Army Intelligence Service, Eli Zorea. They knew, that morning, that the war would break out the same night. They also knew Kissinger's decision. Israel would not move.

The night before, Israeli Air Force Commander General Elezar asked Dayan for authorization to carry out a preventive operation "like the last time." Without meeting Elezar's eyes, Dayan replied simply, "No. That wouldn't be intelligent on our part." He refused to answer any further questions.

On Saturday morning, while there was still time, Elezar, who now knew the time and place of the impending attack, entered the Prime Minister's office. He went straight up to her with tears in his eyes, asking for permission to strike first: "Why should we wait to be attacked if we know that their attack is coming? Why not use our one element of superiority, the air force, as in 1967? What difference is there now?"

Golda Meir looked straight at him. "What difference? I'm the one who knows about the difference. For a long time I thought that what had happened in 1967 was clear to everyone, that people knew that we'd been encircled, threatened, that we'd used our only option by striking first at their airfields. But I was wrong. Everybody criticized us for the Six-Day War. And Israel's isolation, which was bad enough then, has been growing steadily worse. What good came of our military exploits? Look at our position today! This time it's got to be perfectly clear for everybody. I understand your point of view very well. You have the right to expect a frank answer—it's no."

General Dayan would add later on, "We had been advised that, in launching an attack, we'd be destroying our relationship with the United States. So what do you expect?" General Rabin, Dayan's successor as chief of staff and the former ambassador to Washington, added, "If Israel had opened the hostilities, America would have ended its support. We knew that."

At 10 A.M. that Saturday, the ambassador of the United States handed a last message to Golda Meir. It confirmed everything. The tactics worked out by Kissinger and approved by Israeli leaders in exchange for future support remained unchanged. The message said wait, whatever you do, wait.

Late that morning, alone in her office which she kept locked, a seventy-five-year-old woman now had to search her heart and soul. Could she maintain her silence right up to.the end of the day of the Sabbath? Could she keep her people and her army immobilized until the very hour when their borders had been crossed, their territory invaded? Or, as she was later to recount, should she consider a preemptive strike and take the risk of confronting her one ally, the United States, with a fait accompli?

Golda Meir had weighed over and over what Kissinger had explained to her during the past few weeks: The battle for and the fate of the Middle East no longer depended strictly on the balance of military power or the occupation of territories. At stake now were oil and an embargo. That was the new field on which, she had to realize, everything could be lost. And nothing else counted. Nothing else should be allowed to count.

In 1973 Arab oil countries had the means to impose an embargo. America, with its own production and its reserves, could hold out for a long time. Europe and Japan could not. In the face of a true embargo, they would be forced to give in immediately, for they had neither the means to withstand an embargo nor to circumvent it. At stake was the cohesion of the industrial world.

Kissinger thought he saw his personal chance to cope with the situation and turn it to his advantage, even after the inevitable embargo was declared. He would stall for time, recreate a kind of unity, and exert counterpressures on the Persian Gulf. A *modus vivendi* was possible, he thought, but on one condition: under no circumstances could Israel lay herself open to a charge of aggression. Confidently he explained this to Golda Meir and Moshe Dayan, even though he knew the sacrifices that it would entail.

Kissinger showed them the other side of the question. The United States depended on Arab oil (in that autumn of 1973) for only 10 percent of its supplies. It was therefore hardly vulnerable to pressure. But Europe depended on Middle East oil for 75 percent of her needs, and Japan for 80 percent. These two pillars of the American system in the Atlantic and the Pacific had become worse than fragile—they had been undermined. And America would not consider breaking its alliances, Kissinger explained. That would mean disaster.

For this reason, he concluded, an appropriate response was necessary. Initially the Israeli Army would have to bear the brunt on the local front, but it would right the situation later. On the world front, that of energy, the United States would have to let Faisal impose his embargo, for he wanted to gain durable control of OPEC. America, not threatened by an oil shortage, would then emerge as the protector of its allies and negotiate directly with Saudi Arabia for the interests of the West as a whole. That was Kissinger's strategy.

If Kissinger was so sure it would work, it was because he held a trump card for the final showdown with the King of Saudi Arabia: the Shah of Iran.

The attack came on Saturday night. None of Israel's reservists had been called up. None of its outposts along the borders had been alerted. None of its planes were in the sky. Its lines, both north and south, along the Canal and on the Golan Heights, were pierced. The Jewish state was undergoing the first hours of defeat and retreat since its creation twenty-five years before.

On the day after the initial onslaught, Faisal's overall program, far away from the battlefield, began to gear up smoothly. The vicissitudes of the fight would be of major concern only briefly. The great game had begun.

On Sunday, October 7, the OPEC delegates began arriving at Vienna to attend a meeting with the representatives of the oil companies that had been planned a month earlier. Even before the slightest rumor of war, OPEC had announced that on October 7 the price of oil would be doubled—at least.

In a brief memo, Sheikh Yamani explained the reasons for this decision. The rate of inflation in the industrial countries from 1970 to 1973 was canceling out OPEC's benefits from the oil, both in terms of current income and in the value of its huge investments. This could not go on. Despite new prices, the market was so strained by rising demand that the spot prices in Rotterdam had already jumped to $5.00 a barrel at the end of September—while the official price remained set at only $2.50.

The ministers of the two most influential producer countries chaired the Vienna meeting: Yamani, the Saudi, and Amouzegar, the Iranian. This was a clever move on Faisal's part, for it showed the oil companies that OPEC solidarity was not strictly limited to the Arab countries.

Amouzegar was the first to speak. Ignoring the news from the battlefield, where there was bitter fighting, he talked oil, and stated at the outset that any agreement based on a figure lower than $6.00 was out of the question. These were the personal instructions of the Shah.

That evening he confided to a British observer, Anthony Sampson, "We became disgusted by their mercenary approach, bickering over every penny. Then we realized that the companies were now in a position of weakness even if they weren't admitting it. Deep down, they were beginning to panic at the idea that they might not be getting enough oil to supply their customers, no matter *what* price they paid for it. They no longer had the strength to resist."

Speaking after Amouzegar, Sheikh Yamani confirmed OPEC's decision to go to $6.oo a barrel. The oil companies were stunned. None of them was willing to accept an increase that high.

Yamani said later, "They thought they could start the bargaining as usual by offering us about forty to forty-five cents a barrel more, hoping to reach a compromise at an increase of about a dollar. They made a terrible mistake."

The representatives of the companies requested an adjournment to phone New York and London. Then two of them, delegated by the others—American George Piercy of Exxon and Frenchman André Bénard of Shell—expressed the wish to meet with Yamani alone at the Intercontinental Hotel. Hoping to get Yamani's support, they indicated that if a two-week delay were granted they might be able to come to terms on the price. But the Saudi had precise instructions from Faisal. He knew the sequence of upcoming events. Quickly he broke off the talks, refusing a delay "which would be utterly useless." He let Piercy and Bénard know that "it would be to their advantage to be more understanding" right away, before the Vienna meeting ended on the following night. For the time being he would go no further.

The following morning when the representatives of the big companies arrived at the conference hall, they found no one. During the night, Sheikh Yamani and the other oil ministers had left to attend the meeting of the Organization of Arab Petroleum Exporting Countries (OAPEC) in Kuwait, on Tuesday, October

9. The break had finally come. There would be no more dialogue with the companies. They would have to negotiate directly with governments.

Only London's *Financial Times* devoted a few lines on page 13 to the event, an event which would shake the foundations of the world economy. Reporters from the world press were all covering the military conflict in Israel—as if it were still a time when arms determined the future.

In the meeting hall of the Sheraton Hotel in downtown Kuwait, OAPEC was holding the most important meeting in its history.

The ministers of Saudi Arabia and Kuwait opened the session with an immediate demand for a general embargo, a proposal that caught many delegates off guard. The discussions grew heated. They tried to gauge the impact of this crucial decision. There was some wavering. At that point, as Faisal and Sadat had arranged in advance, the arrival of Egypt's new Oil Minister, Mohammad Hillal, was announced. His plane had just come in from Cairo.

Hillal had risen rapidly in his country's governmental ranks after his return from the United States with a degree in chemical engineering. A senior adviser to Egypt's President, he was also an excellent speaker. He brought to the meeting a personal message from Sadat calling for complete Arab solidarity. In particular, the Egyptian leader was urging an embargo for that very afternoon, in the name of those who were dying in battle against Israel along a front that widened with each passing hour.

Hillal was driven from the airport in his Kuwaiti colleague's powerful American car, preceded by an official escort, along the broad avenues of the clean modern city, brightened by the pastel colors of the famous double-domed water towers. In less than ten minutes he was in the Sheraton's lobby, identical to those in Houston or Dallas. When he reached the conference hall, all his colleagues rose to their feet.

Deeply moved, Hillal had time only to say a few words— nothing more was necessary. Without a moment's delay, Sheikh Yamani put to a vote the motion proposing that the Arab heads of state decree an oil embargo and invite OPEC as a whole to join in this move. There was neither deliberation nor abstention. The decision was unanimously adopted.

Iraq was the first to act. Along with restrictions on deliveries, that country also announced the nationalization of Exxon and Mobil Oil installations in Iraq's Basra oil field.

On the following day, Saudi Arabia, Kuwait and the United Arab Emirates jointly announced an immediate cutback in their production and the gradual halting of shipments to the ports of Europe, America and Japan.

In Washington, President Nixon was living through the lonely hours of the Watergate affair. He emerged from seclusion for a few moments to chair an emergency session of the National Security Council, which decided to declare a general nuclear alert—the first since the Cuban Missile Crisis of 1962. The alert was a warning to the Russians to stay out of the Middle East battleground. At the same meeting it was also decided to prepare a presidential message to the nation on the austerity measures required by the embargo.

On the following day an exhausted, hardly recognizable Nixon appeared on the TV screens of the United States. He spoke about the state of the nation at a tragic moment in world history.

"The United States of America," Nixon began, stumbling over the printed text he was reading because he was no longer in condition to memorize the words, "the United States will have to face the harshest energy curtailments that it has ever experienced, including those of World War II." He sketched out the main lines of a series of measures to be placed before Congress without delay—a fifty-mile-an-hour speed limit on the roads, reduced heating in all buildings and the preparation of a fuel-rationing plan.

Senator William Fulbright, chairman of the Foreign Relations Committee, was the first to ask for the floor. Known for his moderation, his openness to the outside world, his support for great international causes, the Senator expressed himself in unusual terms:

"Fellow Senators, it's my duty to tell you what I think without beating around the bush. The Arab oil producers are militarily insignificant in today's world. They are something like weak gazelles in the jungle of lions. We should remind them of this fact so that they make no mistake about it. They would be exposing themselves to terrible risks if things got to the point where they really threatened the economic and social balance of the great industrial powers, ours in particular. They must realize before it's too late what would hit them if this ever happened."

The fact that Fulbright had criticized the use of military force throughout the entire Vietnam War, under Johnson as well as under Nixon, lent a special impact to his words and tone of voice. Two years before, he had written a clear and convincing book, *The Arrogance of Power,* in which he denounced the illusion that America could dominate the world, settling problems everywhere through its intervention, taking upon itself the task of imposing international order. "Such presumption and arrogance," he wrote, "could only lead to the worst disappointments and to catastrophe."

Confronted with OPEC and the embargo, he appeared to change his mind. The use of force that Fulbright advocated on the first day of the embargo would soon become a respectable "option" even among liberals who had deplored its use elsewhere. In Southeast Asia only politics had been at stake. Now, in the Middle East, oil was at stake—and oil was a matter of survival.

On the other side of the Atlantic, Britain's prestigious business weekly *The Economist* published a solemn editorial that led off a special issue: "The idea is absurd that North America, Western Europe, and Japan—which possess about 70 percent of the world's industrial power—will agree to let their economic growth be halted by Arab potentates who between them rule about 1 percent of the world's population."

This "absurdity" nevertheless gained ground—and rapidly —in the minds of leaders in Japan and Europe. They were gripped by panic.

The Japanese government reacted first by announcing "an immediate initial reduction of 10 percent on deliveries of oil to the following industries: automobile, steel, electric machinery, aluminum, cement, tires, synthetic fibers, paper and petrochemicals." At a Cabinet meeting, Prime Minister Fukuda reported that if the embargo were to last more than a few weeks, Japanese industry would be brought to a standstill.

In Germany too the reaction was quick. On that last weekend in October, the Federal Republic's famous highway system, the Autobahn, was deserted.

On November 15, heads of state and government from the Common Market's nine members met in Copenhagen for an extraordinary session. They listened to a report presented by their experts on "the aggravation of inflation, trade deficits and unemployment foreseeable as a result of the embargo." The report predicted that the number of workers idled in the European Economic Community the following year would be four million if the embargo continued. In less than two hours the representatives of the nine agreed on a declaration "of European identity" regarding Middle East questions and called for "a direct dialogue between Europe and the Arab countries."

Three days later, still in Copenhagen, the EEC ministers of foreign affairs received emissaries from the Arab countries. The session was chaired by Danish Prime Minister Joergensen. He led the oil-state envoys into the Danish parliament's largest assembly hall and began his address by apologizing "for the fact that it was so cold in that room which, like the rest of the building, was no longer being heated—for reasons that everyone knows."

On leaving, the Arab delegation held a news conference. Its spokesman was Algerian Minister Abdel Aziz Bouteflika. He declared himself satisfied: "I can assure you that contacts between Europe and us will not cease. This meeting has been a very good start toward what can be called an 'intensification' of relations between Europe and the Arab countries."

Intensification of contacts was the least the Europeans were aiming for in their discussions. What they wanted was an end to the embargo as soon as possible. Their reserves were dwindling, prices were rising and production was falling rapidly. They simply wanted to know what was expected of them in exchange for oil.

Before leaving Copenhagen, the Arab emissaries received a visit from the president of the EEC's council. He had come to speak to them, he said, "man to man and in friendship." His message was the following: "Don't you see that we can do nothing in the Middle East? The embargo is actually aimed at America. But America is scarcely affected, and it's Europe that you're hitting. Tell us what you hope to achieve."

Impressed by the European Community's helplessness, the Arab ministers flew to Vienna to report to their colleagues. The OPEC secretary general announced at the close of the oil ministers' meeting that the Organization "had decided to reward the European Community for its attitude and to make a gesture."

The gesture was by no means extravagant. The machinery set up by OAPEC to enforce the embargo consisted of reducing deliveries by 5 percent each month. OAPEC then announced that "with regard to the month of December this reduction will no longer apply to the countries of the European Community." Holland, which had been alone in rallying to the side of the United States, was made an exception.

Europe offered no more resistance. Japan was next.

Japan was the most threatened of all nations. Knuckling under to OPEC pressure meant risking something that for thirty years had seemed inconceivable—a break with Japan's protector, the United States. But rejecting the Arabs would invite disaster. Without regular, daily replenishment by the supertankers that sailed halfway round the world from the Strait of Hormuz to the port of Yokohama, Japanese industry would collapse.

The Japanese Prime Minister sent an emissary to the King of Saudi Arabia and the Emir of Kuwait—the mysterious and skillful chairman of Japan's only oil company, Arabian Oil, Sohei Mizuno, who knew both Arab leaders well.

A man who said little, Mizuno traveled regularly between Tokyo and the Arabian Gulf. Whenever he returned to his homeland he was received immediately by the president of the Keidanren, Japan's forceful manufacturers' association, and by the Prime Minister. This time, Mizuno came back from Riyadh and Kuwait with a message that shook up the nation's two most powerful men: Unless Japan announced its solidarity with the Arabs that week, before the next OAPEC meeting, it would be deprived of oil supplies. There were only three days left.

On November 21 Sheikh Yamani declared: "Japan must define its policy. If it wishes to be exempted from a further oil supply reduction for the month of December it must follow the European Community countries. Japan must endeavor to show that she can be considered a friend of the Arab cause, and declare her readiness to support it."

On the eve of the Arab meeting, the new Japanese Prime Minister declared before the parliament that his country was willing to reach an agreement with the Arabs "with a view to supporting Arab policy in the UN regarding special assistance to the Palestinians, as well as direct economic and technical cooperation with the developing countries of the Arab world as a whole."

The primary objectives had been achieved: Europe had yielded; so had Japan. This is what Faisal had been expecting. But so had Henry Kissinger.

Now that he had a clear field before him, the Secretary of State was ready to make his entrance.

KISSINGER HAD WAITED PATIENTLY for the right moment. He was now the only person with the power and the freedom of action to deal personally with the one man who controlled events—the King of Saudi Arabia.

For months before the October war, Kissinger rarely left Washington. He put his personal plane, Air Force II, on standby status. When the Egyptians and the Syrians invaded Israel he requested an audience with Faisal in Riyadh. Another round of the game was beginning.

The United States, still the strongest industrial and military Western power, waded into the strange fray. The situation was exactly the one Kissinger had imagined as soon as he spotted the word "embargo" in an interview given to the *Washington Post* by Yamani several months before. All the conditions that he would need in order to act had been met. He was ready for a showdown.

King Faisal, however, even before the Secretary of State landed in Saudi Arabia, had sent Yamani to Washington to address the American people from the National Press Club. Before a forest of TV and newsreel cameras Yamani declared, "The changes that have taken place in the world oil situation will have repercussions for all aspects of life: industry, economy, finance and politics. The new world situation will scarcely resemble the earlier one. The power to make decisions regarding energy, a power that for so long belonged to the Western companies, is now entirely in the hands of the producing countries. Beyond oil, there is the question of the transfer of financial power that will begin to reverse the situation. Up to now it was a one-way street—toward the industrial countries. Now we are going to witness a radical reversal for all countries concerned. The balance of power in the world will never again be what it was.''

Kissinger read Yamani's statement before he met with Faisal. But he was hardly concerned by the price of oil or by financial transfers. He had a very different question on his mind: On whom could the United States rely as military guardian of the Gulf against Soviet intervention?

Using the tactics of Metternich in his Mideast negotiations, Kissinger had one kind of truth for Sadat in Egypt, another for Assad in Syria, still another for Faisal in Saudi Arabia—but he saved his real secrets for the Shah of Iran. Like Metternich, Kissinger felt sure that these statesmen distrusted one another too much to exchange their secrets. In this way he could put himself in the center of all discussion and retain the upper hand.

Kissinger was successful for several months following the war. When the leaders of the Gulf states did happen to exchange a few confidences, each concluded simply that the other had misunderstood what Kissinger had said. But after two or three slips of this kind, a growing number of indiscretions began to generate a certain mistrust among the Arabs.

This mistrust grew to anger when it became clear that Kissinger was not seeking any real agreement on oil policy. Oil was simply not his problem. He had only one obsession: that Iran become a military bastion powerful enough to "protect the oil fields" from the USSR. To Kissinger only the Iranian Army was capable of doing this.

As far back as 1971 and 1972, Kissinger had had talks with the Shah and had committed himself to providing Iran with all the modern weapons available from the United States. As the Shah's revenues from oil swelled year by year, his appetite for the most sophisticated weapons kept pace. In fact, he no longer bothered even to calculate the price of those arms.

By 1973, this deal between the two men gave rise to a disturbing problem: Iran no longer had enough money to pay for such
fabulous weapons. The Shah could not foot the bill anymore.
The solution was handed to Kissinger and the Shah in 1974 by
the embargo, which tightened the oil market to the point where
prices could be pushed up almost at will. This could allow the
Shah to stay financially afloat—and continue to order U.S.
weapons.

America, Kissinger told the Shah, would not balk when the
Shah asked for a price hike, any price hike. By the end of 1974,
half of all United States arms sales were being funneled into a
single nation, Iran.

The other cornerstone on which Kissinger hoped to build his
Middle East policies was the kingdom of Saudi Arabia. Kissinger wanted Riyadh to use its growing financial power to support
the sagging dollar and help balance the ballooning government
deficit. That is why Secretary of the Treasury Simon was sent
to Taif in 1975 to ask for Saudi help on a regular basis. Following that visit, the kingdom's central bank, the SAMA (Saudi
Arabian Monetary Agency), bought a sizeable quantity of
American government securities each month.

During one talk with Kissinger that year, King Faisal told him
that he hoped to go on supporting the dollar for the time being
—since it was the only reserve currency for the Gulf countries
—but he wouldn't be able to continue if frequent "shocks"
continued to plague the oil market. Accordingly, he urged Kissinger to put serious pressure on the Shah to stop pushing for
ever higher prices.

James Akins, ambassador to Riyadh at that time, wrote:
"The Saudis were very uneasy. The King's emissaries came
constantly to see me saying that Kissinger must absolutely put
pressure on the Shah if we were to avoid economic crises and
social tensions over the 'wild' prices of oil. How is it that he
can't manage to do that?"

In the autumn of 1974 Kissinger made another visit to the
royal palace, to keep Faisal abreast of American diplomatic

progress toward a peaceful settlement in the Middle East. In exchange for U.S. action, he asked if the King would be willing to institute a unilateral reduction in the price of Saudi oil so as to stabilize the market as a whole and avoid panic over prices, which were beginning to have obvious and catastrophic consequences.

After taking off from Riyadh in Air Force II, Kissinger told the reporters accompanying him, "I found the Saudis very understanding. They share our analysis of the need to stabilize oil prices by means of gradual but moderate increases. We sincerely hope that the other producers will follow the kingdom's example."

Kissinger was on his way to Iran, where he held a day-long talk with the Shah at his Saadabad summer palace. They discussed the region's military questions, as well as new equipment for the Iranian Army. *Not a word was said about oil.* When the Shah mentioned in passing that he would need more substantial revenues in coming months, Kissinger acquiesced.

Shortly thereafter, Faisal's advisers received a report on this meeting—delivered by the Shah himself.

The Saudi sovereign could hardly believe it. But it wasn't the first time that this kind of information had reached him. He now began to have serious second thoughts about the State Department's policy, the Shah's ambitions, the balance of economic and military forces in the Middle East, the region's very stability and its future.

He understood that a very high-powered game was being played and that he was being kept out of it. And he disapproved thoroughly of its ground rules. He did not want the Persian Gulf to become the center of military confrontations.

Kissinger returned once more to Riyadh. The price of oil had gone up for the fourth time in six months. He scarcely paid attention. It wasn't his problem.

The King asked Yamani to meet the Secretary of State at the airport to try to find out what was at the root of the American's thinking. Yamani brought Kissinger to the royal palace, accompanied by Ambassador Akins. The sovereign no longer had the slightest doubt about Kissinger's double game with the Shah. He demanded firmly that America take a public position against the Shah's "oil policy," which was breaking up OPEC's unity and threatening the political stability of the region as a whole.

Anthony Sampson, who witnessed part of the encounter, wrote: "I watched the meeting between the two men in the King's big office in Riyadh. With his fascinating face, the bitter lines at the corners of his mouth, his penetrating stare, Faisal did not make the slightest effort to greet his guest [Kissinger] who came toward him smiling. The King told him in no uncertain terms that he was disappointed and that he considered Kissinger's diplomacy a failure."

Sampson could not stay any longer. Akins later supplemented Sampson's information: the King had confirmed Saudi Arabia's determination to keep oil price hikes very moderate, knowing the risks of a "wild" policy. At the same time, the Saudis were determined to use the embargo weapon again if America and the West failed to begin dealing seriously with the "Middle East question."

Three days later, Kissinger joined the Shah—this time in Switzerland. The Shah had received his education at the best schools in Geneva and Zurich, and loved to ski in the Alps. He had even bought a charming chalet in Saint-Moritz, where he spent long and frequent vacations. Tanned and smiling after three weeks in the mountains, he arrived by helicopter.

The meeting with Kissinger was warm. American Ambassador to Iran Richard Helms, former director of the Central Intelligence Agency, also attended. He said later on, "The question of oil prices was never raised by the two men. On that question Kissinger told the Shah to do what seemed best to him."

Later that year Yamani wrote a personal letter to the Secretary of the Treasury in Washington: "I should like you to know that we aren't alone in drawing a conclusion that we wouldn't have expected in the light of current events. I am referring to the fact that American policy doesn't seem at all geared to a moderation of oil-price increases. There are even those among us who feel that, for political reasons which remain partially obscure, American diplomacy consistently supports those who demand the speeding-up of price increases. We are no longer convinced by the American government's public statements to the contrary."

Nixon had by now been replaced in the White House by Gerald Ford, who gave Kissinger an ever freer hand to do as he pleased with the Middle East, oil, the Shah's army and the game with Saudi Arabia.

By the end of Kissinger's reign, in the winter of 1976, his policy had profoundly poisoned the Middle East's relations with the West and largely contributed to sealing the Shah's fate. Political chaos, financial chaos, social chaos all would follow. And the United States and the entire world would soon be able to measure the extent of the disaster.

O N THE EVENING OF THE SECOND DAY of the now famous Taif seminar, the oil ministers reached agreement on the main lines of their report, i.e., worldwide redistribution of income and, above all, the transfer of technological capacity. Technology was to be the real price of oil from now on.

They decided to meet again in Algiers late in the summer, and in Geneva in the fall. If necessary, they were prepared to meet a third time; it would be in Bali, Indonesia, in the winter, and again in Geneva and Vienna in the spring and summer of 1981. They had to be ready, with the Third World, for the upcoming dialogue in order to "change the economic order radically."

After devoting twenty years to gaining control over oil and its revenues—and succeeding—the "Yamani committee" had reached a new agreement for a "leap forward" toward a world economic policy.

The ministers ended the session. With these weighty problems resting on their shoulders, they had the feeling that the course of world events for years to come would be tied to the forty-five pages of the Taif Report and to the "international order" it described. As the sun was setting behind the mountains in Taif most of them left on a pilgrimage to Mecca.

Mecca is the center of life for Islam's millions of people. They turn to face it three times a day for prayer wherever they live around the world. Every Moslem man is commanded to visit it at least once during his lifetime. The city and its holy Grand Mosque are the very core of Islam and are held in trust by the rulers of Saudi Arabia, who reap the symbolic strength and stability that come with its sacred protectorate.

But the symbolism of Mecca also makes the Saudis vulnerable in the modern world. The massive changes sweeping through the Arabian Peninsula as ancient nomadic tribes use their petrodollars to convert themselves into twentieth-century peoples spark their own reaction. Just as the leaders of Asia, Africa and Latin America must face the boiling cauldron of social upheaval unleashed by development, so, too, must Saudi Arabia and other oil-producing nations face the masses. That which unites the OPEC countries and the Third World is the race to survive and harness social change—a race they now seek to speed up through the Taif Report. And nothing so highlights the need for speed as the shattering events in Mecca in 1979 when the holy city became a symbol of revolt against the Saudi rulers.

At dawn on a very cold November morning in 1979, the immense mosque of Mecca was already crowded with more than ten thousand pilgrims. Suddenly they were deafened by an explosion. Five hundred men armed with grenades and machine guns came from nowhere to flank the legendary Black Stone of Mecca, al-Hadjar al-Aswad. Gunmen burst in through each doorway and, with bullhorns, ordered the crowd to stand still and remain silent. Thirty men rushed to the top of the outer minarets of the Grand Mosque commanding the entire square.

Their twenty-six-year-old leader took up a position where he could be seen and heard by all the pilgrims. Someone handed him a bullhorn. When he introduced himself, the crowd was stunned. He was a pure Saudi, and an Oteiba, a member of one of the first tribes in the kingdom to help Ibn Saud take the throne.

Juhayman al-Oteibi shouted his name proudly, well aware of the effect that it would produce. He told the worshipers that he was the leader of a legion of Saudi volunteers, accompanied by militants from Yemen, Kuwait and Egypt; his companions even included members of the royal family's illustrious "White Guard," the personal bodyguards of the King. One of his group, he said, was Mohammad al-Qahtani, who had been designated by the Prophet to "save the Kingdom from materialistic corruption, by means of an Islamic revival."

Al-Oteibi and al-Qahtani were names well known to Saudi security agencies and to everyone in the government. The pair had been arrested several times for political activities during the two preceding years, and each time, to the dismay of the authorities, had been released at the demand of the mullahs, Saudi Arabia's keepers of the faith.

As the rebels took over the mosque, fragmentary news reports began to reach the office of Prince Turki al-Faisal, son of the dead King Faisal and brother of Prince Saudi al-Faisal, Minister of Foreign Affairs.

Turki, Faisal's second son, is in charge of Saudi Arabia's intelligence operations. Secretive and pious, Turki Faisal works ten hours a day in a highly secluded place, far away from Riyadh's great ministry buildings with their modern communications. Turki Faisal's office is so remote and unpretentious that no taxi driver can ever find it. The building is unmarked. Whenever he sets up an appointment, he sends one of his own cars to fetch the visitor. The entrance to the building looks like a small military headquarters in the provinces and overlooks a dark, narrow street. There Turki Faisal can work without being disturbed. In addition to a vast room furnished simply, decorated only with a photo of his father and the green Saudi flag with its crossed sabers, his suite includes a smaller room in which he reads.

Turki Faisal has a warm personality; his manners are simple, straightforward. Interested in everything, he keeps abreast of events by endless reading. He clearly believes that Saudi Arabia is the guardian of a world and that its responsibilities grow with each passing day. Although he keeps in close touch with key members of the government, he himself almost never stirs from his place. While the Saudi ministers travel far and wide, he stays at home.

When the phone in Turki al-Faisal's office rang at 6:30 A.M. on the day of the insurrection, he first alerted Prince Fadh, the Prime Minister, then went to meet him at once at his palace. Together, the two men began to command the operations on a round-the-clock basis. First they isolated Saudi Arabia from the rest of the world. All telecommunications were forbidden, both incoming and outgoing, and the airports were closed to all traffic. Telex lines were then disconnected by the central system. Before 8:30 A.M. the usual clacking of Teletype messages between Riyadh and the rest of the world was replaced by total silence. It was a silence that spread fear in the other capitals, fear no one will ever forget. It had happened so quickly, only a few months after the Shah's disintegration in Iran and the sudden accession of the Ayatollah Khomeini in Teheran. Was Saudi Arabia going to be next?

In one time zone after another, governments were placed on the alert. Saudi Arabia remained silent.

For ten interminable hours, the outside world knew nothing. There, in the heart of the Middle East, the entire world economy might be on the verge of collapse. The next morning, a few words filtered out. These were hardly reassuring: "Armed uprising in Mecca."

At the end of two weeks, the five hundred heavily armed rebels were liquidated by Riyadh's security forces. The job was a difficult one, for they had to avoid slaughtering thousands of pilgrims while exchanging fire with the insurgents. By early December it was over. The Minister of the Interior explained the high death toll by saying, "In the first few days of the criminal incident, the bandit group that carried out the operation hadn't hesitated to fire all its weapons and in every direction, wounding and killing many men and women inside the sacred temple and in the square surrounding it."

The greatest casualty of the "criminal incident" (the term officially used) was the security and stability for which the kingdom of Saudi Arabia had been known. Now everybody was afraid. Just how deep did the sickness go? Could Saudi Arabia still be counted on and, if so, for how long?

"How fragile it all is," exclaimed an Iranian Minister—who knew at first hand. Even if Saudi Arabia was able to return to calm and order, the bid for power made in the heart of the kingdom was not an isolated episode. It was, on the contrary, an ominous sign of the tremendous difficulties facing all of the oil-producing countries of the region.

The leaders of OPEC get very angry when Westerners display skepticism about their "so-called" alliance with the Third World. Westerners see this alliance as only a facade, a clever maneuver for OPEC countries to ease their consciences. They see everything in it except one simple truth: oil countries *are underdeveloped countries,* with all of their economic, social, human and political weaknesses. The Arabian Gulf is faced with a colossal transfer of wealth that flows to it every day from the entire world, and it is not equipped to convert this capital into human and economic development.

For eight years, from the first oil crisis of 1970 until the Shah's downfall, most OPEC countries have done little except accumulate revenues in Western banks—where they vanish. It is what has been discreetly called "recycling."

By 1978 the situation was critical: OPEC's financial surplus had melted under the heat of inflation; the real price of exported oil had declined in value with the fall of the dollar; and, at the same time, the prices of industrial and food imports had risen sharply. The gains of previous years were slipping away. OPEC countries had to change their policies. The Taif Report is vital to make those changes coherent and give them a long-term goal. OPEC has no margin for maneuver. Its oil reserves will be dissipated within one generation.

The Algerian Mohammed Bedjaoui, former ambassador to Paris and now his country's representative at the United Nations, expresses the predicament as follows: "Our states are living under a sentence. They risk having only two, perhaps three pathetic decades of existence ahead of them—*if, in sowing oil, they do not reap development.*"

In recent years, the same conclusions have been reached by two very different men: Belkacem Nabi, the Algerian Oil Minister, and Professor Karl Schiller, former Minister of Finance of West Germany.

In the summer of 1980, lunching in the sun on the terrace of his offices which overlook the harbor of Algiers, Nabi discussed his thoughts just before the meeting in Taif. With him were two colleagues, officials of the Algerian National Society of Oil and Gas, and two friends from France.

In contrast to the deep concerns he expressed, Nabi showed great calm and simplicity, and projected an image of a devoted and competent servant of the people.

Nabi explained: "Since the end of the war, in 1962, Algeria's population has gone from ten to twenty million. Innumerable young people there are all asking, at the same time, for housing, education, training, work, jobs with a future. Algeria has oil reserves for no more than about fifteen years. So the problem to be solved is gigantic—to use this very short time and the little oil that we have left to turn Algeria, already drained by the war of independence and the exodus of the French colonizers, into a developed industrial country that can support thirty million men and women."

At Taif, Nabi spoke for the Third World, for if anyone is part of it he is. To walk with him in the suburbs of Algiers, among the endless procession of children on their way to school or the stadium, is to be in the heart of the Third World, and in the heart of OPEC.

Nabi was therefore an ardent advocate of OPEC's "long-term plan," to get the industrial nations to pay for oil not only with money but with unlimited "transfers of technology," which would hasten the development of the Third World.

Nabi also served as a permanent intermediary between the richest and most conservative Gulf countries (Saudi Arabia and Kuwait) and the most underdeveloped and most revolutionary (Iran, Libya) regimes.

On the morning of his last day in Taif, the day after the pilgrimage to Mecca, Sheikh Yamani went to a working breakfast at Nabi's villa. Having seen Calderón-Berti off at the airport, he and Nabi set up the summer and fall meetings by going over once again the delicate points of the long-term report.

They agreed with the basic thrust of the report: the new distribution of resources and productive capacity between the North and the South in exchange for oil.

The other personality to play a major role in helping to shape Arab economic thinking was the German Karl Schiller.

After Ludwig Erhard, it is Schiller who is most responsible for West Germany's economic miracle. For seven years he was Minister of Economy and Finance under Willy Brandt. He left the government because of a disagreement over monetary policy, and became a professor of economics. Years later he was sought out by Saudi Arabia and other Gulf countries when economic and social tensions began to endanger their stability. He was asked to become the adviser of the leading governments of the Persian Gulf. A man of the North, with bright eyes, few gestures, and precision, Professor Schiller hesitated a long time before accepting such an unexpected mission and plunging into the din and torrid heat of the Persian Gulf.

Schiller in 1970 helped put together the system of "floating rates of exchange," which replaced the postwar monetary system, and he was more aware than anyone else of the fragility of the international monetary and industrial order. He could not refuse the request. And for a Social Democrat, the investment of part of the fantastic oil revenues for the benefit of the people of these countries was something that could not be undertaken too soon. Schiller went to Riyadh.

For months he lived in a room in the Intercontinental Hotel.

Every morning a car from the Ministry of Finance or the Ministry of Planning came for him. The great capacity for work, the integrity and detachment and the charm displayed by this apostle of modern economics earned him the friendship of the leading technocrats in power in Riyadh. Abah al-Khail, Minister of Finance, Hisham Nazer, Minister of the Plan, Ghasi al-Gosaibi, Minister of Industry, were more than colleagues for him. They became friends.

Schiller advised them to proceed very gradually along the road to industrialization, "by beginning with the infrastructure first so as not to take the risks that Iran has taken." Schiller said this three years before the fall of the Shah.

Schiller trembled at the thought that Saudi Arabia's ports could quickly be blocked, and its few towns submerged by the innumerable projects that industrialists from all over the world proposed to Riyadh daily. He called for restraint. But the Saudis couldn't resist the temptations of fast development.

So Karl Schiller saw huge industrial complexes rise from the east on the Gulf, to the west on the Red Sea, around two small towns: Jubail and Yanbu.

In 1978 Jubail was a fishing town of three thousand inhabitants. By the end of 1980 it was an industrial city of more than fifty thousand inhabitants. It is expected to reach 200,000 before 1987 and 300,000 in twenty years. Housing, factories, roads, railroads, loading platforms, equipment—everything must come from the outside, and be built in the desert.

In Yanbu, at the other end of the peninsula, where two thousand fishermen and pearl divers lived two years ago, there are now twenty thousand workers employed. And 100,000 inhabitants are expected there within three years in what is rapidly becoming Saudi Arabia's second industrial metropolis.

Five giant petrochemical complexes are under construction at Jubail and Yanbu, which will be linked by two huge pipelines for oil and gas. There are also five oil refineries, two modern steelworks and three fertilizer plants.

Around these two gigantic work sites are rows of military camps where thousands of tents shelter the foreign workers who had to be recruited. Among them are Koreans, Yemenites, Palestinians, Malians, Egyptians and Sudanese.

Hisham Nazer, Minister of the Plan, explained the huge projects this way: "People believe that we are rich in Saudi Arabia. But we are not really. We are selling oil which will not be replaced. And what will we have left? So we need industries. And we need them before 'oil power' loses its power—very fast."

Following a new appraisal of Saudi Arabia's problems, Nazer decided to shift gears. In a meeting at the University of Riyadh, at the end of 1980, he concluded: "Saudi Arabia should reduce the number of projects and expenditures for factories and infrastructures of communication and urbanization to direct our priorities to *education and training*. Our next 'plan for development' will be centered on exploiting what we lack most, human capital."

At a seminar in Zurich devoted to Arabian Gulf problems held around the same time, Karl Schiller went further:

> To attain the objectives of a developed economy, the Saudis must learn that it is not enough to watch foreign managers and technicians: They must take their place. Local manpower composed only of merchants, bankers, store owners, is not sufficient. There are not enough business leaders either. The "noncommissioned officers" of industry must be available to assume the vital posts of plant managers, foremen, etc. So there must be a massive, carefully adapted training and educational effort.

This new outlook spread in the Gulf. Kuwait's Ali Khalifa al-Saba clarified it: "As long as creative outlets are not proposed for our oil revenues, it will be necessary for us to curb production. Otherwise, we will be signing away our entire future."

Two years ago, Kuwait began reducing its production from

2.5 million to a little over 1 million barrels a day. And if there is no constructive attempt to come to grips with the fundamental problems and goals underlying the Taif Report, all of the Gulf's production may be even more drastically reduced with disastrous consequences for the rest of the world.

I N 1977, the CIA began to receive a whole string of reports about Siberia. For a long time the CIA had perfected intelligence teams specializing in industry and economics to the point where they had become better than its military research teams. The agency's reputation has seriously suffered from errors in strategic evaluations over the years and from charges of political manipulation by the White House, but no one has yet meddled with its economic analyses. Experts place great confidence in them.

In the mid-'70s, agents began to analyze information received from Tyumen, the most desolate, most inaccessible region in Russia. A vast, icy area, largely unknown, Tyumen is in fact the second largest reservoir of oil in the world after the Persian Gulf. The largest Russian oil field under production, Samotiar, is at Tyumen. In 1974, thanks to Samotiar and a few other important deposits, the Soviet Union became the world's leading producer of oil. By 1979, Soviet production was about 11.5 million barrels a day—more than Saudi Arabia. That, in turn, made the USSR one of the biggest exporters of oil: 3 million barrels a day.

Soviet oil reserves were thus large enough to supply Russia's army, its industry and most of the Eastern-bloc countries (at the world market price) and still leave enough over to export to the West, especially to use on the "spot" markets of Rotterdam. These exports were crucial to Moscow because they earned precious hard currency needed to pay for imports of food and industrial equipment.

It was at Samotiar that the first hints of something going wrong were detected. The high pressure in the wells, which allowed for simple and profitable pumping, began to decline. The same phenomenon soon appeared in other fields of the Tyumen region, indicating that the entire chain of wells under exploitation was nearing exhaustion. Since Moscow hadn't begun exploiting other reserves in the vast territory, it became clear that in the years ahead the USSR's production would level off while the Soviet bloc's consumption continued to rise.

The CIA estimated that the annual growth of Soviet production, which was around 10 percent in the 1960s, had declined to a growth of 5 percent in the 1970s, and then to less than 4 percent in 1979. At the same time, the Soviet bloc continued to increase its energy consumption while Moscow accelerated its exports. Russia made billions on the oil markets thanks to the efforts of OPEC. Exploiting Iran's difficulties, the Soviets began to supply oil to many of the Western European countries, especially West Germany.

The CIA's report indicated that sometime in the 1980s the USSR would become an importer of oil. Specialized Soviet publications confirm these indications.

The CIA said:

> Our estimate now indicates that in the mid-80s, the USSR will have ceased to be an exporting power, that the import needs of the Eastern bloc as a whole will increase to 3.5 million barrels a day, at least. If the recent difficulties indicated in the Russian oil fields should become prolonged, the needs for oil imports could even rise to 4.5 million barrels per day.

A whole series of events were triggered by this information.

In an attempt to make Congress accept the gravity of the oil crisis, President Carter, in 1979, made the CIA's secret report public. It had a tremendous effect. The Soviet Union would soon be a new and formidable customer on the oil markets in the Persian Gulf. In addition to political reasons, Russia now had economic interests in the region. This could lead the USSR to exert pressure in the strategic location of the Gulf countries as its vital oil needs increased.

Without waiting for the 1980s, Moscow began to tell the leaders of Eastern Europe to begin to make commercial contacts with OPEC countries. Moscow told its Eastern-bloc satellites that it would no longer supply all their oil needs.

Kuwait announced that it would not discriminate between oil customers as long as they paid the official price. Saudi Arabia's Foreign Minister, Saudi Faisal, declared that his country would deliver to the East as well as to the West. Libya and Iran soon adopted the same policy.

Nevertheless, the problem was not solved. Washington was faced with the full-blown dilemma of how to deal with the prospect of an energy-dependent Soviet Union.

As always, with regard to the challenge of Soviet-American coexistence, two fundamentally different attitudes emerged in the United States. One was to gloat over Russia's economic problems, and if possible to aggravate them, in the hope that the Soviet system would explode from the inside and that we in the West would remain unscathed by such an explosion.

The other strategy was an effort to draw the poison out of the East-West confrontation by engaging the Soviet Union in a constructive dialogue, and by knitting a web of economic agreements with new forms of commercial and industrial cooperation. These are the terms in which international lawyer Samuel Pisar has repeatedly defined the historic dilemma of East-West coexistence before policymakers in America and Europe and in his new book, *Of Blood and Hope*.

This crucial debate has raged indecisively for more than three decades among the political and economic leaders of the West.

Today, it takes on an added dimension not only because America and Russia must find a way to live together less dangerously, but because of the specific problem of oil, coupled with the strategic situation of the Gulf. "Given the likelihood of increased pressure on supplies, prices and the political soft spots of the Middle East, are we really enhancing the security of America, Europe and Japan," asks Pisar, "by denying an energy-hungry Russia the technology that would enable her to get her own oil from her own, plentiful Siberian reserves?"

Without consulting its European and Japanese allies or the OPEC countries, the Carter Administration, which had long kept one foot on the accelerator and the other on the brake in regard to this vital issue, made a fateful decision. A few months after Chairman Brezhnev declared before the Supreme Soviet that the USSR would not hesitate to import foreign equipment and knowhow for drilling and exploration, National Security Adviser Brzezinski persuaded President Carter to embargo the sale of oil technology to the USSR and other Eastern-bloc countries.

This decision may have long-lasting effects. It can prevent, for many years, the exploitation of the vast reserves of oil that have been discovered in the Soviet Union, beyond Tyumen itself, under the Arctic Ocean, in the Barents Sea and around the Caspian Sea.

Geologists say that access to these reserves is much more difficult and costly than was exploitation of Tyumen, and is beyond current Soviet technology. The USSR's technological backwardness in this vital sector is so immense that it cannot be overcome before the 1990s without the cooperation of the West.

Arthur Meyerhoff of Tulsa, Oklahoma, a specialist who has been studying the USSR's oil situation for almost thirty years, considers the level of Soviet technology in the exploration of oil to be thirty years behind the West. He gives the following information: "The Western companies' geophysical equipment enables them to bore to depths of from 15 to 25 kilometers under the earth, in search of deep layers of oil. That of the Soviets has never gone beyond a capacity of 5 kilometers, which makes them blind to all deep exploration and, consequently, to the study of underground layers of regions other than Tyumen."

Laurent Zwadyinski, an expert of Petroconsultants S.A. of Geneva, concludes in his latest study that the Soviets know the theories that govern seismic methods of oil drilling but they are far from being capable of manufacturing the equipment.

The new Soviet thirst for oil worries Arab leaders. Says one: "If they are confirmed, the new Soviet need for oil could lead to major risks of military confrontation in the Middle East."

West Germany and Japan tried to get Washington to see the risk involved in its policy of embargo on transfers of oil technology to the USSR. They wanted to sell Moscow their own equipment. These attempts were not very successful. The boring and drilling technologies perfected by West Germany and Japan are superior to those of the Soviets—though not equal to those of the United States—but the Americans repeated their wish to see this equipment excluded from all trade with Moscow, and the Germans and the Japanese had to agree. They must adhere to the "agreements on the delivery of strategic material" which bind the two countries by treaty to America.

The formidable link between the USSR's needs in oil and its maneuvers in the Persian Gulf has been taking shape for a long time. In Bénoist-Méchin's work on Ibn Saud and Saudi Arabia we find this passage:

When Molotov went to see Hitler in 1940, one of the conditions for the conclusion of the German-Russian Pact was a free hand in Iran and Iraq as well as a rather large part of Saudi Arabia to ensure Russian control of the Persian Gulf and the Gulf of Aden.

Since then, the leaders of the Kremlin have not changed their doctrine. At the November 1948 meeting of the Soviet military staff and the Politburo a plan for a lightning attack on the Persian Gulf by fifty divisions was placed before Stalin.

Two years later, in November 1950, the Russians called a conference on the Middle East in Batum, where delegates and observers from Turkey, Palestine, Iran, Iraq, Syria, Lebanon, Jordan and Egypt studied ways to protect the USSR's oil zone and the "annexation of sources of fuel located in border countries."

The Americans, newly arrived in this region of the world, finally grasped the importance of Saudi Arabia. Pentagon experts reached the conclusion that whoever held this bastion would have a great advantage. They even went so far as to say that in ten years the master of Saudi Arabia and the Middle East would be the master of the entire European continent.

The American embargo, in depriving the USSR, at the dawn of the 1980s, of the means of intensifying its oil production, has, by a disturbing paradox, contributed to acceleration of the Soviets' long-term movements in the direction of the Gulf. American leaders respond to this danger, not with a change of economic policy, but by intensifying military preparations and warnings in the region. Thus a vicious circle seems to be closing around both of the superpowers, and in a way that is vital to the rest of the world.

When the Soviet military moved into Afghanistan (where in the spring of 1981 the occupation army came to exceed 150,000 men) on the border of Iran, the Pentagon ordered its air and naval units, spread out from the Mediterranean to the Pacific, to send large detachments to the Middle East.

Declaring that the Soviet Union had engaged in a series of military movements which created a serious threat to freedom of movement in the straits of the vital region of the Middle East, the President set forth what would be called the Carter Doctrine. It warned that any attempt by external forces to seize control of the Gulf would be considered to be directed against the vital interests of the United States of America. All measures, including military force, would be used against such a threat.

As soon as it was announced, the policy ran into a series of difficulties that would make the Western position in the oil empire even more fragile.

First of all, there was the immediate reaction of the Gulf countries themselves, beginning with those considered to be "moderate." Saudi Arabia set the tone without delay. Crown Prince Fahd personally saw to it that three confidential messages were taken to the White House; to the Pentagon; and to the State Department.

Crown Prince Fahd clearly stated that in no case would he consider the presence of American military forces in Arabia reasonable or acceptable. He could not foresee any situation in which they could be used effectively, and he believed that they would serve only to precipitate crises and risks of confrontation which the oil countries of the Gulf could not afford.

At the same time, Prince Fahd granted an interview to the *Middle East Economic Survey*. Founded in the 1960s and today published in Nicosia, Cyprus, by two well-known journalists, the Lebanese Fuad W. Itayim and the Englishman Ian Seymour, the *Middle East Economic Survey* has become required reading for all economic and political leaders of powers concerned with the Gulf.

Interviewed in the spring of 1980, the day after receiving a delegation from the Pentagon, Prince Fahd made it clear that all that had been discussed with the American mission was the delivery of modern equipment to Saudi forces. There had been no discussion of the possibility of American bases of any kind in Saudi Arabia or surrounding territory. He told the journalists that they could affirm categorically, and in his name, that Saudi

Arabia would not accept any foreign military installation on its soil and would not grant military facilities to America or any other forces.

The first part of the statement by the Crown Prince, who is known for his moderation and for his American friendships, was an event. But he did not stop there. He explained himself with greater precision when answering a question about his attitude toward the Carter Doctrine. He replied that those who express such threats themselves create the risks that they profess to fear. The Saudis would blow up the oil fields if any military action were taken.

Following the Saudi leader, other political officials of the Gulf spoke out in the same terms. Their language became harsher after the American attempt to free the hostages, which was launched from American bases in Egypt and aircraft carriers in the Gulf.

The oil countries' attitude of reserve or hostility as far as any "military protection" is concerned was not the most unfortunate result. It was the Pentagon that delivered the most severe blow to the credibility of this botched militarization of the very complex question of the relations between oil and the West.

The press published a basic document which had been prepared after an eighteen-month study by Paul Wolfowitz, then one of the directors of the Pentagon's planning services. The report states that America does not have the means for a confrontation in the Gulf. If such a case arose, the United States would be unable to oppose a Soviet invasion of Iran, following the invasion of Afghanistan.

After examining the various cases that could arise, the Wolfowitz report concludes that the United States would have to reach the point of threatening to use nuclear weapons before it could face a military operation in the Gulf.

The very idea of exploding nuclear devices in the midst of oil fields boggles the mind.

Walter J. Levy, the American expert, writes in *Foreign Af-*

fairs that the only thing that military action in the Gulf would allow us to count on would be the destruction of the very oil fields which we are seeking to protect and preserve.

Stripped of fantasy, the truth about the crisis begins to emerge more clearly. It is to be found less on distant borders than in the fabric of industrial society itself—as it is coming to an end.

But still . . . Even after a momentous change in American politics, from Carter to Reagan, the mission to the Middle East, in the spring of '81, of Secretary of State Alexander Haig showed all the old "geopolitical" illusions of his former boss, Henry Kissinger, revived.

"**B**REAK OPEC!" . . . "Stand up to Moscow!" All through the seventies, slogans such as these were coined to calm the nervous, troubled public in Western countries. Now the age of illusions is over. Because of their lack of imagination, courage and above all will, each of the great industrial democracies now finds its social fabric under pressure because of the oil crisis. The chief cause is neither Soviet policy nor OPEC—but the absence of a coherent American foreign policy.

More than Europe or Japan, the United States has been afflicted with lack of foresight, as if this great country, which has carried the world on its shoulders for so long, and performed so many miracles, had suddenly run out of breath. Acting as if American oil reserves—and, in the last resort, military power —would protect it, the United States ignored all warnings, paid little or no attention to the North–South dialogue (in which the danger signs could easily have been detected) and failed to measure the social consequences of the technological revolution.

After the third oil crisis and the collapse of Iran, the record shows that during the seventies, American oil production *fell* from 3 to 4 percent *every year,* while consumption continued to increase; that the United States still imported *half* of the oil it consumes—of which *two-thirds* came from the Middle East; and that, according to the U.S. Geological Survey's latest estimate, the country's total oil reserves added up to 28 billion barrels, or only nine years of consumption at the present rate.

America is committed to developing energy substitutes. No doubt they will come, but on two conditions: they must be competitive with the price per barrel of oil, and they must become available as quickly as possible.

Experts agree that the price of oil would have to rise to at least $50 a barrel before substitute energies would be profitable. Out of its present consumption of twenty million barrels a day, it is estimated that the United States could replace two million barrels of imported oil with synthetic fuel by 1995, provided the program is launched immediately.

There is no doubt that *some* oil can be replaced by other energy sources (nuclear, synthetic fuel and, above all, solar power) in ten to fifteen years. It is less certain that there can be any real substitute for oil—more precisely Middle Eastern oil —now, or during the rest of this decade. As the Egyptian economist Charles Issawi emphasized in his talk at a recent oil symposium in Vienna, this is a fact which the world must accept. "It should be neither a dream for some, nor a nightmare for others."

We must adopt measures designed to conserve energy. We must find a model for social change, a model of activity and employment, and a way of life that uses less energy, less oil. John Winger, vice-president for energy at the Chase Manhattan Bank, notes that, during the years of expansion, equipment based on the use of expensive manpower was replaced with equipment based on cheap energy. But with the cost of energy continuing to rise, our only choice is to consume less. We must be prepared for a general reduction in our standard of living, at least during the transition to the postindustrial society. The objective is not zero growth, with the unemployment and other social consequences it entails, but *zero energy growth*—as soon as possible.

The most complete study of the social and industrial changes that would facilitate moderate but stable energy growth has been published by the Ford Foundation. The study notes that, in the past, growth was considered to be the solution to all of society's economic and social problems—that is, until growth itself became a problem. Now we are trying to find ways to resume reasonable growth *without increasing our consumption of energy*. The Ford Foundation study concludes that it is possible—but not before 1985.

Meanwhile not only are the instruments of modern technology needed, but a radical change in life-style as well. An example of this is to be found in the drama of the automobile industry. As the leading industry of yesterday's social model, it developed at a phenomenal rate, particularly in the United States. Today, 362 million vehicles are on the road. And a hundred thousand more come off the assembly lines *every day*. Eighty-eight percent of the world's automobiles are in the hands of 10 percent of the population. Forty percent of these are in the United States, 30 percent in Europe and 18 percent in the other industrial countries. The remainder (about one-tenth) are scattered among the three billion inhabitants of the Third World.

If the Soviet Union has been less affected by the oil crisis than the West, it is primarily because it has only three million automobiles for 250 million inhabitants. By comparison, the United States, with 220 million inhabitants, has 115 million automobiles.

Between 1950 and 1970, all the countries of Western Europe followed the American example, though fortunately for them, with a certain delay and with cars that consume less gasoline. But in the final analysis the difference is not significant. At the beginning of the eighties, the automobile industry and its subcontractors employed almost 20 percent of the active population of the United States; the figure is about 15 percent for European countries—an enormous number in both cases. Massive numbers of men and women are dependent on the industry, which has been severely affected by the first cracks in the old order. With the occurrence of the third oil crisis in 1979, it was hardly possible to prevent a collapse in the automobile industry. In the United States, Chrysler found itself insolent. And in the course of a year and a half, the vast industrial complex around Detroit and across Michigan, Ohio, Illinois and New Jersey had been struck by the implacable combination of recession and rising costs.

Steel, tire, glass, aluminum and other industries are dependent on the automobile industry; and 85 percent of American workers use their cars for transportation to and from their places of employment, morning and evening. During the last year before this brutal crisis, Americans traveled 16 billion miles in their cars and consumed 10 percent of the world's total production of oil every day. As for the truck, it has surged ahead to become the major freight carrier. Of all the goods transported within a radius of 125 miles around the cities of the United States, 88 percent are transported by truck and only 7 percent by railroad.

Detroit, the capital of this industrial empire, became a focal point during World War II, turning out jeeps, trucks, tanks and motors for aircraft and victory ships. Today, Detroit and the automobile manufacturing centers are experiencing the most painful crisis in their history. The drama began in 1980 when 30 percent fewer cars were manufactured than in the previous year because of a decrease in demand and the importation of small, electronically controlled Japanese cars that are half as expensive to build and to run. Automobile assembly-line workers were the first victims. By the spring of 1981, fully *one third* of the United Automobile Workers' membership was unemployed.

That represents only a part of the general industrial crisis. As the secretary of a subcontractors' organization points out, for every automobile assembly-line worker laid off, at least two workers in firms of subcontractors and suppliers lose their jobs. In other words, about 750,000 are now unemployed in the devastated Detroit area.

After the banks had finally turned their backs on them, Chrysler's executives, including its president, Lee J. Iaccoca (who developed the Mustang in the 1960s) appealed to their last possible creditor: the United States government. This was an unprecedented step. An even greater impact was felt when the other two giants, Ford and General Motors, without having reached the extreme straits in which Chrysler found itself, announced considerable declines in sales and began closing plants. Chrysler's 1980 deficit rose to $1.7 billion. After a long and difficult debate in Congress, the American government agreed to an unprecedented $1.5 billion loan for the firm. Tomorrow, how much will Ford and General Motors need for new investments?

Douglas Fraser, president of the United Automobile Workers, was invited to become a member of Chrysler's board of directors. Iaccoca then made the logical move and declared that he was not at all certain that the American automobile industry still had a future in the private sector. Studies of the Japanese case convinced him that the transformation of Japan's automobile industry owes its success to general planning between the government and industrial leaders. Americans will have to learn to practice something different from the free enterprise to which they have been so wholeheartedly committed in the past.

The real problem, then, is not so much the present crisis, bad as it is, but the future. American and European automobile industries will have to be completely restructured before they can be revived. Retooling along the lines of systematic electronization, to which the Japanese have been committed for several years, implies a long delay and the investment of tens of billions of dollars. No single firm in Europe or America has that much money at its disposal.

The American automobile industry's manufacturers' association estimates that modernization of the three leading producers to the point where they would be on a level with the Japanese would require a commitment of $75 billion between now and 1985 ($35 billion for General Motors, $30 billion for

Ford, $10 billion for Chrysler)—double the amount spent on the entire Apollo space program in the 1960s. Where is the money to come from?

Even General Motors, America's most powerful corporate giant, announced a loss and began to close plants, with dramatic social and human consequences for entire towns. In Anderson, Indiana, for example, General Motors is responsible for the unemployment rate rising to 17.5 percent. Robert Hooker, an automobile worker who is also a member of the Anderson City Council, notes that every worker he hired between 1965 and 1978, when he was the personnel director, has been fired. The shock was so great in Anderson that many of its 71,000 inhabitants have succumbed to despair and depression.

At the same time in Dearborn, Michigan, Ford's board of directors announced, for the first time in thirty-five years, a loss for the year. The early figures placed it at $1.5 billion. Ford's future is hardly assured. Its share of the American market fell to 21 percent in 1979. The following year it dropped to 18 percent, the level which Chrysler had reached when its debacle began. As soon as these figures were known, Ford immediately moved to close three plants, including its giant plant at Mahwah, New Jersey. Ford's total reductions in work force have now reached 12 percent in six months. The decline in sales for the first quarter of 1981 was one third compared to the preceding year.

Faced with these appalling figures, the American public is forced to ask how this could have happened without being anticipated. Why did Japanese manufacturers alone sell more cars to Americans than all of the Ford factories combined?

It is at this point that discussion of modernization begins— automation, microelectronics, energy controls, the new lightweight metals, the reduction in the size of cars, less powerful fuel—everything, in fact, that could be achieved with $75 billion if we exhaust all of the funds earmarked for many other sectors. In any case, it may already be too late to solve the problem.

The automobile as it is now produced in the United States is condemned because of its high price and the cost of keeping it on the road. With complete retooling, it could still be adapted to the needs of today. But what will be the needs of tomorrow? Will the automobile, the symbol of industrial society in its use as individual transportation to and from work, have any place in the computerized society?

In the future, the automobile industry in developed countries will no longer employ one third of the manpower that works for it today. And how many people will still be employed by the iron and steel industry, which is constantly reducing its work force? How many will work in petrochemicals and metallurgy? This evolution is inevitable—and it must be understood before we can begin to plan for the future.

No one has the courage to face the fact that certain occupations must disappear to be transformed into new ones. We must assure the success of this transition with all of the economic and social effort necessary—with different politics, with a different society.

Modernizing industry entails replacing man's physical strength with machines—changing the nature of modes of production and work. It will be a revolutionary and fruitful change, one that is already under way in Japan where an industrial society is being transformed into a computer society. Industrial employment will be replaced by employment created by this society of intelligence, for already there is a shortage of men and women trained for the new tasks.

The industrial world has lost precious time, almost ten years, through fear of change. We no longer have ten years to bring about the transformation of the industrial society, based on *energy*, into the computer society, based on *information*.

PART-II

THE TAIF REPORT HAS BEEN APPROVED in Saudi Arabia from a mountain town surrounded by vast, arid deserts, empty of people except for the ever-roving nomads. After the meetings planned for the spring and summer of 1981 by the Taif Committee, a new and radical reshuffling of power is inevitable between the industrial West and the new Third World alliance over the economic destiny of the world. The massive power of oil, transformed at frightening speed into hundreds of billions of petrodollars flowing into Arab coffers, can hardly be resisted by the bled-white industrial nations.

Ironically, twenty-six years ago, in the steamy islands of Southeast Asia, there was a time when the West was given a chance to avoid the fight. Then, in another mountain resort like Taif, delegates from all over the Third World gathered to form a new alliance aligned to neither West nor East. Unlike the empty, dry desert and nomadic population of Saudi Arabia, this city sits atop a wet lowland rice plain, amazingly fertile, and in one of the most densely populated regions of the globe. The city is Bandung, the country Indonesia, and the men and women who joined in the Bandung Conference in April 1955, represented the burst of freedom, the thrill of nationalism, and the desperate hope that came with the postwar breakup of the British, Dutch, French and even the prosperous American empires. At Bandung these men and women turned to the West for help in building their new countries—and the West ignored them.

The West was too absorbed in confronting the Soviet Union

and waging a cold war to take the nonaligned nations seriously. As far as America was concerned, no country could be neutral in the global conflict with Communism. And the same for Russia, Khrushchev told Walter Lippmann. "There are no neutrals —they can't and mustn't exist," he said. Of course, the Soviet Union would support nationalism when it suited its interests. But only opportunistically.

For the Third World, of course, the East–West military confrontation is a civil war among the industrial countries. That civil war is sterilizing the creative forces of progress and is gutting the economies of both camps. With economic growth grinding to a halt, not only in the West but in the East as well, this "civil war" must end if the economic and social advancement of the poor is to proceed. A North–South dialogue must replace the East–West obsession, and now the investment monopoly of oil has the capacity to force such a dialogue.

It took the Arab nations a quarter of a century to gather the power—the oil power—to make up for their early humiliation and impotence. Had the rich nations greeted the newly emerged poor peoples of the world decades ago with greater understanding, the present conflict would not be taking place. But they did not, and the gauntlet of Taif is being thrown at their feet. The sad history of Bandung can be a guide to what the West must *not* now do in its second encounter with the Third World.

The Bandung Conference of twenty-nine nations, representing 500 million people, was called by Ahmed Sukarno, the first President of Indonesia. In 1949 he had successfully wrested the independence of his country from the Dutch after a long, bloody rebellion. Indonesia then joined India, Pakistan, the Philippines, Ceylon, Laos, Cambodia, Vietnam and Singapore in the move to freedom from colonial rule. They would soon be joined by the peoples of Africa.

Sukarno wanted a conference "where the nations of Asia and Africa could pool their thinking and shape a unified policy." At the opening ceremony the participants shared the feeling that this was the eve of a global Fourth of July. They were free and their time had come. "The wretched, humiliated, despised, insulted, oppressed of the human race," wrote black American novelist Richard Wright, who attended the conference, "left their calling cards on the table of history, announcing their entrance on the international scene."

The Bandung Conference opened after an astonishing military event on the plains of Indochina. At Dien Bien Phu in May 1954, in a battle waged with modern weapons, whites were defeated for the first time in the twentieth century by a "colored" army.

The famed General Giap had deliberately drawn his French adversaries into the basin of Dien Bien Phu. The French army —with seventeen battalions, 22,000 tons of equipment, heavy artillery, tanks, 173 combat aircraft, 71 transport planes—lost everything.

It was inconceivable to the French that a little yellow man, especially one who had never gone through Saint-Cyr or Sandhurst or West Point, possessed military genius. The French generals could not imagine twelve battalions of soldiers, dragging twenty-eight cannons and sixteen mortars through two hundred miles of jungle tunnels to fire on an allegedly inpregnable fortress.

The white, Western chiefs of staff were unable to conceive of a Vietnamese army supplied by fifty thousand coolies, each transporting over 150 pounds of rice on bicycles manufactured at the Peugeot factories in France. The French paid a horrendous price for their contempt. Dien Bien Phu was the first modern victory of a Third World army against the West.

The lesson spread quickly through the Third World: colonial powers could be defeated, despite their superior weapons. The key was in organizing local nationalist forces, then deciding when and where they should be committed to battle.

Three leaders who symbolized Third World emancipation arrived in Bandung on the same day. They scarcely knew each other. One was Gamal Abdel Nasser, the Egyptian colonel who had succeeded the puppet of the British, King Farouk. Nasser did not trust Western airlines, and worried about an American and British attempt to prevent him from attending the conference. So to go from Cairo to Bandung he chartered an Air-India plane. En route, he landed in New Delhi to pick up Jawaharlal Nehru.

Everything possible separated these two men: race, religion, class, style. Gloomy and zealous, Nasser was a tall man with the gait of a powerful animal. A career soldier and a visionary, he nourished a great dream—to forge a union of 400 million Moslems. That gigantic historic mission waited only for a qualified leader, and he saw himself as fully qualified. "We alone in Egypt are designated by the past to play that role . . . and oil will be the world's sword."

Nehru, on the other hand, was an Indian of noble caste, an "Oxford gentleman." Actually, it was at Harrow that he (like Churchill) learned the intricacies of cricket and Latin declensions, while Cambridge gave him a love for the sciences. At Oxford he studied law before returning to India to serve the cause of nonviolence under Gandhi. The agnostic Nehru, by then sixty-five years old, was frail, almost effete.

The Eastern quality in Nehru was deeply buried under his British veneer. But even this Anglophile could not forgive England for some of the things it had done in his country. He could not forgive the British practice of amputating fingers of young country girls—a mutilation, or so the legend goes, designed to prevent the girls from weaving and eliminate Indian competition with the textile factories of Manchester. The personal assistant of Indira Gandhi, Nehru's daughter, reminisced about this "protectionist" mutilation fifty years later, during the victory parties of the 1980 election campaign.

Nehru's father had been the leader of the nationalist movement, and Nehru succeeded him at the head of that movement. This won him nine years in prison.

In 1939 the British Viceroy of India announced India's entry into the Second World War alongside the rest of the British Empire—without so much as consulting native leaders. As Rommel's troops were battering Montgomery's army in North Africa, and as the last British garrisons surrendered to the Japanese at Singapore, Nehru joined Mahatma Gandhi in launching India's first independence movement by threatening "absolute disobedience if Great Britain does not leave the country immediately." This was in August 1942.

Once more Nehru was arrested, with his daughter Indira, as the Indian people responded with insurrection, ravaging every part of the immense country—train stations, tax bureaus, post offices, telephone exchanges, schools. Two thousand people were killed, and the police made 100,000 arrests. The uprising was quelled in six weeks, and India was forced by the British to mobilize for its defense against the Japanese.

Yet the British were not able to hold on to India or their empire once the war was over. The end of three hundred years of colonial rule ushered in a period of great hope.

Nehru went to the Bandung Conference ten years later because he believed that a new era had dawned, one in which the West would join with the Third World to end its poverty.

Nehru, along with all the other delegates to Bandung, fervently believed that with the West's technology the famine that always followed each period of drought could be conquered. He believed in the intelligence of the developed, "civilized" world to which so many ties connected him. And that belief forged a bond between Nehru and Nasser. Despite their many differences, both belonged to the Third World and both had a powerful, almost religious faith in the West's technological genius. They would be right, as we shall see, but decades later.

When the Air-India plane landed at the airport in Rangoon, Burma, for refueling, Nasser and Nehru saw through their side window a lithe, slender man wearing a gray tunic, smiling as he came toward them on the runway. It was Chou En-lai, the new

Prime Minister of the People's Republic of China. He too had stopped in Burma for a visit en route to Bandung, and when he learned about the other two leaders' layover he had postponed his own departure in order to meet them.

"Need I introduce you to each other?" asked Nehru. He then asked Nasser if he wanted to arrange an immediate talk with the Chinese Prime Minister.

"Yes," Nasser replied, and the meeting took place there at the airport.

Nasser let Chou know that he was obsessed by the "plotting of the West." He feared attack and wanted arms to defend Egypt. He explained that Paris had refused and Washington had made any such arms deliveries contingent on the signing of a military agreement. Then Nasser dropped the shoe: "I don't know," he said, "if the USSR would be willing to sell us arms. Would it?"

Chou En-lai offered to serve as intermediary with the Soviets. "I think that they will give you a positive answer," he said. Then and there, the Chinese Prime Minister wrote up a report which he sent to Mao Tse-tung with the suggestion that it be forwarded to Moscow.

Chou En-lai's text made three points: "I think that Nasser firmly believes in the policy of nonalignment as a long-term strategy. . . . If his disagreement with the West were merely tactical, it would not have provoked the present crisis. . . . Nasser asked me if the Soviet Union in the socialist camp could give him the aid that he can no longer obtain from the United States and the West. In my opinion, it is impossible for the socialist camp to limit itself to the role of a spectator."

The following day, the three leaders landed in Bandung. The planes were besieged by reporters. One of them asked Nehru, "Some people wonder if the meeting isn't the beginning of a racist movement against the West. What is your opinion?"

"It is possible that this may come about," replied Nehru. "There is racial feeling among these people, and if the West continues to oppress them a racism will be created that can never be extinguished.''

As the Indian Prime Minister made his way back toward his official car, he turned around and added, ''I belong to those who seek to avoid irreparable damage. It must be understood that Bandung is the last *appeal* of the poor countries to the West's moral conscience.'' And it was—until Taif would open the real era of Third World *demands* on the West.

At the opening session in Bandung, Sukarno—dressed in the white uniform and black velvet kepi of an Indonesian officer—gave a stirring ninety-minute speech that caught the spirit of the times. ''We are now masters of our countries,'' he said. ''Nations and states have awakened after a sleep of several centuries. We are no longer the tools of others or the toys of foreign powers.''

Sukarno then began pounding his fist on the lectern. ''But we still live in a world of fear! Fear of ideologies, fear of the hydrogen bomb, fear of remaining poor. There are things that separate us here artificially—our ways of life, race, national character, skin color. But what are these differences compared to our common aversion to racism and our hatred of colonialism?''

Thunderous applause punctuated Sukarno's speech. Once the calm had been restored, the session's chairman read the telegrams of congratulation received by the conference. There were only a few and they all came from the same camp—from the Moslem republics of the Soviet Union, from North Korea, from East Germany. None of the greetings came from the West.

American Secretary of State John Foster Dulles had described Bandung as a ''pseudo-conference'' and had issued orders that no American observer was to attend. Anthony Eden's Conservative government in Great Britain treated it with the same hostility and contempt. France, having learned nothing from Dien Bien Phu, was already bogged down in another ''pacification'' program, this time in Algeria. And Germany, Japan and Italy, still rebuilding from the war, were completely indifferent.

In Bandung, Chou En-lai made a daring proposal, one that could have changed world politics twenty years before Nixon went to China. He declared, "We are ready to negotiate with the United States," and proposed "a seven-point peace declaration, embodying the principles of coexistence, racial equality and the right of peoples to self-determination." But less than two hours later the American government said no. John Foster Dulles, who just weeks before had refused to go to Geneva for the signing of the Indochina armistice to avoid shaking hands with Chou En-lai, saw nothing that merited attention in any proposal made by the "Red Chinese."

America missed its rendezvous with China, and the industrialized West missed its chance with the world's poor. Bandung did indeed make the headlines in the world press, but only to emphasize the participants' "weakness." These twenty-nine states, who spoke on behalf of two thirds of the world's population, were seen abroad as representing no more than eight percent of the world's wealth. Bandung was "a spectacle put on by the inhabitants of the hunger zone to hide their wretchedness," said one U.S. official at the time.

The tragedy resulting from this shortsighted policy would be staggering. It would lead to three conflicts in the Middle East, to two Vietnam wars, and to dozens of revolutions and counterrevolutions around the world. Nasser would make war—and lose. But oil, just as he had warned, would become the weapon to avenge him when Taif replaced Bandung as the new cradle of North–South confrontation.

THE DEAL BETWEEN NASSER AND THE SOVIETS went through. With Chou En-lai's help, Egypt received from Czechoslovakia the weapons that the West had refused to supply. As soon as he heard about it, Secretary of State John Foster Dulles sent his right-hand man, Kermit Roosevelt, to Cairo with a message for Nasser: If Egypt went through with the arms deal, the United States would retaliate: technical and economic assistance would be stopped, diplomatic relations would be broken off, ships carrying the weapons might even be intercepted on the high seas. Again Nasser was facing threats.

Nasser's grand dream, his overriding ambition, was to build the Middle East's greatest economic-development project, the Aswan Dam. The waters of the Nile would be diverted from their course to provide irrigation and reclaim land for millions of peasants. The estimated cost of the project was $500 million.

Before the arms deal the United States had said it was willing to place $54 million at his disposal, no strings attached. This was to cover the preliminary work of construction. Britain would add another $16 million. For his part, the president of the World Bank proposed a soft $200-million loan at 3.5 percent interest, payable over twenty years. All this was now in jeopardy.

In the summer of 1956, Tito, Nehru and Nasser spent several days together at Tito's home on the island of Brijuni. They were now the leaders of the nonaligned group of nations that came into being after Bandung.

The three men spoke easily. Despite coming from different cultures, they shared the same aspirations and saw the same looming difficulties. First there was the problem of the East and West blocs. The nonaligned nations had to avoid joining one camp or the other. There was also the industrialized world's ignorance of and contempt for the underdeveloped countries. This wall had to be demolished.

Tito read to Nasser and Nehru messages that came in from various parts of the world. Waving one of them, he said, "This one was sent to me by a man who wants to take part in our talks. I won't tell you his name—I want to see President Nasser's reaction." He handed him the letter. It contained a request for Marshal Tito to mediate the Israeli–Arab conflict. The sender was willing to fly to Brijuni and *join the nonaligned group*. He was Israel's Prime Minister, David Ben-Gurion.

Ben-Gurion and the Israeli Labor Party were serious. They didn't want to be pawns in the East–West struggle; they wanted to develop their country among Arabs and with them. But Israel was never admitted to the new group of nonaligned nations. Had it been allowed to do so, there might never have been a 1967 or a 1973 war.

On the island of Brijuni, as everywhere else, Tito lived high and handsomely. He enjoyed taking his visitors to Vanga, a tiny island just behind his villa, which he kept stocked with animals and birds. There he released the monkeys given to him by Nehru as a gift. His best wine cellars were also located on Vanga. A great connoisseur, he often carried on discussions over a rare bottle brought up for the occasion.

Tito was admirably informed about everything that went on in the Soviet bloc. The Yugoslav leader got into the habit of sending Nasser and Nehru copies of any documents he thought might interest them. In the margin he would scrawl "Interesting reading" and then add his signature. Tito also kept himself informed about the Vatican, a political and diplomatic relay station he regarded as important for obtaining firsthand information on the West.

At the end of their stay in Brijuni the three leaders reached a joint conclusion, which they drafted and signed. The concept sketched out at Bandung, i.e., that of "positive neutralism," was now published in the following terms: "Peaceful coexistence was formulated to govern *relations between the two giants, allowing each to spend billions to equip itself with bombs, ballistic missiles and artificial satellites.* These nations are advanced, industrialized nations. Positive neutralism is to be used as the policy of the smaller proletarian countries."

This positive neutralism proved detestable to both the U.S. and Russia. Khrushchev and Dulles immediately went after the person among the new force's leaders who seemed the most vulnerable at the most sensitive point—Nasser in the heart of the Middle East.

As Nasser was leaving his meeting with Tito, the Egyptian ambassador to Washington was summoned by John Foster Dulles.

"Mr. Ambassador," said the Secretary of State, "we aren't going to help you concerning the dam, and we plan to issue a statement to make that fact known." To the astonished diplomat, who had had no advance notice of this development, he read a statement that had already been turned over to the press. He pulled no punches: American aid would not be granted, because "the Egyptian economy was not ready for such a project." And it concluded threateningly: "We believe that anyone who does build the dam will be hated by the Egyptian people because this burden will be overwhelming for them . . . especially when added to arms purchases."

Nasser was with Nehru aboard the Egyptian airplane that was flying him back to Cairo, where Nehru planned to spend a few days. Suddenly the liaison officer emerged from the cockpit with a radiogram—John Foster Dulles' declaration. Nasser read it. Without sharing the contents with Nehru, he excused himself and got to his feet to show it to Heikal, who was accompanying him. "This is no simple retreat from their former position," said Nasser. "This is an attack against our regime. The people of Egypt are being called upon by the U.S. to overthrow their government."

Nasser withdrew for a quarter of an hour. Then he rejoined Nehru and told him what had happened. Nehru read the message attentively. "Those people," he said, "how arrogant they are!" Nothing else was said. This first blow against the movement of nonaligned countries demanded their intense concentration. The fate of what they termed "all the proletarian countries" was at stake.

It was midnight when the airplane landed at Cairo airport. All of the diplomatic corps, including the ambassor of the United States, had come to welcome Nasser. He greeted them but said nothing and drove his own car home. On the following day Nehru cut short his visit and left. Between 10 and 11 A.M., Nasser drafted his reply. He would *nationalize the Suez Canal* and use canal revenue for the construction of the Aswan Dam, crucial to Egypt's future. Before making his decision public, he sought information about the exact status of British forces on Cyprus, on Malta, in Libya and in Greece. If these forces were strong, the British might be tempted to intervene militarily immediately. But by the next day he knew enough to be convinced that the British did *not* have sufficient troops in the zone to invade Egypt and that it would take them two months to assemble the needed men. "A month—that is all I need," concluded Nasser.

His advisers were uneasy about the possibility of French military intervention. "No, they have enough to do in Algeria," he told them. "And if the British need two months for the buildup, the French certainly need just as much time." Nasser was scheduled to make a speech in Alexandria the next day on the anniversary of King Farouk's exile from Egypt. The ceremony took place—but the speech was not as originally planned. Nasser sent a team of soldiers to Ismailia. There they were to listen to him on the radio. As soon as he uttered the name Ferdinand de Lesseps, the French engineer who had built the Suez Canal, the team of commandos were to go into action.

Before a crowd of 250,000 people massed on Alexandria's Liberation Square, Nasser began to speak. For once this shy man spoke boldly. He mesmerized the crowd and even provoked laughter by telling about his struggles with the American diplomats, with that gentleman who reminded him, he said, "of Ferdinand de Lesseps." As Nasser spoke the code word the operation began.

Nasser went on: "As I speak to you this very moment, the official newspaper is publishing the law nationalizing the Suez Canal Company . . ." And then, laughing heartily, he said, "The Canal is going to pay for the dam. Today, in the name of the people, I am taking over the canal. Tonight, this very night, the canal will be Egyptian, run by Egyptians!"

The announcement was greeted with wild enthusiasm. The people were overjoyed. For Nasser, it was a consecration. In the eyes of the people, the canal was the greatest symbol of colonial domination. Thousands of Egyptians had died building it. Even after independence, the Suez Canal Company had remained a state within a state—with its own flag. Now, while the commando team which had gone into action on hearing the name de Lesseps seized the canal installations, the police in Cairo occupied the Suez Canal Company's offices.

What began in Cairo after Nasser's nationalization of the Suez Canal was the next-to-last Western military expedition into the Third World, the next-to-last attempt to maintain the status quo by force. It would end in fiasco.

Nasser had miscalculated the military risks. He failed to see the passion and fury his move would trigger in Britain and France, the co-owners of the Suez Canal. Two great statesmen, Churchill in London and Mendes-France in Paris, had been replaced at the helm of their governments by two men of limited world vision. They were nationalist politicians who lived timidly in the shadows of their great predecessors.

Anthony Eden believed that "the Suez Canal is the British Empire." Britain's flag and presence in the world, its future on the seas, its prestige, were symbolized by the canal. An attempt had to be made to get it back from "that bandit Nasser," he said.

Meanwhile, France's Guy Mollet, the Premier and leader of the Socialist Party, was bogged down in the Algerian people's rebellion. Nobody in his government or in French ruling circles had taken that revolt seriously when it began in November 1954. But, despite increasing commitments of troops and, finally, the complete mobilization of France's young men to "keep Algeria French," the rebellion spread. Soon France had an army of one million men in Algeria. But the bigger that army grew, the more the Algerian population protected the rebels, encouraged them and joined them—and the more the Algerian guerrillas armed themselves by stealing rifles and machine guns from the expeditionary corps. Guy Mollet and his government began to panic.

These circumstances prompted the rapprochement with Britain. Anthony Eden didn't want to be considered any less concerned about the greatness of the British Empire than his illustrious predecessors. Eden and Mollet met in secret and decided to embark on punitive military action against Nasser.

Mollet believed that the "Algerian rebellion" would collapse if no longer supported from abroad—that is, by Egypt. He was pleased by Eden's determination. All that remained was to find the means for a victory on the ground. England and France could indeed mount air attacks and a naval blockade against hopelessly inferior Egyptian defenses, but where could they find ground troops?

This hole in European planning against the first bid for Arab power led to the plotting and implementing of a tragic idea. It would continue to trigger a chain reaction for decades to come. Britain and France decided to send *Israel's army* into battle.

Since the creation of Israel in 1948, the tiny but modern Israeli Army had never gone beyond its own borders. It was a truly defensive army, flexible and motorized, designed to protect extremely vulnerable borders. Israel had never envisioned using this army as a tool of conquest. The Israelis were far too absorbed in turning the bit of desert allotted to them into farmland, too busy modernizing their industries.

The French and the British summoned Ben-Gurion, Israel's head of state. A secret meeting was held in an abandoned hangar at Bourget Airport near Paris. They offered Ben-Gurion a deal: If Israel's army joined the Franco-British coalition and made a lightning strike on the Suez Canal, it would be protected by the air forces of both countries and supported by paratroops. In return, Ben-Gurion would rid himself of the "one Arab political leader who represented a threat for Israel," as Anthony Eden put it.

The British and the French also told Ben-Gurion he could extend his country's sovereignty over Egyptian soil in the Sinai Desert.

The Israeli leader was amazed and embarrassed. He could not imagine Europe in such a state of panic, or in such an aggressive mood toward Egypt. He had been convinced that colonial militarism was over for the two aging empires. What, he asked the Anglo-French leaders, did the United States think about their invasion plans?

Eden and Mollet guaranteed Ben-Gurion that since the public break between Dulles and Nasser the U.S. wanted nothing more than to see the Arab leader fall. Once the operation began, America would do nothing. Furthermore, the whole business would be over in a matter of days. Egypt would collapse immediately.

JEAN-JACQUES SERVAN-SCHREIBER

Returning to Tel Aviv, Ben-Gurion had trouble explaining to his government what he had heard. The only thing clear in his mind was the West's determination to get rid of Nasser. For Israel, didn't this opportunity represent a unique chance to improve her own security?

The operation was set in motion on October 29. The Israeli divisions raced toward the canal. The British air force bombed and the French paratroopers jumped. Egyptian defenses were quickly breached. But while Nasser had miscalculated the balance of power on the ground, the British and the French had made an even bigger mistake about the balance of power in the world.

In less than two days—even before Moscow reacted—Washington brought the invasion to a jolting halt. An ultimatum from President Eisenhower was telephoned to London and Paris: The French and the British had forty-eight hours to declare a cease-fire and to withdraw from Egypt. As the hours went by, Eisenhower himself phoned the British Prime Minister, saying: "Anthony, what's got into you? Have you gone crazy? I want this insane adventure stopped right away. If not, *American military power will go to Nasser's aid.* Kindly transmit this information to your colleague in Paris. We'll let the Israeli government know about this ourselves."

It ended the next day. Nasser had been saved in the nick of time by America. The whole world watched the spectacle of two old and glorious European powers, England and France, cowering before the U.S. It took Europe nearly twenty years to get over this humiliation—twenty years before the American dollar became anemic, American goods shoddy and expensive, and American military power so weak that its helicopters broke down in an attempt to rescue fifty-two hostages held in Iran. For Israel, dragged into a military adventure, the tragedy acquired historic proportions. Mollet and Eden had struck the tiny nation a terrible blow by giving the valiant Jewish state the appearance of being the imperial West's outpost in the heart of the Middle East—the Arab empire of oil.

Although saved by America, Nasser once again approached the USSR for help to build the great Aswan Dam, and the Soviets furnished engineers and money. Eight years later, Khrushchev inaugurated the completed dam. The fact that Egyptian Communist leaders were in prison did not bother Moscow unduly. In the end, Nasser emerged from the Suez test with tremendous popularity; he was seen throughout the Middle East as standing up to the European and Israeli imperialists and surviving. Until Suez, Egyptian nationalist leaders had believed neither in Arabs nor in Arabism. But Suez changed all that. Suez made Nasser into a hero of the Arab masses who shared "the humiliation felt by colonized peoples forged in one melting pot by injustice," according to one Arab official. Arabism gripped Nasser as much as he gripped it; it would shape his strategy from then on. And just as important, the same feeling of shared humiliation that was at the core of Nasser's support would soon become the center of the new alliance against the West. Oil would soon provide the weapon to "ask" the West to hand over its technology, and the colonial experience provided the cement to bind the Arabs to the world's poor.

THE GRAND STRATEGY OF THE UNITED STATES, Europe and Japan today is to cut down on their dependence on imported OPEC oil. Every industrial nation is striving to build up its coal production, its synthetic-fuels production, its gas output and, despite objections, its nuclear power. The West believes that if it could only cut its dependence on imported Mideast oil, life would return to the high levels of the 1960s, inflation would subside and the bothersome demands of Taif in the name of the Third World would fade away.

This myopia could prove fatal. For it is not only imported oil that industrial nations have now become addicted to, but a whole list of other crucial materials that are absolutely needed to keep the factories operating.

Take, for example, a typical day in the life of an American businessman. He wakes up, showers and heads for his breakfast in the kitchen. This breakfast may be accompanied by toast made on an *imported* asbestos grill. Will he have his breakfast before or after shaving? No doubt about it, he'll shave before a mirror made of silver or aluminum—both of which have been *imported*. He'll be using an electric razor with *imported* lithium batteries, equipped with an *imported* copper wire; or with an electric razor whose blades are made of an alloy of tungsten and vanadium steel—both *imported*. He may even want to dry his hair with a dryer made of *imported* steel. While eating, he may listen to the news over a transistor radio that has silicon circuits and batteries made of lithium (both *imported*).

Now he goes out—dressed in *imported* wool or cotton, after turning off the heating unit, in which the *imported* copper piping brings steam to *(imported)* nickel or chromium radiators.

It's raining. Water is spouting from the *(imported)* zinc rain-pipe. Should he take the car? It's hard to start—something wrong with the battery, which is made of a combination of lithium, manganese and lead (all *imported*) surrounded by *(imported)* antimony plates.

Finally, he's in the office elevator which has been fire-proofed with *imported* antimony. It takes him to the sixth floor where his office is located. The telephone (with a receiver that employs thin strips of *imported* aluminum and *imported* copper wiring) starts ringing. It's a cloudy day and he needs light, so he switches on a bulb that has an *imported* tungsten filament—or neon lights having long bulbs with filaments made of magnesium tungstenate, zinc mercurate—all *imported*.

Obviously, the West's economic and political problems do *not* only revolve around imported oil. These other imported raw materials creep into every phase of its people's daily lives. Only now are governments learning that jobs, the standard of living of their citizens, the bulk of their nations' industries and even the safety of their people depend—even more than on oil—on these imported raw materials.

West German Chancellor Helmut Schmidt commissioned, in 1978, a report on the consequences for the German economy of a possible cutoff of raw materials. The conclusions of that report were so shocking that the government banned its publication. It revealed that several million jobs would be eliminated in the steel, automobile, aircraft and shipbuilding industries if just five of the mineral ores Germany imported from southern Africa became scarce. These are chromium, indispensable in the production of special steels; molybdenum, needed for the

JEAN-JACQUES SERVAN-SCHREIBER

manufacture of refractory alloys used in the construction of jet
aircraft engines; vanadium, essential for sheathing bars of nuclear fuel; asbestos, in insulating material for auto brake linings,
battery cases, oil piping; and manganese, needed in metallurgy
for every aluminum alloy. The same study estimated that a 30
percent reduction in chromium imports during any one year
would produce a 25 percent drop in Germany's gross national
product.

In June 1977 the German government decided to stockpile at
least a year's supply of the five vital raw materials. These stock-
piles are being set up by the private sector with the aid of public
funds. The German central bank is investing $1.5 billion in this
life-insurance operation.

A second report, this one commissioned by the British government at the request of Industry Minister Keith Joseph, said
that if the supply of manganese were cut off by one of the five
producing countries—Gabon, South Africa, Australia, India,
Brazil—"major disorders would be created for the Western
economy."

Right now, however, all eyes in Washington and Moscow are
on Africa and its enormous mineral resources. If South Africa
were to be led into a black revolution against the white rulers,
and raw-material exports were cut off, the West could be devastated. If Zaire tilts toward the Soviet sphere of influence like
Mozambique, Ethiopia and Angola, the continent could be split
in two. Zaire, or the Congo as it was known under the Belgians,
has already come extremely close to falling under Soviet influence.

"There are no neutrals. They can't and mustn't exist." Such
were Khrushchev's views on nonalignment. All the same,
eighty "neutrals" met ten years later in 1970 at the third nonaligned summit held in Lusaka, the capital of Zambia. But the
men holding forth with unheard of virulence were not the same.

The "charismatic" leaders were now Boumédienne, Qaddafi, Fidel Castro.

In Belgrade, Cuba's young premier had said that under capitalism men can die of hunger, but Communism can destroy them by suppressing their freedom. How then did Castro become the Soviet proxy in the Caribbean?

A then little-known American Senator described the process in strong terms. The United States had ignored Cuba's desperate need for economic reform. Government influence had served the interests and increased the profits of the American firms that controlled the island's economy. American spokesmen had hailed Batista publicly as a loyal ally and a good friend at a time when he was slaughtering hundreds of people, destroying the last traces of freedom and stealing millions of dollars from the Cuban people. The Senator went on to declare that it was America's own policy, not Castro's, that had turned her old friend against her.

The Senator's name was John F. Kennedy.

When the second decade of development ended, the Third World still represented less than 10 percent of world industrial production. Nevertheless, a new meeting between the West and the Third World, the first conference for development, was held under the auspices of the United Nations in 1964. There, from the poorest Africans to the semi-industrialized countries of Latin America, from the Upper Volta to Mexico, the nonaligned joined forces to demand that the conditions of international commerce be established on a more equitable basis. It was the first manifestation of the North–South confrontation, the first cry for a "new world order." It would be heard constantly in the future.

The West replied with a cold refusal. Its own prices—but not those of its suppliers—increased with the rate of inflation. In 1960, Malaysia could buy a Jeep with four tons of

JEAN-JACQUES SERVAN-SCHREIBER

rubber; in 1970, it had to pay ten. In 1960, the copper-producing countries could purchase a Jeep with 190 tons of copper; eight years later the price was 300 tons. The poor countries wore themselves out producing raw materials in order to buy converted products and even basic foodstuffs at higher and higher prices.

In certain areas of Java the population was forced to give work on tea or rubber plantations priority over the satisfaction of their own food needs. In Senegal, peanut plantations were enlarged because of the export value of peanuts. At the same time, the production of dried vegetables and sorghum, staples in the Senegalese diet, fell well below the needs of the country. During a twelve-year period in Jamaica, the areas planted in sugarcane, bananas and lemons, all destined for export, increased respectively by 50, 30 and 100 percent. At the same time, the cereal harvest dropped from nineteen to four kilograms per person.

It fell to a Westerner to sound a cry of alarm: Robert McNamara, who after eight years as U.S. Secretary of Defense became president of the World Bank. A hardworking, methodical, self-disciplined man with a remarkable mind, McNamara controlled the most modern and complex computers, systems and machines while at the Pentagon. Absorbed in his work, he forgot that men, by virtue of their courage and their brains, are superior to machines.

But human nature was avenged. In spite of himself, McNamara the war leader became a sort of apostle. He issued a solemn warning, in 1972, to alert the world to the growing economic schism between the North and the South. If the rich nations did not fill the gap between the prosperous northern half of the planet and the starving southern hemisphere, no one would be safe in the long run—however many weapons they stockpiled.

"Development" became the theme of conference after conference, each more futile than the other, attended by men who were either disenchanted or resigned, for power remained in the hands of the Westerners who, obsessed by Moscow, had little time for the problems of the vast North–South frontier. In the meantime, the Third World no longer harbored any illusions. It sank into bitterness.

At the conference on world trade held in Nairobi, Kenya, in the mid-seventies, Westerners failed again to live up to the expectations of the 120 delegates from the Third World. The American delegation, led by Elliot Richardson, announced one refusal after another, even over minor matters. One disenchanted African delegate murmured, "The Americans are substituting arrogant diplomacy for gunboat policy."

The Japanese maneuvered with the same caution to extricate themselves. The Soviets, working the corridors as usual, succeeded in blocking any recommendation that would indict them for their notoriously inadequate financial efforts on behalf of poor countries. The European representatives remained silent and subdued. The delegates observed with mixed feelings the self-destructive actions of the United States—though it was the height of irony to see the only noncolonial Western power, the country that alone supplied 30 to 40 percent of the credits granted by the World Bank, attract the combined resentment of the Third World.

At the close of this meeting Philippine President Ferdinand Marcos, one of Washington's most loyal allies, remarked in his concluding speech that the Third World no longer had any choice except war or death. The audience was dumbfounded. If Marcos had abandoned all reserve just as the meeting was coming to an end, it was because he was completely exasperated. The rich nations were doing too little, too late. Those leaders, like him, who had counted on enlightened reformism from the industrialized West, now felt deceived and embittered. Marcos spoke about it with Jomo Kenyatta, on the latter's farm facing Mount Kenya. The old leader confided that until then he had believed that all African attempts at Socialism were a dead end.

Now he wondered if it was not they, the Kenyans, who had chosen the wrong path.

Frantz Fanon's prediction had come true. He had noted that certain underdeveloped countries were moving strongly in the direction of Socialism. With great enthusiasm men and women, old and young, undertook what amounted to forced labor and proclaimed themselves slaves of the nation. Yet this common human investment, he knew, was not sufficient—capital, technicians, engineers, mechanics, were also required. "The colossal efforts to which leaders summon their peoples will not produce the results expected," he wrote, yet for the Third World there seemed no other choice.

Zaire's troubles date back at least twenty-one years, when almost a century of the worst type of colonization under Belgium ended, and Zaire, a country half the size of the United States, began its independence with a handful of doctors and university graduates.

On June 30, 1960, the colonization of the Belgian Congo formally ended. Baudouin, King of the Belgians, came to the independence celebration. No sooner had his speech ended when Patrice Lumumba, the new Premier, jumped up onto the dais and shouted, "No Congolese worthy of the name will ever forget that independence was won by fighting. It was an unending struggle that we waged. It was a struggle in which we gave our effort and our blood." The astonished Africans applauded frenziedly. The King turned white as a sheet. Lumumba went on: "We have known the brutal work demanded for wages that did not allow us to eat our fill or buy clothes or have decent shelter or raise our children as loved ones should be raised. We have known derision, insults, and the blows that we had to take morning, noon and night—because we were niggers!

"In our cities there have been magnificent houses for whites and decrepit shacks for blacks. A black was not allowed in the cinemas or the restaurants or so-called 'European shops.' A black had to travel below the waterline in riverboats, at the feet of a white who sat in his luxurious cabin. Who can ever forget the shooting? Who will ever forget the dungeons? Who will ever forget?"

There was silence, then an endless ovation. "In this moment of truth," said Lumumba, "we're getting even for eighty years of domination." They were living out an extraordinary dream —only to awake amid tragedy.

On the following day, July 1, General Janssens, commander in chief of the police force (and maintained by Lumumba as head of the army), summoned his African officers and chalked the following formula on the blackboard: "After independence = before independence." For those who still did not understand him he added, "The first one who doesn't obey will hear from me."

Unfortunately, Janssens' bravado didn't work. Four days after independence was proclaimed, mutinies broke out all over the country. The army marched on the capital, soldiers massacred Europeans and laid siege to the missions. Then the province of Katanga seceded, taken out of the crumbling country by a local merchant, Moïse Tshombe.

Katanga's main city of Elisabethville lay 1,200 miles from Lumumba's capital of Brazzaville. It was in Elisabethville that the core of Zaire's real financial power, the Upper Katanga Mining Union Company, was located. In 1960 the Belgian-owned Mining Union produced 70 percent of the world's copper, 60 percent of its cobalt, 16 percent of its germanium and much of its manganese and zinc. Belgian interests were concentrated in Katanga, and Belgium supported Moïse Tshombe.

At first, Belgian troops actually protected Tshombe's new regime. But they were soon relieved by the first Katangese gendarmes, commanded by two French officers from Algeria, Colonels Faulques and Trinquier.

Another mining province, the Kasai, rich in diamonds, also

seceded. Patrice Lumumba no longer was able to control anything. The Congo wallowed in anarchy. The United Nations sent in its "Blue Helmets," who restored a little order. Later the Congolese Army regained some discipline under the command of a former payroll sergeant, the son of a white cook, Joseph Désiré Mobutu.

Mobutu had been a brilliant pupil of the missionaries. They taught him French and soccer, but failed to convince him to become a priest. He preferred being a soldier. As his assistant, Mobutu chose his ex-superior, a Belgian, Colonel Marlière, who would remain senior adviser for years along with Moroccan General Kettani, a graduate of Saint-Cyr. Backed by the CIA, Mobutu decided to stage a coup to "neutralize" Lumumba and to "call in foreign specialists to save the country from chaos." After one escape attempt, Lumumba was recaptured and imprisoned in the lower Congo. He was turned over to the Katangese by Mobutu as a gesture of reconciliation. On his arrival at Elisabethville's airport he was killed by Tshombe's men, and his body was never found.

Meanwhile, someone else was reorganizing Lumumba's defeated forces. It was Che Guevara. Sometime in the mid-1960's he made a clandestine trip to the Congo, then went secretly to Cairo to see Nasser. On one particular evening, rolling tobacco leaves into long cigars, Guevara told Nasser of his journey—and his vision.

"To work at world revolution," he said, "I believe that we must first operate in Africa, where the situation has ripened. The Congo is a trouble spot and I think we should strike the imperialists in Katanga, at the very heart of their interests."

Nasser was fond of Guevara, but he was also less of a dreamer and more of a realist. Pensively he looked at his friend. "You really surprise me. What's happened to you in Cuba? You haven't quarreled with Castro, have you? I wouldn't want to get involved in that. But if you're out to become a new Tarzan, a white leading the blacks and protecting them, that's out of the question!"

Guevara laughed, but to Nasser he looked like a disillusioned man stricken with despair. He had left Cuba to fight alongside the Congolese guerrillas, on the very day that Fidel Castro received his farewell letter. Che gave up his rank as commandant and everything that connected him legally to the Cuban government before venturing into the African jungles.

Guevara confided to Nasser, "I'm a great believer in the transformation of society, but the 'competent' people that we put into office in Cuba quickly forgot their revolutionary fervor in the arms of beautiful secretaries, or in their automobiles, or in their privileges, or their air-conditioning. They began closing the doors of their offices to keep in the cool air instead of opening those doors to the working people. I realized that we were promoting opportunism."

Che's Egyptian host tried to comfort him. But he went on: "And then, there's a paradox in Communism. When I do business with the Soviet Union, I find the Russians trying to buy our raw materials at prices set by imperialism. I can't accept that from a socialist country. I've discussed this with them and they told me that they were forced to sell at competitive prices. So I asked them, 'What's the difference between you and the imperialists?' They told me they understood my point of view but then said the same old thing—'We have to sell at competitive prices.'

"So I asked them questions about the manufactured goods that they sold us. I told them, 'You have automation, you don't pay high salaries, yet you sell us your products at higher than market prices.' We're overwhelmed. There's no solution for us in this course."

Alone, Che took a regularly scheduled airline under a false name. He carried an attaché case full of literary works, plus inhalators for his stubborn case of asthma. During his layovers, he killed time by playing interminable games of chess with himself. Three months later two hundred Cuban soldiers joined him in the Congo.

Moïse Tshombe was quickly overthrown and fled. But he was

kidnapped when his plane was hijacked. The diverted aircraft landed in Algiers, where he later died in one of President Houari Boumédienne's prisons. Having rid themselves of Tshombe in this way, the Congolese asked Guevara to leave.

The chief of state, Mobutu, began making a show of nationalization. The Mining Union became a public corporation, with 100 percent of its capital belonging to the state, which turned over its management at once to the Belgians. Then Mobutu launched his "authenticity" program: he Africanized European names. The Congo became Zaire, and Katanga was baptized Shaba; Léopoldville was transformed into Kinshasa; Elisabethville became Lubumbashi. As for Mobutu himself, he was no longer Joseph Désiré, but Sese Seko N'Gbendu Wa Za Bangu, "the intrepid warrior, terror of hens and other females."

Mobutu became America's man in Africa. In twelve years Zaire received more than $800 million in U.S. economic and military aid. The head of the State Department's African Section told the *New York Times:* "The United States sees Zaire's position in Africa like Brazil's in South America. The trend in favor of supporting Zaire makes it possible to hope that the country will be able to extend its hegemony over the continent." When Zaire's debt reached $3 billion, the international Monetary Fund granted new credits, despite a rate of 100 percent inflation annually. And then, in June 1977, there was another invasion.

Two thousand men, Che's heirs, crossed the border from Angola. They marched into Shaba, once Katanga, led by their Cuban advisers, and attacked the mining city of Kolwezi.

It took General Mobutu's regime forty-eight hours to learn of the attack. It took three days for the foreign chancelleries to announce the event to their governments. A week later the scope of the disaster became known: mines had been looted and installations destroyed. All the white supervisory personnel left. Mining could not be resumed for months. Copper prices skyrocketed on the London Metal Exchange, and cobalt became practically unobtainable.

Official representatives from France, Belgium, the United States, Great Britain and Germany met in Paris to discuss military support for Zaire. Then another meeting was held in Brussels, with Mobutu attending. Besides the countries represented at the earlier Paris meeting, this one brought together emissaries from the Netherlands, Canada, Japan and Saudi Arabia, as well as the European Commission and the International Monetary Fund. Zaire, it seemed, was "indispensable" to everyone.

A third meeting took place in Mobutu's own apartment on the luxurious Avenue Foch in Paris. Zaire's creditors then demanded that the price of further aid must be complete control of Zaire's financial system. A delegate of the International Monetary Fund would have to take over as director of Zaire's Central Bank. Once again Zaire had to give up its sovereignty.

Mobutu got the foreign money and then set up a household guard of Europeans and South African mercenaries. This topsecret operation was coordinated by Colonel Mike Hoare, former commanding officer of the famous Sixth Commando unit which, with CIA help, had put Mobutu in power. A large number of the South Africans recruited came from the motorized column which in 1975 had pushed nearly six hundred miles into Angola to stop the combined Cuban-Soviet advance into Shaba. Mobutu turned these men into the nucleus of a "strike force" intended to maintain public order and cope with any new "coup" triggered from Angola. Mobutu had no choice. Neither did the West.

THE MAIN PHASE of the industrialized world's development occurred over the past thirty years. During this period, the North systematically exploited the South's (Third World's) resources and sold its products on its own markets, which were the only expanding markets in existence.

Now the developed countries, all of whose markets are saturated, must constantly increase their exports in order to pay for oil and the raw materials essential to their industries. As a result, a fierce economic war has started between Japan, the United States and Europe. Each time one wins a particular market through superior skill, ingenuity or equipment, it is to the detriment of the others' exports—in other words by eliminating jobs in the others' areas. Thus, it is no longer possible for industrial countries to maintain their expansion by trading among themselves. They are all together on the path of economic chaos.

There is no doubt that the industrial world must adapt to a new era. Regression might be appealing to people who dream of bucolic societies. But "regression" also means doing away with hospitals, schools, social services, the most skilled and highly paid occupations.

Whether we deliberately choose this path or simply allow ourselves to drift, we must invent another cycle of development, one that will pass through and only succeed with the Third World, the last "new frontier" on the planet.

The repeated failures of North–South dialogues have given rise to suicidal temptations.

For the North, the temptation is protectionism. The Southern countries are accused of creating difficulties for Western industries by flooding their markets with goods manufactured with cheap labor. It is economic war, the Northern countries declare. Close the borders. The spread of unemployment feeds this argument, but the figures refute it.

In six years, French imports from the Third World, which are limited to fourteen products, have brought about the disappearance of fewer than 25,000 jobs, chiefly in the textile and clothing industries. During that same period, French exports to the Third World created 100,000 jobs, notably in mechanical construction and the electrical and electronic sectors.

Without exception, every time a Southern nation develops and becomes a producer, it buys more, *it creates more jobs in the North than it eliminates.*

All of the experts denounce the danger and the illusion of neo-protectionism.

Roy Jenkins, former president of the European Commission in Brussels, declared that we cannot separate our economic recovery from the development of the poorest nations and a worldwide increase in demand. According to the International Labor Organization in Geneva, the interdependence between North and South risks being forgotten because of the present state of confusion and alarm in the North. But it would be to our detriment. In 1981, the OECD stated: "Nothing would be more dangerous than to forget the enormous potential market for industrial products represented by the ill-satisfied demands of an enormous segment of mankind. Developed and Third World countries do not have to divide up fixed global demand. They have to build a new industry to the new scale of billions of men and women."

The temptation to break away is just as strong in the South. Nations of the South notice how the West practices interdependence when it talks about it, and the bases on which it establishes interdependence when it is in control. Many representatives of the Third World have lost faith in the institution of a new economic order. They see in the North's arguments a desire to divide underdeveloped countries, and they argue in favor of a policy of "collective autonomy," that is, for breaking off relations with the North as far as direct investments, international commerce and raw materials are concerned.

At the time of the opening of the last United Nations session on development, Pierre Drouin wrote that, in keeping with this strategy of "collective autonomy," in which the notion of "counting on one's own strength" prevailed, a movement coming from the depths of the Third World was pushing toward the development of a South–South dialogue.

To abandon the dangerous illusion that we can tack onto the Third World the model of development followed by the West during the last two centuries, a model which a number of Third World forces reject, is not to abandon development, but to invent a new model, worldwide.

We can trace other paths, invent other methods and bring other forces into play.

At a time when the world is trembling at the thought of a fundamental crisis, scientific and human ways of forging a common future are now appearing.

PART-III

PARIS HAD NOT SEEN A JULY AS COLD as this one in fifty years. But then the mild weather returned, and the August light bathed the city in the languor of the summer holidays. Strollers returned to the banks of the Seine, and the public squares, from the Etoile to the Carrousel, were crowded with tourists. Yet beneath the lazy calm, signs of danger were gathering from all over the world.

The anxiety hanging over the city was different from that of August 1914 or May 1940. It was the awareness of an impending upheaval of another sort, one already building momentum. Autumn 1980 was the watershed.

Few responsible world leaders were in a holiday mood, least of all the eighty-five-year-old Toshiwa Doko, the quiet master of Japan's economic power and president of the Keidanren, Japan's national federation of industries.* He had just sent a special envoy to Paris with a 280-page report entitled "The Scientific Revolution and the Information Society." Produced under Doko's authority and supervision, drafted in five weeks by six separate teams, this document was delivered to the "Paris Group," the team of men methodically seeking a new direction for a world paralyzed by fear.

The Paris Group was formed in the summer of 1979 by the

---

* Dr. Doko has now chosen to concentrate his energies on "the new world order" and has asked to be replaced as president of the Keidanren by Dr. Inayama, chief executive of Nippon Steel and Number 1 expert on China for the past twenty-five years.

author of this book, the West German Minister, Karl Schiller, and the Paris-based American lawyer, Samuel Pisar. Month after month, several top economists, politicians and scientists from Japan, the United States, the Arabian Gulf and the Third World joined them in analyzing the new multipolar situation in which the world finds itself.

The Group grew out of the belief that, although the problems facing the world are complex, *every man and woman is capable of understanding them.* Solutions will be found only if everyone, wherever he or she may be, is informed and made to understand what is at stake.

The basic premises that have guided the Group's actions and deliberations may be summarized as follows:

—For more than thirty years, the international scene has been dominated by a sharp East-West antagonism which has drained energies and sterilized imaginations that should have been channeled into constructive initiatives. Current world tensions are indications of the serious consequences that may result from this state of affairs.

—The escalating arms race has reduced to nothing all attempts to correct the abysmal inequality between the northern and southern regions of the planet. Yet it is this basic split, more than anything else, that has given rise to the present crisis.

—The era of the "American Challenge," or the economic and scientific supremacy of one country is now over. New spheres of power and influence have appeared: the European Community, Japan, Southeast Asia and the Arabian Gulf. The world has become multipolar.

Will this world remain fragmented, violent and helpless, or will it find a way to unite its forces by intelligent means? The Paris Group has set for itself the task of finding the means of putting into effect a new dynamic of development.

The message was delivered to the Paris Group by one of Doko's closest lieutenants, Masaki Nakajima, president of the Mitsubishi Research Institute. The "Mitsubishi Report" supplied essential material for a plan of action to check the disintegration of the world's economy, incorporating the latest technological data that the group needed in order to formulate a concept.

At Taif the OPEC leaders' long-term-strategy report raised basic questions and formulated firm demands. It did not pretend to offer answers. This time there would be no waiting for plans for meetings, for endless negotiations. In the past, the oil countries had experienced the futility of such discussions with the West. Now they demanded action.

In June, the determination to act before it was too late had prompted a thorough exchange, all day one Sunday, between Sheikh Ali of Kuwait and the only Westerner who had followed the final discussion on the Third World at Taif.

The heart of the Taif Report is what the Yamani committee called "transfers of technology" to the undeveloped countries, including those of OPEC, in exchange for oil. It was the Kuwaiti leader's exceptional boldness that unleashed the chain reaction that followed and continued in Paris. When his French guest asked him, "Do you know exactly which technologies the report wants to transfer, by what priorities and by what means?" the young Minister, who holds a U.S. university degree in mathematics, simply replied, "No."

So the common task began, and continued with one meeting after another during the year 1980, and then in 1981 in Paris, in Zurich, Hamburg, Tokyo, Riyadh, Kuwait. Under the pressure of events, the principal organizers of the Paris Group followed Doko's example: no vacations. It was crucial to define the transfer of technology, to outline a vision that would match the "*spirit* of Taif."

The fact that Nakajima had arrived in Paris on exactly the date agreed upon months before reflected Doko's refusal to ease the pressure for one moment. From week to week his messages, telephone calls and Telexes were relayed across continents. During the six days that Nakajima spent in Paris and the days he stayed on the Persian Gulf, he was in regular telephone contact with Tokyo for Doko's approval.

When he returned to Japan on August 11, and again on September 10, he immediately reported to Doko at a special meeting of the men who make all of Japan's important economic decisions—decisions always made by consensus. Among those present were the members of the Keidanren, including the leading figures in industry and banking, representatives of the Ministry of International Trade and Industry (MITI), whose powerful bureaucratic apparatus has been organizing Japanese-style economic planning for thirty years, and leading international economists who are official advisers of the government.

The task involved nothing less than the development of a global plan for the Third World.

Toshiwa Doko's unique authority is based on the fact that he has a gift for translating concepts and theories into concrete actions. If he is listened to so attentively, it is because over the past thirty years he has won every battle he has waged to shape his country, with the result that Japan today is the leading worldwide technological power. Doko knows that the West must accept the urgent challenge from the Persian Gulf to the industrialized nations: develop the world, or we perish together.

A stocky, broad man with a square head, slow gestures and a penetrating stare, Doko resembles a judo expert. At the beginning of the summer, while all of the MITI officials were busy working on their final document, "Industrial Policy for the 1980s," he told them: "After ten years of the oil crisis, the procedure we must follow seems clear: we must be the pioneers of a new technological era which must be extended to the entire world, *but in organic partnership with the other advanced countries, without exception.* We must enhance the abilities of the world, across all borders. The means are there. It is a matter of putting them into operation. The objective for all of us is simple: create, spread, organize technological power."

The men to whom Doko made this speech have already, in less than thirty years, made Japan the world's most advanced industrial power, through the application of scientific discoveries and innovations to naval construction, cameras, motorcycles, steel production, petrochemicals, watches, television, videotape recorders, automobiles, machine tools and electronics. They are now focusing on genetic-engineering information processing and on one of the last industries dominated by the United States, aeronautics.

Nikon, Cannon, Honda, Seiko, Mitsubishi, Sony, Toyota, Hitachi, Matsushita have all become first in their respective fields. But Doko, the strategist of their victory, knows that Japan must now change direction. The Japanese industrial giants can no longer concentrate simply on expanding overseas and conquering foreign markets. They must become more closely integrated with the world. And the new "technological revolution" provides the opportunity.

Behind this major shift in Japanese strategy is the knowledge that oil, the basic source of energy, is no longer cheap and inexhaustible, and that the entire industrial base of the world *must be rebuilt* with another kind of raw material: the microchip. The chip will eventually replace the barrel of oil as the basis for a new kind of "information society," succeeding the industrial era, with one crucial range of development, one basic raw material: the trained human brain. And this time the Japanese know they must share their knowledge with others.

Japan is ready. Europe and the United States are still fearful. But there is no choice. The formal demand by OPEC, whose members hold the key to energy *and* investment for at least several years, can be met only by a global plan in which the industrial powers place their technology and knowledge at the service of the world.

THE METHODICAL RISE of Japanese power held no mysteries for Doko. An engineer trained at the Institute of Technology in Tokyo and later at the Brown-Bovéri works in Switzerland, Doko took charge of the maritime division of Ishikawajima-Harima, a firm that was barely recovering from the ruins of war when he joined it in 1950.

Brazil, then determined to become a major exporting nation, had decided to build itself a merchant fleet. Doko won the contract for two huge vessels. They were delivered four years later.

At that time an unforeseen incident occurred which determined the engineer's career. On leaving port, one of the Brazilian pilots of the ships that Ishikawajima had delivered made an error in navigation and crashed his vessel into the pier. The pier collapsed, but the Japanese-built cargo ship suffered only a few scratches. It went back to sea the very next day. That was the beginning of the rise of Japanese naval construction. The reputation of Japanese ships for strength and quality spread around the world, and orders poured in. In ten years, with Ishikawajima leading the way, Japanese penetration in this field was such that by 1975 eight out of ten vessels in the world came from Japanese shipyards.

As for the Brazilians, they were so impressed that they asked Doko and his firm to establish a local maritime industry. Thus was born "Ishikawajima do Brasil," which combined Brazilian and Japanese capital and engineers and, by 1958, had gathered 3,500 Brazilian trainees around the best technicians from Yokohama. Today it is the leading maritime-construction firm in South America.

The government of Singapore, encouraged by the rapid success of the Brazilian venture, sought the same kind of arrangement. Doko decided to assume responsibility for it. By 1963, the Jurang Shipyard had become the most modern in Southeast Asia, competing with the Japanese shipyards themselves in cost and productivity.

Doko had already moved on. He was builidng an aluminum factory in the Amazon that would become the leading rival of the North American giants. By then Doko had personally come to symbolize the Japanese saga.

Interviewed by the press while visiting New York at the end of the '60s, he said, "We have no natural resource, no military power. We have only one resource: the inventive capacity of our brains. It has no limits. We must make use of it. We must educate, train, equip. In the very near future, this mental power will become the most creative common good of all humanity."

With his vision of the future and his faith in scientific invention, Doko left Ishikawajima and shipping to join one of the new industries that would soon raise Japan to its zenith: electronics.

The directors of Toshiba (competitor of Hitachi, Matsushita, and Sony) hired him. He became president of the company and turned Toshiba, with its calculators, its transistors, its integrated circuits, into a worldwide concern. In 1974 he was offered command of the entire Japanese economic machine—the Keidanren.

Although he was at the center of Japan's industrial and scientific empire, Doko himself remained a discreet, almost secretive man. Almost nothing was known of his private life. Until the day in 1976 when the police paid a visit to his home.

For almost a week there had been an active government investigation aimed at tracking down anyone in the administration or in business who might have been involved in one of the numerous financial scandals which regularly occur in Tokyo because of the extreme overlapping of government and private industry. During the inquiry it was suggested that Doko might be involved, so the Tokyo police sent an inspector to the residence of the president of the Keidanren, in a suburb of the capital.

At the address indicated, the inspector found only a small house with a wooden door opening onto the street. The Doko family's residence was probably protected by a curtain of trees. He looked for an entrance, but without success. When he rang the doorbell of the small house, an elderly woman came to the door wearing house clothes. It was seven o'clock in the morning.

The inspector asked her to show him the path to President Doko's villa.

"There is no Doko villa," the woman replied. "I am Mrs. Doko. This is where we live."

The inspector and his colleagues couldn't have been more astonished. Would Mrs. Doko ask her husband to come to the door?

"Oh," she replied, "he left a long time ago. He takes the six-thirty train every morning to his office. Can you come back tomorrow? You are sure to find him before six o'clock."

Doko was already eighty years old and had been president of the Keidanren for two years when this incident occurred. The "Doko investigation" was dropped. The report made the rounds of Tokyo and was taken up by the press, which circulated the formidable image of this taciturn, modest, austere man at the summit of power. Japan adopted him and took him as a model. He became a legend, a symbol: a sort of new emperor in the era of computers and energy economies.

The speed of deployment, the technological quality, of Japan's industrial force, already impressive before 1970, increased under the impact of each "oil shock" in 1970, 1973 and

1979. They are called *shoku*s in Japan, and their dates are engraved in the nation's memory.

Each *shoku* marked an immediate, sharp check to the growth of consumption and buying power. And each one produced a new acceleration of rationalization, innovation, greater productivity, and stronger competitiveness. Thus, up to now,* Japan has come out of each *shoku* performing better than any other industrial power, including the United States and Germany. The standards of living and consumption were often cruelly sacrificed to investment; but it was a crucial effort, and nothing was allowed to get in its way. By 1981, the situation called for a national reexamination, which was undertaken by a group of MITI and Keidanren officials known as the "Group of 60." The group turned in its report in the spring. Its conclusions were revolutionary:

1. Between 1960 and 1980, Japan had succeeded in taking the lead in most "traditional" industrial sectors (naval construction, photo supplies, motorbikes, steel, television, electrical equipment, consumer electronics, automobiles). But it was no longer enough to confront the energy crisis.

2. Most, if not all, of Japan's success had been achieved through the intensive application of "imported technologies," mainly from the United States but also from Europe. This reservoir dried up as soon as Japan took the lead in these industries. Henceforth, the future can only be ensured by new inventions and technologies, in sectors where innovation can rapidly promise industrial applications—*and employment.*

3. In the 1980s, then, everything will depend on moving away from energy-intensive industries, such as steel, toward energy-efficient industries based on combining scientific computers and data processing. In other words, the future depends on the mastery of computers, semiconductors, microprocessors, industrial robots, optic fibers, bioengineering. These new technologies

---

*We will see the exact measure of it later.

must be applied to accelerated programs in education and medicine. Finally, the microprocessor—a complete, programmable computer engraved on a silicone-from-sand chip one millimeter square—must be linked to worldwide modern telecommunications networks.

4. No industrialized country will survive the upheaval unless it makes use of this technological revolution to create the jobs of the future. At the same time, it will be necessary to apply these technologies on a global scale; the old notions of nationalism and division of labor will no longer have any meaning in a world in which all work, creative energy and information can be instantly available. Everything will depend on the quality of human resources: education, training, communication—a new social fabric.

5. This new stage of development constitutes a "qualitative leap" compared to those that preceded it. Automation, because of microprocessors, will shortly be able to perform all the laborious tasks that do not depend on the active working of the human brain. This will force the human race to develop the capacities of its collective mind—capacities greatly underdeveloped in industrial countries and completely fallow in the Third World.

This new computer-based information-focused social system will permit the personalization and decentralization of all work. It may mean the end to mass society with computerized, information-based cottage industries growing up in the homes of individuals—homes that will be linked to the outside world by computer terminals. In the end, this will mean the generalization, the globalization, of educational and training systems, with tasks equally distributed.

This last point—the newest—is also the least debatable. Japan is setting up training institutes first for its Southeast Asian neighbors Singapore, Hong Kong, Korea and Taiwan. Then Indonesia, the Philippines and finally, on Doko's and Inayama's initiative, China. The institute encourages entire classes

of Japanese technicians and engineers to get their career training in other countries, for the industries of the future will have
no national boundaries. They will exist wherever human brains
link up with computer terminals.

These guidelines, taken together, constitute the new charter
for Japanese industry, which will be entirely overhauled so that
it can be rebuilt on microprocessors, the nerve cells of the future.

Strictly speaking, there is no "Japanese challenge." In the
1960s and 1970s there was an *American* challenge which was a
management challenge of discovering the best organization possible to generate innovation. By the mid-1970s Japan and some
European countries, such as France and Germany, had learned
what America had to offer and reached the same level of efficiency. At the same time, the United States, for reasons linked
to its military and monetary policies, saw its own vitality dry
up. Thus, in 1981, there is no longer an "American challenge."
And because we are dealing with another time and another
world, there is no challenge from Japan. The technological revolution under way and the emerging information society are not
linked to any one country. The Japanese are in the vanguard of
the world, not challenging it. The object is not to imitate the
Japanese but to adapt to each culture the approach to technology. It is a human challenge extended to the entire planet.

Perhaps the future is best described by the formula advanced
by Dr. Uenohara, director of research of the Nippon Electric
Company, one of Japan's leading firms in telecommunications
and electronics, as stated in the conclusion of the Mitsubishi
Report: "In the considerable field of all the industrial activities
that are going to be computerized, in the field of 'software,'
microprocessors and robots, if we employ the five billion inhabitants of the planet we will still be short of personnel."

This prophecy is confirmed by scientists, industrialists, and academicians who have assimilated what the revolution in microprocessors represents, be they Americans, Frenchmen, Germans or Swedes. It is the hope of tomorrow, it is the world we are entering in ignorance and anxiety.

The deep crisis of the eighties obscures this future. It is up to us to give it shape during the coming years. Besides, there is proof that it has already taken shape in Japanese industry, which is undergoing technological change *without creating unemployment*. If this radically new phenomenon has occurred in Japan first, it is because under the brutal pressure of successive oil crises the country has journeyed the most rapidly and the farthest into the new society.

Just how and why events pushed Japan to a position of world leadership deserves to be recalled and understood before we examine this revolution in detail—one in which society will offer *not only full employment, but the full employment of each individual's human capacities,* by means of the application of microprocessors and computerized human learning.

THROUGH AN EXTRAORDINARY SERIES of historical accidents, the Japan of the eighties, a compact, isolated island without resources, on the edge of the great Soviet plain, 7,500 miles from Europe and 5,600 miles from America, has become a technological superpower. Modern Japan is paradoxically the product of a Western mind. The mind was American: Franklin D. Roosevelt.

One summer day, in the south of Newfoundland, in Placentia Bay, one of the most magnificent and deserted places in the world, two men sailed toward each other on their respective ships: Winston S. Churchill and Franklin D. Roosevelt.

It was August 14, 1941. Churchill, on the battleship H.M.S. *Prince of Wales*, was then the Prime Minister of Great Britain, at war against a Germany at the summit of its conquests and power. Harry Hopkins, close friend and confidant of the American President, had visited Churchill several times at 10 Downing Street to work out the delicate relations between heroic, impoverished England and remote, neutral America, whose leader wanted at all costs to contribute to the survival of the British, and with them to a world free from totalitarianism.

During his last visit, Hopkins had handed Churchill a message from Roosevelt indicating that "he would be happy to meet him somewhere, in private, in a tranquil bay if possible." So there was Roosevelt aboard the cruiser U.S.S. *Augusta* making his way to a rendezvous with the *Prince of Wales*.

The American President, confined to his wheelchair by the

poliomyelitis that had paralyzed his legs for twenty years, admired Churchill's personality and temperament, even though he and the Prime Minister disagreed on certain political matters, particularly on the imperial colonies and possessions.

As a courtesy to the President, the Prime Minister decided that each morning and evening he would go aboard the American cruiser during the three days that their talks would last. Only on the last day did Roosevelt take the opposite route. Through a complex system of chains and pulleys which were standard equipment on his travels by sea, he was hoisted aboard the *Prince of Wales* to say goodbye to Churchill.

Neither knew whether or not they would see each other again, but each had an instinctive faith in the future. And to establish clearly what they had worked out together, the Atlantic Charter, each one kept a handwritten draft. There was never an official text.

In the Charter, Roosevelt persuaded Churchill to accept the principle of the emancipation of the colonized, exploited peoples of the world, much as Lincoln had done in the preceding century in the Civil War. "Each people will have the right to freely choose its own government and to obtain the independence of its territory; *each will also have the right of access, on an equal footing, to the sources of raw materials and must participate in a collective effort, in aid to countries still underdeveloped.*"*

Thus in a distant bay in the North Atlantic, Roosevelt helped put an end to centuries of imperialism and colonialism. It would be many years before total political independence occurred, but the path was already traced.

Roosevelt was delighted with the Charter, although he was unaware that Churchill had not the slightest intention of "presiding over the demise of the British Empire." But the President

---

* A striking instance of what would be rediscovered, and demanded, in Taif—some forty years later.

was obsessed by a problem. He had promised to keep America out of the war, and the country had no intention of freeing him from this promise. Roosevelt knew well, however, that America could not influence the future unless it were a partner in victory and peace. To enter the war, which only the United States could win, he would have to use cunning. Roosevelt acted so boldly, and with such steadfast determination, that even today, forty years later, many of the decisions that he took to involve America in the war remain a secret.

Despite public statements to the contrary, Hitler feared America. He was a gambler, but a shrewd one. Given enough time, he could hope to isolate and blockade England. Given enough luck, he had a reasonable chance of defeating the Soviet Union. The winning card was American neutrality. Hitler made no mistake about it. Neither did Roosevelt.

The President did everything possible to circumvent neutrality. He delivered first destroyers, then fighter planes, to England. Congress supported him by the slimmest margin. Before long, he decided to hand over the entire production of American P-40 fighter planes, and opened credits for Britain so that the agreement would have the appearance of an industrial-export operation rather than an act of belligerence. He persuaded Congress not to veto the agreement by publicly explaining that "the more one aids England to resist, the less one risks seeing America involved in helping directly."

By 1941 German submarine packs were doing terrible damage. Roosevelt, on one occasion, said to Harry Hopkins and General Marshall, "My God, the Atlantic is becoming a German ocean."

One of the first Gallup polls asked the American public whether its ships should be allowed to escort convoys taking supplies to Britain. The reply revealed massive opposition. Clearly the American public didn't care if the Atlantic became "a German ocean," even if Roosevelt opposed it.

A few months later, Roosevelt considered the growing losses

— 147

of U.S. ships in the Atlantic and simply decided to ignore public opinion. He issued an order permitting the American Navy to escort convoys to waters off the English coasts, but forbidding them to open fire. Hitler responded by ordering his submarines to avoid American ships and not to fire unless fired upon.

Two accidents occurred. On October 17, 1941, a British convoy was attacked by a group of German submarines. An American escort ship, the U.S.S. *Kearney*, was hit by torpedoes. Eleven men were reported missing. American newspapers published their names.

Roosevelt studied the public's reaction. There was no softening of its opposition to the war.

Three weeks later, the U.S.S. *Reuben James*, an American destroyer escorting a merchant convoy, was sunk by German submarines off Iceland. She went down with all hands on board —one hundred men.

Reaction in America was strong, but confused and ambiguous. Part of the public passionately blamed the Germans. The majority blamed the President.

Then Roosevelt went ahead and asked Congress for authorization to arm American merchant vessels so that they could defend themselves if attacked on the high seas. The debate was bitter in both the House and the Senate, and though Congress finally agreed it was by a very narrow margin—a majority of only eighteen votes in the House and thirteen in the Senate.

Roosevelt understood what this meant. He confided to Harry Hopkins, "It is clear to me now that, except for a tragic occurrence, we will never get Congress and the country to engage in war against Germany." Only an error by Hitler could bring about such a tragic occurrence.

But Hitler was careful. In three interviews with the Führer, Grossadmiral Erich Raeder, Kriegsmarine Chief of Staff, threatened to resign if he was not given permission to open fire on American ships, which were destroying the blockade. Hitler refused.

A little later, Raeder drew up a formal list of "twenty acts of war against Germany by American vessels in the Atlantic." Warning the Führer that ample supplies were reaching Britain, he concluded by insisting on the German Navy's right to attack. Hitler stood by his refusal. He knew where his enemy was: in the White House. He was determined to keep Roosevelt and America out of the war.

Meanwhile, at the end of the summer of 1941, American intelligence had begun to decipher the "Purple Code" which the Japanese used for transmissions between Tokyo and their air and naval bases in the Pacific. Roosevelt marked the transmissions carefully. They were beginning to signal, at last, a historic opportunity.

Americans who refused to risk their sons in Europe were even less concerned about the Pacific and the Far East. Most Americans were not disposed to take the Japanese seriously as enemies.

But Japan was on the move. When Japanese troops occupied Indochina without a struggle, Roosevelt froze Japanese assets in the United States and persuaded the governor of the Dutch East Indies to suspend all oil shipments to Yokohama and Nagasaki. In the Japanese Diet, Prince Konoye, the Prime Minister, declared that the situation was intolerable and that the country's Army and Navy were running out of fuel.

Roosevelt was encouraged. It came as no surprise to the President when his ambassador to Japan, Joseph C. Grew, cabled him that gasoline rationing was in effect all over the country and that there was not a single taxi to be found in all of Tokyo.

The U.S. ambassador soon warned the President of the risk of a government crisis in Tokyo "which would lead to the replacement of Prime Minister Konoye, who is relatively moderate and opposed to war, by a much tougher man from whom Americans could expect the worst."

Polls indicated that Americans would remain indifferent and still opposed to their country's entry into the war if the Japanese attacked Indonesia or any other territory in Asia or the Pacific, including America's own Asian colony, the Philippines. An attack on only one place could trigger an American reaction.

The crisis in Tokyo's government predicted by Ambassador Grew came about on October 16, 1941, when the Konoye government, faced with increasing economic difficulties, was replaced by a government of hawks. It was led by the fiercest hawk of all, General Tojo, a man who wanted war.

American intelligence had been deciphering Japanese messages since the summer, and in November they recorded preparations for war. But the Americans did not know what the target was.

Two Japanese diplomats, Nomura and Kurusu, were in Washington in December 1941 to negotiate the lifting of the embargo and the release of Japanese assets. During that time, Roosevelt personally received deciphered copies of all cables between Tokyo and the two diplomats. He refused to discuss the cables with anyone. Secretary of State Cordell Hull carried on negotiations with the two envoys without any instructions from the President.

Only one target within reach could trigger war if it were attacked by the Japanese: Pearl Harbor. Sometime in 1941, Richmond Turner, chief of the Bureau of Naval Intelligence in the Pacific, informed the White House that "Hawaii and Pearl Harbor should be considered *possible* targets of the first Japanese offensive."

Ambassador Grew cabled, "to the personal attention of the President, that, according to rumors circulating in military circles in Tokyo, the Japanese could launch an offensive against Pearl Harbor if negotiations going on with the Americans in Washington were broken off."

In November, Admiral Husband E. Kimmel, commander of the American fleet based in Pearl Harbor, advised Washington, in a special message, that "the Japanese could well launch a surprise attack on Pearl Harbor before an official declaration of war could intervene.'' The White House's intelligence sources already knew that and more.

On November 29, faced with an impasse in the negotiations in Washington and the hardening of the American position, the secretary of the Japanese diplomatic mission cabled Tokyo, under cover of the military code: "Tell us when you expect to program H Hour so that we will know how to bring our talks to an end."

Tokyo hesitated, either because of worry over the security of the code or because it didn't immediately know what to reply. Washington's decoding service had to wait for what seemed an interminably long time. Then, on November 29, the critical message arrived. Tokyo's reply: "We can tell you. Hour H is fixed for Sunday, December 7, at dawn. It will be at Pearl Harbor."

Washington confined itself to listening. In Pearl Harbor no one suspected anything.

On Friday, December 5, Mrs. Roosevelt telephoned Edward R. Murrow, one of the best-known journalists in the United States, to invite him "to an informal and friendly dinner with the President at the White House on the evening of Sunday the 7."

The weekend began quietly. On Saturday, December 6, Brigadier General Dwight D. Eisenhower was given leave to go to Fort Sam Houston, Texas, for a rest. Harold Ickes, the Secretary of the Interior, was entertaining friends on his Maryland farm. Dean Acheson, after going with his family to pay respects to the remains of Supreme Court Justice Louis D. Brandeis, went off into the woods to rest and meditate.

On Saturday evening and Sunday morning, contrary to his usual routine, the President was in his office on the first floor of the White House.

On Sunday, December 7, at 10:20 A.M. Washington time, the two Japanese diplomats, acting on instructions from Tokyo, telephoned the State Department to request a meeting with the

Secretary of State at one o'clock. The Secretary was away, but officials promised to find him and give the Japanese an answer.

Roosevelt was informed of the Japanese diplomats' request for an audience. He calculated the time. It was one o'clock in Washington, eight o'clock in the morning at Pearl Harbor. Cordell Hull called to ask him if he had any instructions concerning the Japanese request for a meeting. "Nothing special," was the reply. At 1:20 P.M. Washington time—8:20 A.M. in Hawaii—the Japanese attacked, in three waves.

With a military dispatch in front of him, Roosevelt called his secretary for the first time that day and dictated an official message to be sent to the news agencies. "From the White House: Japanese air attack against all American installations at Pearl Harbor. The President will make a statement in the late afternoon."

Roosevelt called London and personally gave Churchill the news: "They have attacked Pearl Harbor. . . . From now on, we are in the same boat together."

It would be long and hard, but Roosevelt had no doubt about the outcome. He had gambled with all the boldness and resources of his political skill and knowledge of the world. He had won.

The Japanese who were celebrating their victory had lost. They had struck, without striking a fatal blow, at the one point which was bound to bring America into the war.

But to say "the Japanese" when referring to this people of 1941 is to blame a whole nation for the narrow-mindedness of its leaders. The most striking proof—one rich in lessons for the future—was the struggle between Prime Minister Tojo and Admiral Yamamoto.

Tojo, who had never been outside Japan, wanted war, and he wanted war with the United States. Only America seemed to threaten his own country's power and glory. Yamamoto denounced "this dangerous illusion" week after week. For fifteen years, as a sailor, then as a naval officer, later as an admiral, he had traveled around the world. He knew America from the West Coast to the East Coast. He knew that the wealth and the industrial might of the United States would be irresistible once mobilized. In forcing the United States into war, Japan was committing suicide.

The duel between Yamamoto and Tojo will remain a historic moment in the great Japanese adventure. Both men had gifted minds and bold temperaments. But one had an integrated knowledge of the outside world, whereas the other was immersed only in the Japanese reality. Yamamoto was not only intelligent—he was much better *informed*.

Postwar Japan's secret, the key to its success, would lie in an understanding of Yamamoto's superior intellect. Tojo was buried with the past. Yamamoto, to whom homage is paid in innumerable books, shares with Roosevelt and his military commander MacArthur the paternity of the new Japan.

Pearl Harbor was the decisive, inevitable turn of events. It determined Japan's destiny, and so, to a very large extent, that of the entire modern world.

THE LONG YEARS OF WAR AGAINST JAPAN had an unintended conclusion. The weapon that was built for fear the Germans would develop it first was, in the end, used against people who could not have imagined it.

The success of the Manhattan Project defeated Japan, but also transformed her and the world by revealing the power of science in one spasm. Miraculously, Hitler failed to build the atom bomb first. Yet it was he who initially organized a research team to look into "the possible applications of nuclear physics" and installed it in a section of the Ministry of Science at 69 Unter den Linden, near the Reich Chancellery.

The most brilliant mind of the team was an Austrian physicist named Lise Meitner. As early as 1938, with the aid of two great physicists, Otto Hahn and Fritz Strassman, she carried out the first successful experiments "by bombarding uranium with neutrons." At the time she was far ahead of anyone, including the Americans.

Then came the Anschluss, the occupation of Austria by Nazi divisions. Like all of her fellow Austrians, Lise Meitner became a German citizen. As a Jew she now came under the Third Reich's racial laws. When she was excluded from the laboratory, her colleagues were appalled. Leading German scientists requested a meeting with Hitler to explain that Lise Meitner must be kept at all costs. The Führer flew into one of the blinding rages that obscured his intelligence. He called the two German scientists "dirty white Jews" and dismissed them. When an order for Lise Meitner's arrest was issued, her colleagues organized her escape and she left Germany forever.

In his fanaticism, Hitler gambled against intelligence. Like General Tojo, he lost.

Thus, as early as 1939, two and a half years before Pearl Harbor, the research that would lead to the bomb was already in the hands of the democracies. Germany had lost the race before it was aware it was being run.

The Italian Enrico Fermi, the Frenchman Joliot-Curie, the Swede Niels Bohr, the Hungarians Leo Szilard and Edward Teller arrived at the same conclusion: Roosevelt must be alerted. Only he, if he understood what was at stake, could mobilize the immense resources that would be needed if there was to be any chance of developing the bomb in time—for they were haunted by the fear that the Germans would persist and succeed.

But none of them knew Roosevelt. They had no way of reaching him, or even bringing the information to his attention. Then luck handed them the key. In Berlin, an anti-Nazi German physicist named Flügge decided to publish what he knew about the "capabilities and possibiliities of the chain reaction that could be unleashed with uranium," in the specialized journal *Naturwissenschaften*. Flügge sent a copy of the journal to Zurich, where the local press published essential excerpts from it. Now nothing could dissuade Fermi, Szilard and Teller, for they knew how far their German rivals had progressed.

After thinking about it and meeting with their American colleagues, they concluded that only one man had the reputation and authority to secure an appointment with the President of the United States—Albert Einstein. They decided to go to see him.

At the time, Einstein was vacationing in Peconic, an isolated village on Long Island, where no one was able to direct the scientists to his house. Finally they found him taking a walk, his hair tousled, smoking his pipe and wearing rumpled trousers. With extreme kindness and in poor English, the great man greeted them and led them to his house. He put on his slippers and listened.

Szilard, who made notes of the meeting that evening, was greatly surprised to learn that the scientific genius of the century, whose fundamental equation had established the definition and the measure of nuclear energy thirty years earlier, had not considered the possibility of an explosive reaction.

Szilard wrote: "It seemed to us from the very beginning of this conversation, which fortunately was prolonged, that the possibility of unleashing a chain reaction had never entered Einstein's mind. When I began to explain to him the nature of our information about what was going on in Berlin, he understood the consequences and told us that he was ready to help us if necessary, or as one says: to get his feet wet."

The three men tried to find a way to get Einstein to Roosevelt. One of them suggested that Einstein, who had never met Roosevelt, should write to the Queen of the Belgians, whom he did happen to know. But that did not seem to be the best idea. They got no further.

Two weeks later, Szilard noticed on the restricted list of Roosevelt's regular visitors the name of the banker Alexander Sachs. When Szilard approached him, Sachs agreed to transmit a letter from Einstein.

Accompanied by Teller, Szilard went back to the little village on Long Island. Einstein agreed. He dictated his letter to Roosevelt in German so that he would be surer of each of the terms he would use. In concluding he wrote: ". . . the nuclear chain reaction, whose progress I have just succinctly described, would make it possible, if it occurred, to manufacture a new type of bomb. A single bomb of this type, transported to a port by a ship would suffice to destroy the entire port, as well as much of the surrounding territory."

Sachs translated the letter into English and read it to Roosevelt in his office on October 11. The President found it long and incomprehensible. Sachs was shocked. He implored Roosevelt to give him a breakfast appointment the next morning, when he would explain calmly and more fully the letter's contents and meaning. Roosevelt, acting on instinct, agreed.

At the second meeting Roosevelt was more attentive. Then, without comment, he summoned General Watson, his personal military attaché, and said to him, "This is going to require some measures." He handed him the translation of Einstein's letter, keeping the original for himself. The secret operation baptized S-1 had begun.

Throughout the war Roosevelt made sure that he was kept informed of each stage of the project. Others who knew of the project were thinking of Germany, perhaps not as the eventual target, but as a rival in producing the bomb. The President had a deeper vision of the project.

If Churchill and De Gaulle were certain of victory from the day Pearl Harbor was attacked, it was because both were understandably obsessed with Hitler, who for them was the immediate danger. America's power, in their view, must first be used to secure victory over Germany.

Roosevelt had another obsession: Japan. He had no illusions of white "superiority," he did not underestimate the ingenuity, the courage and the infinite resourcefulness of the Japanese people. Hence the close attention with which he followed the work of the nuclear physicists at Los Alamos.

Before carrying out the last experiment to determine whether the "atomic bomb," as it was beginning to be called, could be exploded, two of the men who had first prompted Roosevelt's historic decision were stricken by remorse. They wanted to share it with the Preident.

The scientist Niels Bohr was first. As soon as he learned through intelligence sources that Germany was far behind in the race, Bohr asked Roosevelt to abandon the project. He argued that it was no longer necessary for victory and that it incurred the risk of a "later nuclear weapons race, which would surely lead to another war, which could mean the end of the world.'' It was his opinion that the order of priorities must be reversed. The experiment must be stopped and the manufacture of atomic weapons banned.

Roosevelt received Bohr for thirty minutes at the White House. The scientist was by then so upset and suddenly so confused that he did not succeed in explaining his viewpoint. With Japan on his mind, Roosevelt did not agree with what he could understand of it.

Next came a more thoughtful and better-prepared intervention by Alexander Sachs, who shared Bohr's obsession with the risks of unleashing a nuclear armaments race. Received by the President in December 1944, he approached the matter quite differently. After a long conversation during which the two men discussed the postwar world, and particularly the question of Japan, Sachs drafted a memorandum that incorporated the conclusion on which he thought they had agreed:

In the case of the success which has not yet occurred at Los Alamos, of a secret experimental explosion, a second will be organized to take place publicly somewhere in the Pacific. It will be attended by neutral and allied scientists and, if necessary, by representatives of the enemy. A detailed report of the capacities and the consequences of this extraordinary weapon will then be drafted in common, transmitted to the Japanese authorities, and the power of the weapon having been demonstrated, we will ask the enemy to surrender—once he has had concrete proof that the other option is annihilation.

Actually, Roosevelt had not decided to explode the bomb. He wanted to use it as a threat to force Japan to capitulate. He would decide when the time came. After a conversation with the President that seemed to confirm Sachs's memorandum, Secretary of War Stimson noted:

I have examined with him the two schools of thought concerning the authority that will be placed in charge of this project: try to keep it in the closet, among a secret circle of those who are running it at present, or put it in the hands of the international community's authority in the name of scientific freedom. I told him that this problem must be settled and that he should have a communiqué ready to be issued when the time came. He agreed.

That was in March 1945. At the beginning of April, the final experiment had not yet taken place at Los Alamos. Roosevelt had still not made his decision. He was obsessed with "thoughts about the Pacific, about Japan, about nuclear science, about the vast workshop in ruins that would have to be rebuilt," as one of the rare persons who spoke to him recorded.

On April 12, at his favorite place, Warm Springs, Georgia, where he had gone for a rest, he found himself wide awake at 6 A.M. His powerful mind, still indifferent to the growing weakness of his body, was haunted by Japan and the question of the nuclear bomb. He got up and asked for the newspapers and the mail.

The newspapers brought only good news: the Allies were no longer meeting any resistance in Europe. The mail was heavy. He looked at it briefly and put aside two documents to study: a personal letter from Einstein (the second) and, accompanying it, a memorandum from Leo Szilard. Deeply opposed to any atomic explosion, which they believed would expose all of humanity to too many risks, they implored Roosevelt to stop everything and spread the scientific information throughout the world. A bomb was no longer necessary.

Roosevelt intended to read these two documents in the afternoon. At twelve-thirty, while waiting for lunch, he agreed to continue sitting for the portrait ordered by his devoted friend Lucy Mercer, who was sitting there with him. He daydreamed during the sitting, lighting one cigarette after another. At one o'clock he said, "Another quarter hour; that will be all."

At one-fifteen he put his hand to his forehead as though a sudden migraine attack had come upon him. A few minutes later he collapsed. Cerebral hemorrhage. The date: April 12, 1945.

TOKYO WAS JUBILANT. Roosevelt was dead. America no longer had a leader. Japan, already knowing that she could not win the war, could now prepare for a negotiated peace with honor among equals. Emperor Hirohito gave thanks to heaven.

In all of Japan there was only one nuclear physicist, Yshio Nishina, who knew the theoretical calculations that could lead to a "chain reaction." But no one had ever summoned him. And he did not complain. He was Japan's leading pacifist.

On April 24, Harry Truman, seated in the armchair that had replaced the invalid's wheelchair in the Oval Office, listened to Secretary Stimson and General Grove's first account of a secret project that no one had ever mentioned to him: the Manhattan Project.

The two men explained to the President of the United States, as best they could, what was at stake. They pointed out that the first experimental bomb, scheduled to be exploded in the desert surrounding Los Alamos, should be ready during the month of July—in a little more than two months.

Truman, calling to mind his experience as an artillery officer, asked them about the explosive's power. Stimson replied that in principle, the first device should activate the equivalent of five hundred tons of conventional TNT. The second, which would be the bomb to launch, could have a capacity of several thousand tons of TNT.

Truman was visibly shaken by these figures and decided to take time to think it over. As a temporary measure, he created an "advisory committee" composed of three nuclear scientists and three government officials, to study all the options that would be presented to him. Members of the government committee were General Marshall, Secretary of War Stimson and Secretary of State Byrnes; from the scientific community came Vannevar Bush, James Conant and Karl Compton.

The first conclusion forwarded to Truman was of great importance. It declared that atomic energy could not be considered only from a military angle. It must also be seen to represent the establishment of a new relationship with the universe.

Numerous reports and meetings followed all during the spring and the beginning of summer. Truman did not want to rush into anything. He arranged for a note to be sent to the Japanese government, politely but firmly calling for cessation of hostilities and capitulation, while alluding to a "fearful threat the nature of which he did not specify."

The Prime Minister of Japan was now Admiral Suzuki, a man more open-minded than Tojo, but confident that it would be many years before the Americans could launch an attack against the island nation itself. On July 28 Admiral Suzuki let a few foreign journalists in on the secret of the "ultimatum from the Americans, which is only a familiar refrain to be treated with contempt."

The remark was reported in Washington to Secretary of State Byrnes, who, commenting on it in President Truman's presence, pronounced it "discouraging." They had to act. Truman asked for a slight delay. On August 2, he made the decision.

On the morning of August 6, at 1:45 A.M., then at 2:56, two squadrons of three B-29 bombers took off, one after the other, from their respective bases in the west of Guam, and came together again directly above Iwo Jima, an hour away from the Japanese coast, which had been inviolate for seven hundred years.

Among the six B-29s was one that was identical to the others —the *Enola Gay*. Its hold carried a device known as "Thin Man," the first atomic bomb.

At eight-fifteen, directly above the industrial area of the great port of Hiroshima, the mechanism was set in motion and the bomb dropped.

Since then the story of the indescribable phenomenon has been told many times. It continues to defy the imagination. The shock struck the minds of the Japanese leaders with a violence that surpassed all human faculties of apprehension.

To make them aware of what had happened, the White House immediately issued a communiqué: "This morning an American plane dropped a bomb, a single bomb, on Hiroshima . . . We have mastered an elementary force of the physical universe, that from which the sun draws its own power. This power has been unleashed against those who have put the Far East to fire and the sword."

In Tokyo, General Kawabe, Chief of Staff of the Army, read a telegram from his intelligence services: "The city of Hiroshima has just been destroyed in one blow by a single bomb."

Kawabe could not believe it.

In return, he asked about the condition of the powerful Japanese Second Army, whose headquarters were in Hiroshima. He was told that at eight-fifteen that day most of the troops had assembled on the city's parade ground for their hour of exercises, and that three minutes later there was nothing left of them.

Belatedly, the physicist Yshio Nishina was summoned to the Ministry of War to meet with the entire general staff. He confirmed that this was indeed what a nuclear bomb would be like.

The horror was imprinted on everyone's mind. No one talked about it, there were no discussions. It was as if a natural disaster had occurred—an earthquake or a hurricane. The government and the military officials returned to their routines. But they were no longer the same men. Every one of the leaders who survived confirmed it: they were unable to think or plan logically.

Hours, days passed. Japan was silent, paralyzed.

On Thursday, August 9, the Supreme Council of War, the

body that brought together government and military leaders, held its usual meeting. During the discussion a message arrived. It read: "A second device, the same as the one that destroyed Hiroshima, has just exploded, at 11:01, in the port of Nagasaki" —Japan's legendary, sacred ancient door to the world.

The Council decided to go in a body to the Imperial Palace to speak with the Emperor.

The Emperor never left the Imperial Palace. He never spoke in public. He took no part in government meetings. He was the incarnation of Japan. But if he were to speak or give a command, there was no precedent for not obeying him immediately.

The Emperor spoke. More precisely, alone in his office, he dictated a message for the Prime Minister instructing him to accept the American ultimatum immediately and end the war. The Prime Minister called a Cabinet meeting. The ministers agreed to obey the Emperor. Responsibility for the request to surrender would be assumed by the government and the government alone, enabling the Emperor to remain aloof in the silence of his palace.

It was then that the consequences of the nuclear explosions first shattered the deepest foundation of Japanese tradition. In the Imperial Staff's great conference room, General Anami, the Minister of War, General Umezu, now Chief of Staff, and Admiral Toyoda, Chief of Staff of the Navy, stood up one by one and declared that they refused to accept capitulation. They refused to obey the Emperor, an event as unthinkable as the atomic bomb itself—and as revolutionary.

Hirohito learned of the unprecedented action and asked the Prime Minister to call a meeting of the entire government for that very evening, the ninth of August, in the Imperial Palace's underground shelter.

The meeting began at eight-thirty. The generals were intransigent. General Anami declared in the Emperor's presence, "The hour of glory has just sounded for Japan. We must let the Americans come to assault the Empire itself, on our archipelago's three islands. And Japanese power will annihilate them as in 1281 the divine kamikaze wind stopped the forces of Kublai Khan, the only one who ever attempted this impossible assault.''

Prime Minister Suzuki turned toward the Emperor and asked him to speak. Stunned by what he had just heard, the Emperor, who had suddenly become a man among others, without hesitation and without protocol curtly repeated his order to cease hostilities. The meeting was ended.

The Emperor realized that nothing had been settled, and so he decided on a course of action that would have irrevocable consequences. For the first time in the history of the dynasty, his people would hear his voice.

He sent for a recording machine. It was heavy and difficult to operate, but he recorded a brief message to be broadcast an hour later over all Japanese radio stations. He asked the nation to accept the decision of fate and give up the armed struggle. He concluded, ''We charge you, you our loyal subjects, to faithfully carry out our will.''

Before the voice which had never before been heard reached the people, there was an attempt at insurrection. Two generals, accompanied by their guards, entered the Imperial Palace and ordered the chief of the Emperor's personal guard to surrender and hand over the recording. When he refused he was dispatched by two sword thrusts. Another officer burst into the room, and he too was killed.

When Admiral Takigishi, a former associate of Admiral Yamamoto's in the Navy's high command, learned of the madness that had taken hold of the entire military command, he intervened to protect the Emperor. He ordered the rebels arrested and saw to the broadcast of the recording.

General Anami committed hara-kiri. Within an hour, the four remaining army chiefs followed his example. Then it was Admiral Takigishi's turn to commit hara-kiri. It was all over.

No people had ever known such an end, such annihilation. If

the country were to rise again one day, it would have to be a different Japan. The past must be erased, the future invented.

The next day, August 15, Nippon Kogaku's board of directors met in Tokyo. It was their firm which had equipped the Imperial Navy's cruisers with long-range optical instruments. The men and the instruments were lost in the Pacific, but the technology remained—in the minds of the engineers. Nippon Kogaku's directors decided to put it to civilian uses. They would begin with the manufacture of cameras. They would be called "Nikons."

It was Japan's first act of rebirth—the first step on the road to the scientific adventure, technological conquest, a new planet. . . .

O N AUGUST 7, 1980, the front page of most of the world's newspapers headlined the official observance of the thirty-fifth anniversary of the nuclear explosion at Hiroshima. Certain other news items reported that day were particularly relevant.

For the first time, Switzerland's famous watch industry was forced to request a subsidy from the Swiss federal government in Berne. Not even among their traditional banking allies could the watchmakers raise the fifteen million Swiss francs needed to enable the Swiss to catch up with Japan's booming electronic-watch industry. In 1975, when the Japanese entered the market, the Swiss, long the undisputed leaders in the marketplace, did not believe that the Japanese effort would last long. In 1980 the number of watches (mostly electronic) made in Japan far outnumbered those made in Switzerland. A "relief plan" was urgently needed; the Swiss watch industry was in danger of being destroyed by the Japanese, who had revolutionized the business by relying on modern technology in the form of microcircuits instead of the traditional "mechanical" movements, which still require precise hand labor.

At the same time, the directors of Germany's leading automobile manufacturers jointly announced a "five-year plan," calling for an investment of unprecedented size "in order to catch up with Japanese automotive technology, which is now the most advanced in the world." Volkswagen and Mercedes Benz, which held the lead in Europe, thus made it known publicly that between 1980 and 1984 they each intended to spend ten billion deutsche marks on the electronic transformation of their factories. BMW also announced it would spend five billion marks.

West Germany's employers' federation announced several months later: "It is not so much a question of expanding our industry's capacity as it is of rationalizing it by means of modern electronics, so that between now and 1985 it will be competitive with the Japanese who have become its masters." In Frankfurt it was pointed out that imports of Japanese cars into West Germany had doubled compared to the preceding year. In 1980, Japan took 10 percent of the *domestic* German car market and was pushing German cars out of export markets in the United States and the Third World. In 1981, this blitz accelerated even further.

Officials of the European Economic Community, which has come to rely on Germany as the most powerful European producer and consumer, were alarmed by Germany's decline, especially since they could no longer count on exporting to the American market, which was already depressed and where the little room available for imports had already become a Japanese preserve.

England, having abandoned the idea of going it alone against Japan, and at the bottom of her postwar economic curve of activity, asked the Japanese to participate directly in her leading industries. So did Italy. But this increasing trend toward collaboration unleashed passions in Brussels, where high-ranking officials of the EEC were under instructions from their governments to "find urgent ways to check Japanese penetration into the Community."

In London, agreement was reached between British General Electric and the Japanese Hitachi group for the manufacture of television sets and a whole range of hi-fi systems. In commenting on the new partnership, which followed by a few months Honda's invasion of the British automobile market, a spokesman for Hitachi said to the press, "Why would you waste your money making strictly English products as far as television sets, radios, tape recorders, calculators, computers, etc., are concerned? Because of our concentration on microprocessors, Japanese industry, which is only too pleased to enter into partnership, can produce enough to satisfy the world's needs."

With Saudi Arabia leading the way, the Persian Gulf countries have contracted with a Japanese team, which has been working on the spot for a year, for the construction of the most powerful petrochemical plant in the world. It will be finished in three years, and its impact will lead to the closing, in Japan alone, of the Mitsubishi group's two petrochemical plants.

The Japanese have come a long way following their tremendous defeat in World War II. How far can be estimated by looking at the country's income. *The Far East Economic Review,* Asia's leading economic journal, published a table which summarized the dimensions of the Japanese epic.

The journal traced the evolution of Japan's "income per inhabitant" from the "zero point" in the summer of 1945 to the summer of 1980:

Income per inhabitant in 1945: $20 per capita.

Ten years later, in 1956: $300—still at the third-world level, but for the last time.

Ten years later, in 1967: $1,000, or the figure that Brazil had reached before the first oil crisis in 1970.

In 1970, at the time of the first oil crisis: $1,800.

After the second oil crisis, in October 1973: $3,600.

At the end of 1979, after the third oil crisis: $10,000. For the first time equality is reached with the West.

Finally at the beginning of 1981: $12,000.

The growth curve of Japan's economy will rise even more rapidly with the recent decisions by the MITI and the Keidanren to make systematic use of so-called "computers on a flea" (computers-on-a-chip). Microprocessors, which were not in existence seven years ago, are now the indispensable cells of all data processing and the building blocks for all industry.

Let us turn again to Japan at the moment of its atomic destruction. Edwin O. Reischauer, American ambassador to Japan right after the war, and author of the classic *Japan: The Story of a Nation,* writes:

> In the late summer of 1945 Japan lay in ruins. Some 2 million of her people had died in the war, a third of them civilians; 40 percent of the aggregate area of the cities had been destroyed, and urban population had dropped by over half; industry was at a standstill; even agriculture, short of equipment, fertilizer, and manpower, had declined. The people had poured all their energies into the war, blindly trusting their leaders and confident that "Japanese spirit" would prevail. Now they were physically and spiritually exhausted. Many were in rags and half-starved, and all were bewildered and mentally numbed. The "divine wind" had failed.

Yet from August 1945, from the "zero point," to the 1980s, Japan was able to transform herself and perform a miracle of change and advance unseen anywhere else in the modern era. Japan stands as a model to the world, especially the Third World, for her success transcends her culture and history. At a time when all the peoples of the world are facing chaos, Japan's example deserves attention only if there is a universal component hidden within it. It must contain a secret that goes beyond Japan. At its very core, the modern Japanese adventure must have a *human basis,* a *human* formula that can be applied elsewhere.

Americans and Europeans are fond of explaining Japan's success in taking away their export markets, and in making superior products, by describing them as "workaholics, living in rabbit warrens" (as cited from a report of the European Economic Community's mission to Japan in 1979). Their success is explained as being due to lower salaries, the absence of a social-security system, severe measures against worker absenteeism, very short vacations, the habit of "blindly copying what others have invented."

These are all clichés which the Western mind continues to cultivate to assure itself of its superiority. The Japanese have done nothing to destroy them. They continue digging, silently, into the one unique and inexhaustible deposit that they discovered by force of circumstances, and which, from year to year, proves to be more productive, richer and more valuable than all the oil of the Middle East: the mine of intelligence.

This resource, of course, is not the monopoly of the Japanese. It is a resource that belongs to the world—to Europeans, Indians, Africans, Latins, Arabs, Americans or Chinese. All of us can share in this resource, because there is no Japanese intelligence, only human intelligence. Japan's only genius is in being the first to exploit it as the major natural resource.

History and circumstance led Japan to turn inward toward the mind. The great island nation contains few natural resources: no oil, little coal, no iron or uranium, no bauxite, and only a tiny amount of agricultural land. Moreover, after Hiroshima and Nagasaki the Japanese were reduced to absolute poverty, with nearly all their factories destroyed. Their humiliating defeat cracked open their rigid social structure, and the voice of the Emperor demanding acceptance of defeat shattered established beliefs and patterns of thinking.

The elementary demands of survival forced them into constant thinking about recovery, what they could produce, improve, exchange, learn, and invent more efficiently and less expensively.

Does it take the agony of Hiroshima to release this creative force in us?

To understand what the human spirit and determination can achieve when necessary it is sufficient to recall the story of

Samuel Pisar, one of the youngest survivors of Auschwitz. With his entire family wiped out, he entered that hell at the age of twelve and remained until he was sixteen. On ten occasions he found himself waiting in the anteroom of the gas chamber; each time he came up with an idea that saved him. When he emerged from this universe of absolute horror and cruelty, he lived like a savage amid the ashes of Europe, rejecting all of the rules of a civilization whose abominable failure he had just experienced. Then gradually he took himself in hand.

Born in Poland, he became a Soviet schoolboy under the Stalinist occupation, a German slave, a British subject, an Australian student and, finally, an American citizen. Pisar is anything but Japanese. But the truth, the message of confidence in the human mind and spirit expressed in his recent work, *Of Blood and Hope,* is of the same nature as the Japanese adventure.

There is no essential difference between a person born in postwar Tokyo and one born in current-day Calcutta, Paris, Lagos or Jerusalem. Each one possesses the same strength that can give rise to unlimited powers of invention—the day his back is to the wall.

And our backs *are* to the wall. Our world is on the edge of disintegration. No one knows what to do to help it regain the collective life force that has left it. The past no longer furnishes us with what we need for the future. We must create our own possibilities of rebirth—our own future.

I F THERE IS ONE FACTOR that explains Japanese success, it is "the permanent and collective quest for knowledge." When Daniel Bell, Peter Drucker, and a few others announced the advent of the postindustrial society in which knowledge would replace capital as the basic resource, they did not imagine the lightning speed with which this new conception would be accepted by Japan's leading circles and soon by the whole country. The national consensus is formed around the supreme importance accorded the permanent pursuit of learning and knowledge throughout one's life. Japanese society is permeated with all forms of information gathering, from the general to the particular, from the short-term to the long-term, from the formal to the informal, in the classrooms and on the golf course, in meetings and conferences, in research institutes and in televised debates. One learns from everyone: from professionals, from amateurs, from friends as well as enemies. New friends are made when it appears that they might be the source of new knowledge.

Study and knowledge extend from one end of life to the other. Upon completing their studies, what young Japanese have acquired is not basically a store of knowledge—they have learned how to learn. Even when they read at home it is in order later to discuss with others what they have learned.

Employees and wage earners are encouraged to ask for supplementary training outside of work. The same is true for young and old women who stay at home. Family and friends are encouraged to bring together persons at home who might be cut off from this permanent circulation of communication and information. Adult-education courses are organized everywhere: by local communities, industrial and commercial firms, local and regional associations, by newspapers and merchants as well as universities.

After work, an employee is first of all looking for opportunities to learn something that will increase his knowledge and improve his efficiency. But he also wants to study whatever interests him, even if it has no direct relationship to his profession. He thinks that he might find this an advantage in the long run. When a foreign visitor comes to Japan, each Japanese he meets instinctively asks himself what he can learn from the stranger. "And the three million who now travel abroad each year look for little hints of new ideas they might apply at home."

Not only do Japanese spend infinitely more time reading than Americans, but the proportion of information in what they read is greater. Each of the two leading Japanese daily newspapers has a circulation of more than six million, four times greater than the largest American daily.

Herbert Passin, chairman of the department of sociology at Columbia University, commented recently that when he wants to see new ideas debated in Japan, he and his Japanese colleagues can find a great number of publications willing to publish them immediately, whereas in the United States it often takes several months to find an outlet for their ideas. Nearly thirty thousand books are now published in Japan each year. In addition, the amount of information translated into English each year is minuscule compared to the volume translated into Japanese.

Japanese bureaucrats, in particular, consider it a prime responsibility to be as knowledgeable as possible about the most recent information in their fields. They do not hesitate to mobilize private institutions to help them.

In the decades after World War II, for example, MITI officials decided that priority must be given to the development of basic Japanese industries such as *steel and electric power.* This decision followed an exhausting, worldwide information-gathering operation. They began a similar process in the late 1960s that resulted in Japan's push in computers. Anything having to do with supplying and saving energy took priority in Japan after the oil crises in the early 1970s; and all the industries were mobilized to find the means of exchange necessary for a regular supply of oil. New technological projects such as huge petrochemical plants were adapted to the Middle East, in order to link the Persian Gulf countries more closely to Japanese technology. For even greater success, a rapidly growing number of students were encouraged to study Arabic and Middle Eastern culture, to establish lasting ties to the Middle East.

The Japanese make a point of listening to foreign experts. Anyone from abroad recognized as an authority is invited by governmental authorities or one of the many private groups to speak or write in Japan. Foreigners who visit Japan are received with truly impressive generosity and interest. On the whole, the Japanese prefer not to spend much time in discussion or argument. They prefer to listen attentively, carefully taking notes. They save discussion and debate for later—among themselves.

Asahi Shimbun is a newspaper whose daily press run of eight million copies holds the world's record. Every day it covers a wide range of subjects in many articles, none of which exceeds four typewritten pages. According to a simple, general principle adopted by the paper, effort should never be demanded of the reader but of the journalist, who must tailor his articles to this compact format designed to attract the reader.

In 1979 *Asahi Shimbun* celebrated its founding one hundred years earlier. Celebrated is not exactly the word. There was no party and no round of laudatory speeches. *Asahi*'s directors

preferred to invite five foreigners, economists and political officials, from Europe, America and Asia, to take part in a public
debate. Five major themes concerning the problems of the
1980s were presented by five professors from the University of
Tokyo.

The audience who attended this symposium were not, for the
most part, distinguished or even specially selected guests. An
announcement of the debate appeared in the newspaper, and
any interested reader was free to enter the hall at any moment
during the discussions.

The day's talks were communicated to the Japanese public as
a whole, first by radio, then by the daily editions of the newspaper itself, every other day, in an inside supplement that carried a summary on its first page. Thus the five foreigners who
had come to talk were heard by all of Japan. And what they said
could be discussed in every town and in every home, during the
evening or on the train.

Of all the lessons drawn from this event, the Japanese retained one that came from a nation that was Japan's greatest
European rival—Germany.

At the end of 1979, at the time this seminar was taking place,
Japan was becoming the target of harsh European and American attacks and criticism for the immodesty with which it pa-
raded, month after month, new records of production and
export. These records were mounting as many European nations were sliding into deficit, with their oil imports surging
ahead of their industrial exports. From all quarters came recommendations, and then demands, that the Japanese take measures "to put the brakes on this serious imbalance." Publicly,
no one raised a dissenting voice in this chorus of complaints
and threats against Japan, which, along with OPEC, was
blamed for world economic decay.

But then a man invited as one of the respected economic
experts in the world spoke in the public forum in Tokyo. He
was Professor Herbert Giersh, president of the World Eco-

nomic Institute, who had come a long distance—from Kiel, a cold port on the Baltic Sea, near the tip of Germany.

Under Professor Giersh the Kiel Institute has acquired respect well beyond Germany's borders for the rigorous independence of its economic analyses and forecasts. In order to remain free of any outside influence, Giersh makes it a rule not to accept private clients. He allows no German or foreign industrialist, no private or public firm, to finance him or hold a contract with the institute. He works only for the public. Day after day he examines the world economic indicators with his specialists and his computers, and he regularly publishes the results of his observations, with comments that he considers necessary for "the public's information and the government's direction."

To fund the monthly budget required to run this powerful machine, Professor Giersh negotiated with the federal government in Bonn an automatic annual subsidy for half of his expenses; the other half is assured by the same sort of arrangement with the regional government of Hamburg. Neither one has the right to interfere with the work or publications of the Kiel Institute.

At the beginning of 1976, when the second oil crisis was smashing the world economy, Professor Giersh and his team published a study disagreeing with the German government's own analysis. As is his custom, he sent it to the various ministries as well as to newspaper and governing boards.

Giersh soon received a message from Bonn indicating that the Kiel Institute's attitude was embarrassing to government policy and suggesting that if he continued along this path he would risk seeing the subsidies cut. Giersh replied immediately that this threat was unacceptable, that it was advisable to withdraw it, and that otherwise he himself would make it public on television at the first opportunity. The threat was withdrawn. Giersh has not received another.

When Giersh took the floor at the *Asahi Shimbun* forum, he astonished the Japanese by declaring, in substance, "Contrary to all the nonsense being spread about the so-called indispensable measures that you should take to reduce your exports in order to relieve your partners and rivals of the industrial world and contribute to world balance, I must say, frankly, that I am of another opinion.

"These braking measures would not be consistent with healthy economic logic and could lead to dangerous results.

"First of all, they would artificially push up domestic consumption and unleash inflationary risks within Japan which have been remarkably curbed up to now.

"Then, by pulling back from foreign expansion, Japan would allow industrial competitors to relax their efforts at rationalizing, modernizing and increasing the competitiveness of their industries. Without Japanese competition overseas, Europeans would curb the development of their own technology and slow down the movement toward increasing the quality of their products.

"It is a cynical proposal to suggest that such a device could promote a healthier world economy. The more the Japanese export, thanks to their technological superiority, the more the other world economic agents are encouraged to make a similar effort.

"Consequently, I will conclude with a different proposal.

"I am strongly in favor of the increasing profit that the Japanese gain from their industrial force, which has been modernized through technological progress. But since this imbalance must evidently be integrated into a world situation that is far from being stabilized and demands corrective measures, I suggest that the Japanese invest a great part of the monetary means that they have accumulated in a vast program of new projects abroad, precisely in countries where investment is declining. I suggest a worldwide dissemination of Japanese profits, in the form of new investments. And if someone tells me that next year or the year after this will increase the profits of the Japanese, I would reply, This is exacly what I hope for—on one condition, that the Japanese continue to reinvest overseas.

"I know that I will not please my European and American colleagues, but that is neither my intention nor my role. I seek whatever measures can contribute to a global stimulation through the creation of new economic activities to replace those that must disappear. I have given you one example of what one can do to succeed."

The Japanese press gave Professor Giersh's simple and courageous statement extensive coverage. The complete text of his remarks was immediately translated into Japanese, and photocopies were made overnight by the technicians whom *Asahi* had placed at the seminar to respond immediately to any requests from the MITI and the Keidanren. The pros and cons of Giersh's speech were discussed by the Keidanren during staff meetings and integrated into that organization's recommendations to the government on policies to be pursued in industry and foreign trade. Giersh's extraordinary speech was closely studied by the Japanese government.

It deeply influenced Tokyo's foreign exchange policy. The yen, which the Bank of Japan allowed to appreciate in value for months dropped for many consecutive months. Whereas a rising yen made exports more expensive, a falling yen made them cheaper and allowed Japan to acquire new markets without worrying about complaints from Europe and the U.S.

In the months following his speech, Sony and Honda announced new decisions to establish factories in the United States. Nissan has followed. The plans were greeted unanimously as "goodwill gestures" and as supports to the American economy that would reduce imports and the outflow of dollars, while creating jobs.

The only cloud on the horizon for Japan's new strategy of investing abroad is protectionism. The increase and deployment of Japanese investments could provoke the erection of capital barriers, just as the invasion of Japanese products induced a wave of trade barriers. Already attempts by Japan to invest in Italy and Britain are being deplored by the French.

If, having increased barriers against better and less expensive products, we begin to raise them against investments themselves, we will be on the edge of economic warfare. And that can only mean disaster for the Third World and general impotence.

S ony, Honda—behind each of these famous labels is a man. Behind the latest-model Honda Accord and the newest Sony stereo set is a Japanese entrepreneurial genius.

In less than two decades, the German, English and American manufacturers of motorbikes (BMW, Harley Davidson, Triumph, BSA), once world leaders, have been entirely crushed by Honda. The Japanese company has conquered the whole range of markets from mopeds for adolescents to the big-engined models used by the police. But how and why?

The hottest-selling consumer electronic product is now the videotape recorder. The VTR was not invented by Sony; nor was the color TV, but the Japanese manufacturers have conquered both the VTR and the color-television markets in America. But how and why?

Masuru Ibuka, the engineer who is the founder and president of Sony, and Soichiro Honda, the cocky youth from a Tokyo suburb who has become the worldwide emperor of motorcycles and small autos and is now beginning to tackle electronic cars, are two friends of the same generation. Each one speaks of the other's genius with sensitivity, insight and frankness.

Sony's Ibuka has the air of an absent-minded professor. Friends who have known him over a period of time notice with surprise that it is always *he* who takes the trouble to come to see *them*. He comes by, drops in, and visits. When his friends go to buy electronic toys for children, he goes along and never hesitates to recommend a product made by Hitachi or Toshiba rather than Sony, if it seems more suitable. He takes his visitors to one of his many experimentation centers for mental development. He is always available, kind and considerate—a warm seventy-three-year-old man who is sometimes almost childlike in his passions or pleasures.

This famous industrialist who has never stopped inventing and perfecting his machines, which are low-priced so that they will be within the reach of young people, no longer takes an interest in objects. He has founded an "Association for Mental Development," and his skill is now devoted to perfecting the intelligence and brainpower of individuals.

For Ibuka, his future objective is the worldwide diffusion of the only Japanese secret that he would like to see introduced to all peoples as quickly as possible: training and improvement of the mind. In his youth Ibuka had no time to write. But at the age of seventy-one he was eager to write a book about his favorite topic—the development of the mind.

Now when he is questioned about Sony's latest breakthrough in France or Brazil, he listens politely but his mind is elsewhere. But whenever the discussion turns to the mental development of the young or the old, Ibuka comes to life. He stands up, walks about, concentrates on the choice of words that will translate his thought exactly.

Ibuka's work, so surprising when one reads it for the first time, is characterized by a simplicity that is difficult to imagine, impossible to describe. It is in rereading it that one discovers its depth. It is the very essence of the new Japan, so foreign to the sophistication of former times. Consider these words from *Kindergarten Is Too Late:*
On himself:

Readers may well wonder why I, an engineer by training and now company president, should happen to step into the field of early development. My reasons are partially "public"—that is, I find myself deeply concerned about the present rebellions of the young, and asking myself how far our present education has contributed to their discontent; and partly private—I have a child who is mentally retarded. While this child was going through the early developing stages, I was totally ignorant of the idea that a child born with such a heavy burden could develop to a remarkable degree, if properly educated from birth. What opened my eyes was the claim of Dr. Shinichi Suzuki that "any child will do well—it all depends on the method of educating." When I witnessed in person the remarkable results of Dr. Suzuki's "Talent Education" method of teaching the violin to very young children, I could not help regretting that I as a parent had not been able to do anything for my own child.

On the brain:

The brain cells of human beings are said to amount to ten billion in number, but most of the brain cells of a newborn baby are not yet in operation. Recent research indicates that the "operative cells" will have been found, however, by the age of three.

Individual brain cells are all separate at birth, and they cannot function individually at all. A microscopic photograph of the brain cells taken right after birth shows that as time goes on and the brain develops, protuberances come increasingly into being, connecting one cell to another, like bridges. That is, brain cells stretch out their hands to one another and then link and cling together, to respond to and correlate information received from outside through the senses. This process is exactly like the working of the transistors in an electronic computer. No individual transistor can function by itself, but when they are connected by a circuit to other transistors, all the transistors together function as an electronic computer.

The period when the brain cells learn most rapidly to make these connections is the period between birth and three years of age. Seventy to eighty percent of the connections are formed by the age of three. And as these connections develop, the capacity of the brain increases. In the first six months after birth, the brain capacity has reached 50 percent of its adult potential, and by age three 80 percent. This, of course, does not mean that the brain cells of the child after age three stop developing: it is the rear part of the brain that develops by the age of three, and at about age four a different part of the brain begins to go through a wiring process. This is the front part, called the "frontal lobes." The difference is in the wiring process during the periods before and after the age of three and is equivalent to the development first of the hardware of the equipment, which is the main circuitry of the machine, and then to the software, which determines the way in which the equipment is used.

The fundamental facility of the brain to catch stimuli from outside, make patterns of them, and then remember is the "hardware," the facility on which all further development depends. Such advanced capacities as thinking, willing, creating, and feeling develop after the age of three; but they use the faculty already formed by that age.

Therefore, unless the "hardware" formed in the first three years is sound, there is no point in repeatedly attempting to train the "how to use" activity in later years; just as there is no point in trying to operate an electronic computer of poor quality and expect to achieve good results.

At the age of seventy-five, Soichiro Honda still resembles a little boy. Strangers who meet him say that he is, of course, a sort of genius but "also a little mad, the proof being his odd habit of bursting out laughing all the time." Even when visiting his factories one notices that he laughs at every turn. Everything amuses him. Life is a pleasure to him.

Dinner at Honda's is a delightful experience. His little place in Tokyo's green suburb looks like a dollhouse, and there are never more than five or six people around his table. He himself composes the menu. And when he entertains a friend who does not read Japanese, he writes it out with an explanation of each dish in English. All during the meal he gives a running comment on the dishes. He talks about several things at once, without losing the thread of any of them. Conversation with him is dazzling.

If you mention the famous method employed in his factories that makes each worker personally responsible for the quality of each piece and even gives him the power to stop the entire factory by simply pressing a white button if he thinks a piece is imperfect, Honda will explain that far from curtailing production this system has contributed to his success. It ensures the flawless quality for which Honda is known. Honda's famous "quality control circles" supplement its technology and are one of the keys to Japanese productivity. The "QCs" are small personal groups, rather than assembly-line masses, who work together on solutions and on the constant improvement of production. So successful are the Japanese QCs that advanced U.S. companies such as the semiconductor-maker Intel have begun using them to raise quality.

Mr. Honda says he owes his success to the confidence he has in each one of his workers. It is because of them that his machines are the best in the world.

Pursuing his human, industrial and philosophical arguments to their logical conclusion, he has gone so far as to disinherit his family. They will never inherit control of his business. He discussed this quite frankly at the dinner table, in front of his wife and his thirty-two-year-old son. His beloved son has had to start his own business. Honda refused to take him in or even to help him gather the capital to create his business.

Bursting out in a loud laugh, Honda said, "You see, they won't get anything. None of that belongs to me. It belongs to those who are responsible for Honda's quality. What does my wife have to do with it? And my son? I have given him the most beautiful gift I could. I have obliged him to make his own way without owing me anything. Imagine how he would have turned out if I had spoiled him."

At the end of dinner Mr. Honda was asked, "In your opinion, what will happen to industrial companies that don't accept the same method you have adopted and remain in the present capitalist system?"

Honda did not hesitate: "They shall all perish."

O F ALL THE FACTORIES IN THE WORLD, the one that receives the most visitors is in the Aichi region of Japan, in the center of the archipelago. It belongs to Toyota. A dual highway links it to the Pacific port of Nagoya, where day after day unassembled parts arrive and finished automobiles are shipped to every country in the world. In 1979, this "Toyota city" became the world's leading exporter of automobiles. A year later, in 1980, Japan surpassed America to become the world's largest producer of cars, with ten million units.

Visitors who make their way to the heart of the Toyota complex are always amazed. As soon as they enter one of the eight plants grouped in cloverleaf fashion, they discover the most highly automated plant in the world: a factory without workers.

From each side of the plant and all along the two assembly lines the robots are at work. They examine the chassis, the exterior and interior parts, assemble them, mount them, connect them, weld them, paint them, check them. Once through to the other end of the line, automobiles emerge ready to be shipped.

These robots are the most recent of the "thinking" machines, resulting from the introduction of "microprocessors" in each instrument at each phase of industrial production. Depending on how they are programmed, they control the most delicate and most complex tasks at a speed far exceeding and a cost far below the most specialized and experienced human teams they replace. While the automobile industry is suffering in both the

U.S. and Europe, it is in full expansion in Japan, because of the robots. Right now all the major European and American car companies are borrowing heavily from the banks, and, like Chrysler, from the government, to launch massive multibillion-dollar modernization programs to replace their old plants and equipment with a new microelectronic base.

A factory without workers does not mean men without work. Although the robots perform all the assembly-line tasks, Toyota employees do not stream to unemployment offices. Instead they go to one of the apprenticeship schools or institutes of training, education or retraining which make up the "internal system of education" developed at Toyota. After suitable education, accelerated by computer assistance, wage earners find another career open to them. The training courses permit them to take higher-paying jobs, above the work done by computers and robots, in the immense "software" areas, where the nourishment of the new machines can be produced only by human minds.

Employment is, therefore, no longer a problem. To respond to the human needs of the computerized data-processing system which is the new basis of production, the internal training complex demands more workers than the assembly lines lay off.

A few figures will clarify this mystery.

Computerized data processing and its robotic systems permit an output of sixty-five cars per year per work station in Toyota factories, against ten to twelve for American and European automakers.

And yet the two hundred robots at work at Toyota are only the beginning. By the end of 1982 the Toyota program will have 720 robots. This development feeds itself: the more one puts robots to work, the more the output rises, the more the car is improved and its price lowered, the more foreign sales and financial benefits increase, the more employees are freed for initiation into the various phases of software, and the more the new robots are improved.

The robot, which must become firmly established everywhere, demands a space of planetary dimensions; otherwise it will suffocate. For this transformation will not occur only on the Japanese archipelago. It will necessarily have to depend on the industrialized world and, before long, on the countries of the Third World.

This change will be a rapid one. The new technological revolution will skip the stages of classical industrialization, such as heavy steel production or large textile manufacturing based on cheap oil, and go directly to computers made from silicon and sand. And while the old industries were dependent on heavy manual labor, the new industries depend on brainpower to conceive and carry out programming.

Japan has paved the way for this transformation. One understands why this is so by looking at the global distribution of robots. Of the 60,000 robots working throughout the world, 6,000 are in West Germany, 3,200 in the United States, 600 in Sweden, 300 in France, 180 in Great Britain, 100 or less in a half dozen other countries, and 47,000 in Japan, states the Mitsubishi Report.

$\mathbf{H}$ONDA AND SONY are not the only Japanese corporations to take the global lead in recent years. The creative spark also kindles the officers and engineers of Fujitsu, the leading Japanese manufacturer of computers. And they set their sights on the impossible: challenging the giant of giants, the only genuine high-tech monopoly in more than a hundred countries; the company that has won the boldest industrial races with financial outlays for research and development that few other nations would dream of spending; the firm that employs the top researchers from every continent, and is constantly breaking new ground in its laboratories: the famous IBM.

There is no example in industrial history of supremacy comparable to IBM's. It is an absolute power, unrivaled in its field for thirty years. It is this global Goliath, whose activities outside the United States have surpassed its American operation for years, at which Fujitsu has hurled its challenge in 1980. But what will this David use for a slingshot?

Compared to IBM, Fujitsu is still only a very small manufacturer of electronic equipment. In the first quarter of 1981, for example, the Japanese firm exported only a few hundred computers. But up to now Fujitsu has not directed its resources toward manufacturing machines and dominating the market for "equipment." It has instead concentrated its priorities on human beings, and especially on the human beings of the Asian Third World.

Seven years ago Fujitsu established two training institutes for persons with no specialization in data processing. One, in Japan, the Fujitsu Computer School, is reserved for persons from other countries in the Pacific. Five first-rate computer scientists are assigned to each group of twenty-five students taking a six-month course—long enough for basic training that will enable them to become involved in computer programming. The other institute is in the Singapore-based Asian Information Processing Center, which serves all of the neighboring countries of Southeast Asia. It trains in their own language future programmers, whose special function, on returning home, is to familiarize others with data processing.

Such is Fujitsu's carefully considered calculation: *people first and foremost*. Programming, software, training in the new technology, the human milieu of machines and their languages, the "transfer of technology" to the level of minds themselves, for peoples who are not yet part of this world and who must be introduced into it by the most efficient methods and with respect for their culture.

An important short cut is occurring here: avoiding the long, expensive and primitive process that the West had to follow and attempting to go directly to the society of tomorrow being built by the information technologies.

Fujitsu has decided to stake everything on people and the essential role they play in technological development. Moreover, the Japanese firm simplifies its task by building equipment that is "IBM compatible"—integrating its own computers exactly with IBM's so that any IBM user can substitute for his accustomed instrument a Fujitsu computer.

In the sober, cautious Mitsubishi Report, Fujitsu has a special place:

On examining Fujitsu's resources and strategy, it is our conclusion that this firm can compete with IBM sooner than imagined. Here are the reasons:

1. The transfers of technology, relating directly to the peo-

— 191

ple that Fujitsu trains in its institutes in Japan and abroad, represent a new factor for essential development. The experience acquired by Fujitsu in this very special area could become a decisive advantage opposite IBM.

2. This same strategy, centered on the human dimension of the progress of computer science, has brought Fujitsu another advantage. Fujitsu's technologies are not felt to be "foreign bodies" in the non-Japanese milieu in which they are beginning to take root. In a way they became integrated in advance due to the fact that human implanting preceded them.

3. On this point, IBM's strategy does not yet seem to have successfully come to terms with the new demands of the Japanese data process competition which is more like an "advance of mobile guerrillas" than a powerful confrontation between huge machines. We see the first sign of this in the fact that since 1979 the share of the market held by IBM computers installed in Japan fell for the first time below the share taken by Fujitsu.

4. This tendency is destined to increase, because IBM still upholds the principle of one hundred percent control of its foreign subsidiaries. This policy has already given rise to a certain number of difficulties and friction in many industrialized countries. They will be even more considerable when data processing is extended to the Third World. All the more so since Fujitsu, all set to enter into competition, will appear with the opposite strategy: local control and minority Japanese participation.

The last factor is the scientific and technical "milieu" in which the mother cell of the IBM empire functions: the American milieu.

There is no doubt that, for a long time, a great part of IBM's vigor and creativity have come from the American milieu. But with the progressive decline of the American economic stock's productivity and forces of innovation in the 1970s, it has become impoverished.

In conclusion: the conditions seem to us right for data processing on a worldwide scale to confirm the value of the choices made by Fujitsu. The present disproportion in strength, still overwhelmingly favorable to IBM in numbers and in equipment, will reverse itself when the predominance of software, based only on human factors, grows.

What this report did not mention was that at the very moment when this forecast was drafted some signs of fragility in IBM's power had begun to appear. For the first time, the preceding summer, the giant had found itself forced to borrow $1.5 billion and float a bond issue of a billion dollars through an investment banking syndicate. IBM also got a private loan of $300 million from Saudi Arabia.

We can judge the importance of these changes by referring to two works published at the beginning of the 1970s that deal with the "IBM case." One is by the American William Rodgers, who wrote in *A Biography of IBM:* "In all of history, no other firm has committed such investments to technological innovations. Such a policy has succeeded only thanks to this firm's enormous financial reserves and its almost unlimited credit."

The other is by the Frenchman Robert Lattès, who, in his *Mille Milliards de dollars,* explaining why, in his view, not so long ago IBM's competitors had no real hope of gaining a major share of the market, wrote: "If one of its competitors only tries to nibble away 1 percent of IBM's market, it means a colossal growth for that firm, more than 35 percent a year. Such growth is impossible to maintain in the long run. On the other hand, for IBM, an increase of 1 percent of its share of the market represents only a marginal effort."

As pointed out by the Mitsubishi Report: "If, with a boldness that even recently was hardly imaginable, Fujitsu can aspire to rank with IBM, it is because Fujitsu has undertaken to get in in an entirely new way. Through preliminary training and preparation of men and teams for programming of future machines, with an eye to a worldwide and unified data processing network, Fujitsu is competing with IBM."

IBM still reigns. But Fujitsu is closing in. If Fujitsu can thus defy IBM, it is because it is prepared to leap over the past to the future opened up by the technological breakthrough of the microprocessors.

The British scientist Christopher Evans wrote the best study on the consequences of the technological revolution. Here is how he sees the Japan of the 1980s:

At a conference in London towards the end of 1977 I was treated to lunch by the vice-president of one of Japan's largest computer companies. In excellent English he gave me a blow-by-blow account of his country's industrial strategy for the 1980s. Japan, he pointed out, has a population of about a hundred million (about twice that of the UK) and few natural resources. It has risen to be the world's most efficient and successful post-war economy on the basis of starting completely afresh with brand new factories and no clogging industrial heritage, a shrewd and nationally determined assessment of what world markets were likely to be in the '50s and '60s, and a deep-seated and universally accepted understanding that without a huge export-based industry it would be unable to feed its population. Britain, he told me, had come out of the war with antiquated factories, a heavy industrial commitment to the past, a misplaced assessment of world markets, or more probably no assessment at all, and a fallacious belief that we would somehow muddle through however rough the economic waters. And without rubbing in how wrong we had been and how right they had been, he went on to say that Japan was now facing up to the next phase of the future.

The oil crisis and the various shifts in the balance of political and economic power throughout the world meant that Japan would be unable to maintain, let alone increase, its standard of living in the years to come if it relied on such archaic means of making money as selling motor cars, cameras, tape recorders and the like. The solution was simple and blazingly unambiguous. His country had to make itself the number one computer power of the 1980s, designing, making and selling the stupendous range of computers and computer-based products which the world of a decade hence would crave. To achieve this end the Japanese Government, in consortium with industrial investors, was injecting about seventy billion dollars into the computer industry in the decade 1975–1985. By the end of 1979 thirty billion of that will already have been invested, and the Japanese thrust—whose rewards one must remember do not mature immediately—will be half way home. Almost half that stupendous budget, incidentally, would be spent on computer training and teaching—about three billion dollars a year. Since that rather unsettling lunch, I have had few doubts that the most striking feature of the short-term future will be the emergence of Japan as the world's dominant computer power.

While explaining Japan's rise to economic power, scientists and economists have tried to understand and explain what happened recently to American industry.

At the end of 1980 the editors of *Business Week* published a report entitled "The Reindustrialization of America," in which a considerable amount of data on the unexpected phenomenon was brought together.

The effects of the obsolescence of economic psychology in the U.S. have been devastating. Overall economic growth slid to 2.9% per year in the 1970s from 4.1% in the 1960s and 3.9% in the 1950s. The U.S. standard of living now ranks only ninth in the world; it ranked the highest as recently as 1972. The U.S. inflation rate was higher than the average of all industrial countries in 1979 for the first time in history.

Nor do these macro statistics tell the whole story. At a deeper level, the U.S. economy is showing signs of the kind of fatigue that causes industrial powers such as 19th century Britain to go into an irreversible slide. . . .

The question of whether the U.S. will reindustrialize depends on whether the business, bureaucratic, and political elites can get together to provide the leadership. An enormous amount has to be done, and the time to do it is running short.

Daniel Yankelovich, chairman of Yankelovich, Skelly and White, says in the same issue of the magazine: "The state of mind of the public is worried sick and in a panic. In that condition, people know there is something wrong. That pushes them into working out accommodations that make economic sense."

Another leader consulted by the *Business Week* team, the chief scientist at Xerox Corporation, notes: "One is hard put to compile a list of innovations in the last few years that matches any equivalent span of time in the 1950s or '60s."

The treasurer of the National Semiconductor Corporation says, referring to federal bailouts of Chrysler Corporation and other ailing "old" industries: "What I find most distressing is that taxpayer dollars are directed toward dying things rather than growing things."

Finally, this diagnosis from Professor Keith Pavitt on the issue, during a seminar organized by the Rand Corporation at the University of Sussex:

America is showing the first symptoms of "the English sickness": weakness in productivity, retreat from world markets, decline in professional competence, reduction of research budgets. Like Great Britain, America has progressively concentrated its research effort on sectors linked to national defense: aerospace, rockets, turbines, etc. But, as regards research and production, research programs create habits and attitudes that are harmful when it is a question of entering into real competition in the world markets of civilian equipment.

During the years of America's decline, Japan noticed signs that were forerunners of the revolution to come. They were the years of the successive oil crises, showing how vulnerable the nation was to them. But Japan used them to speed up its transformation toward an "information society," where *information* is destined to hold the place that *energy* once held in yesterday's industrial society. Thus, once more, external forces pushed Japan toward the future. But this time it was not alone in this situation. How can we explain America's and even Europe's passive acceptance of the past while Japan moved to the future?

In *Freedom's Edge,* a study of this malady of the 1970s, Milton Wessel writes:

The social effects of computer science have almost never been the subject of public debate. Non-computer scientists are loath to show their ignorance of the subject. This attitude explains why the leading economists avoid approaching the subject of the computer industry, in spite of its totally new characteristics. It also explains why sociologists and philosophers whose writings should have long been dealing with computer science avoid this subject and perpetuate their own ignorance as well as that of the public. Finally, it explains why our universities, which should be the centers of intellectual activity around this new technology, allocate so little place to the study of the social effects of computer science.

But all controversy is sterile. The irresistible pressure of expensive energy and the appeal of the developing Third World leave no room for hesitation. *We know now that there is a way.*

The rapid decline of the price of microcomputers, their increasingly smaller size, their greater accessibility to nonspecialized users, should lead to general expansion. Important creative markets must open up in the Third World. Their importance will ensure new growth everywhere. The data-processing industry will follow the path taken in the past by the automobile, which spawned a series of related industries. Electronics will do so with increased vigor and will favor more diversified growth.

We must put an end to hedging and reticence, and do what is necessary. This will be possible only through widely diffused, simple and explicit information about these new technologies. "Too complicated," say the "experts." Yet it is within everyone's reach to understand where this powerful, mysterious *microprocessor* comes from and the formidable prospects it opens up. What is incomprehensible is the refusal to clarify the new truths which hold all the keys to our future.

OURS IS AN AGE OF CONVERGENCE: the coming together of ancient intuitions and new discoveries in the realms of mathematics, logic and physics. Calculation is the starting point as well as the end. Our instruments have been forged through the progressive and difficult mastery of the power enclosed for thousands of years *in numbers*. If the key to their use is found, numbers can translate, express, transmit, restore and diffuse everything—except emotions.

Many men have succeeded one another in this long quest to refine calculation. But the scientific community is unanimous in singling out a few whose activities marked decisive stages—from the abacus of antiquity to the microelectronics of today.

Pythagoras held that man had been "haunted by calculation," the treatment of numbers, since the earliest civilizations. And it is to Pythagoras that is attributed, around the sixth century B.C., the multiplication table, the first true *instrument* of numbers.

Things went no further than that until Pascal. In 1634, by the time he was eleven years old, Blaise Pascal had already composed a "Treatise on Sounds," under the guidance of his father, who was a tax collector in the French state bureaucracy.

The young boy constantly observed the tedious work his father was obliged to perform and attempted to find a way to help him. When he was nineteen he drew up plans for the first mechanical adding machine, equipped with gears and wheels mounted on axles. Pascal's amazing advance was based on his producing "carryovers" in calculation for the first time.

The adding machine was called the "Pascaline," and several copies were built; but its rapid development was interrupted by the bitter hostility of accountants who saw in it a threat to their jobs, and by the premature death of Pascal himself.

Although Pascal's teachings and thought became well known after his death, the world soon forgot his machine. Everyone, that is, except a child prodigy, twenty-five years younger than Pascal, who was born in Leipzig in 1646. Gottfried Wilhelm von Leibniz had heard about the invention and grasped its essential meaning: the growing complexity of European society in the seventeenth century, and the growing *accumulation of knowledge could not be controlled, used and placed in the service of man unless we succeeded in mechanizing, and in automating the treatment of numbers.*

Leibniz boldly enlarged the field and the perspective by introducing astronomical data and trigonometric functions. And he soon brought to it another intuition, which he called "the new system of nature and communication." He was led to it by a fundamental optimism concerning man and his destiny, the dynamism of his nature, his mental capacity and the essential tie which links him to the surrounding universe. In a famous phrase, he wrote: "There is nothing of intelligence that does not come from the senses, unless it is intelligence itself."

To record the external world, to permit the storage, accumulation, retention and transmission of data, he invented a "multiplying wheel," equipped with nine teeth of unequal length. Three centuries later, Leibniz's wheel became the matrix of the first electronic calculators, created in the 1960s.

It was he also who first began the radical simplification of arithmetic which would become the heart of our electronics and telecommunications systems: binary calculation, which replaces all *number signs* by two signs in all and for all: 0 and 1. Zero and one. It was the beginning of a great adventure.

The fundamental working principle of all modern computers is based on this 0 and this 1. No other sign is or will be necessary. The 0 and the 1 suffice to represent all numbers without limit. The simplicity of the principle gives rise to all the capabilities of data-processing technologies.

With binary signs, one begins with 0, which is written 0. One continues with 1, which is written 1. One arrives at 2. To accept the addition of 2 as a third sign would be to stray from the essential simplicity of binary calculation, and lose one's way. Therefore, 2 is refused. It will be written 10. One arrives at 3: it is written 11. The number 4 is written 100. The number 5 is written 101. Number 6: 110. Number 7: 111. Number 8: 1000. Number 9, under the unyielding constraint of the binary: 1001. And so on for 10, 11, 12, 13, 14, 15, (1010, 1011, 1000, 1100, 1101, 1110 and 1111). There are always only two signs. At 16, the combination of the two signs 0 and 1, in groups of four, is exhausted. We have to stretch: 16 is written 10000. 17 becomes 10001. And so on.

Leibniz recognized that this way of binary counting, using only two signs, would enable machines to record, retain, combine, and operate an unlimited load of communication signals, on the simple condition that they be translated first into figures which could then be codified into the two signs 0 and 1.

The next step was to link binary calculation with machines, for it would be impossible for the human brain to begin adding, multiplying and combining such huge numbers of zeros and ones. If 17 is already translated by 10001, one can imagine what 177 or 1017 would be in binary language! Since no more than two signs would ever be needed to express everything, it is a language of infinite properties, but it could be used only by machines made for it, capable of making arithmetic rows of a similar length flash by like a shot. The speed of calculation would become the key to every machine's power and usefulness.

It was the Englishman Charles Babbage, at the end of the

eighteenth century and the beginning of the nineteenth, who first conceived a machine capable of multiplying such signs. He presented it to the Royal Astronomical Society in 1822 with a communication, "Observations on the Application of Machines to the Calculation of Mathematical Tables."

Rapidly improved, his machine became *the* "analytical machine." It contained the elements that would become the programmable computer: the input device, which recorded the binary signs; the arithmetical unit, which was the processor; the control unit, which made sure that the machine carried out the task assigned it; the memory unit, where all the figures could be stored at will to await processing; finally, the output mechanism which gives the result of the operations programmed at the beginning.

One difficulty remained: the huge size of Babbage's machine. A succession of other inventors would apply themselves to the two essential advances that remained to be made: the reduction of the object's size and the increase of the machine's internal speed of calculating, which defined its working power.

The Frenchman Joseph Jacquard, inventor of the automatic control of weaving looms by "perforated cards," applied this same method of cards to Babbage's machine, thanks to the intervention of a young Englishwoman with a passion for mathematics, Ada, Countess of Lovelace, Byron's daughter, who published two essays: *Observations on Mr. Babbage's Analytical Machine* and *Analogy between the weaving, by Mr. Jacquard, of leaves and flowers, and the weaving, by Mr. Babbage, of algebraic patterns.*

Lady Lovelace died young, at the age of thirty-six. In recognition of her help, the Pentagon called the unified computer language, designed to unify the excessive number of languages utilized in the huge missile computers, "Ada."

The last person to contribute to bring us to the electronic computer itself was the Hungarian-born von Neumann, a naturalized American. After working on the nuclear program after the war, he turned his mind to calculating machines and made two decisive inventions for the emerging computers.

Neumann created the mechanism for binary signaling, by using the smallest, the lightest, the most rapid element possible: the tiny electron, which gravitates around a nucleus within the atom. Two thousand times smaller than the atom itself, the electron can, under the impulse of a weak current, move in the circuits of calculators in a to-and-fro movement to simulate 0 and 1. This permitted the birth of "electronics."

Neumann then integrated internal memory capacity into this "electronic computer," so that the programs or instructions given it could be inscribed, combined and modified. The door was opening to the "information society."

Information for calculating machines, for big computers, for microprocessors, and for us is not what is normally called information. It is not the newspaper, radio or television news. It is, actually, one of the three fundamental elements of nature, matter, energy and information, which furnish the materials necessary for man's activities and creations. Therefore, if we want to grasp the role and the essence of information here, we must first make an effort to forget its limited and commonplace meaning. Whatever constitutes a *message* is information. A red light which comes on, the cry or smell of an animal, the twinkling of a star, an electric spark—each constitutes a molecule of information, a data-processing element.

The tiny virus, visible only to the electronic microscope, contains a considerable sum of information in its genetic memory, the equivalent of several typewritten pages. The most productive inventions of recent years, more so even than electronics, and already at the frontiers of application to new and important fields, are due to the discovery *in biology* of links between the properties of living beings and information stored in DNA—just as a program is stored in a computer.

In a sense, therefore, electronic calculators are the domesticated synthesis of nature's capacity to fix and exchange information.

Thus defined and understood, *information* is vital, like *energy,* its twin sister. And it has been possible to summarize the evolution of living species by pointing out that from the beginning of time everything that has been won in the struggle for survival has always been by the species with the richest store of *information.* The French scientist Jacques Ruffié has expressed this with the formula "Evolution coincides with the thrust of complexity and of the psyche."

THE POWER OF COMPUTERS, the masters and cultivators of information, continued to grow with the speed of calculation. They diminished in size as well as cost. The first computer was the size of a large room. This shrank to transistors, to integrated circuits and now to the silicon "chips" of the new and all-powerful microprocessor.

The microprocessor, the basic cell of the new computer universe, is the latest stage in the transistor, which was invented by the American mathematician William Shockley at the Bell Laboratories in 1947. This transistor is a small piece of semiconductor material, with impurities that allow electrons to move under the impulse of an infinitesimal amount of energy. It represents the convergence of a system that now links *matter* (the impurities of the semiconductors), *information* (reduced to the universal simplicity of binary language) and *energy* (which, as in the case of the atom, has electrons as support).

The invention of the transistor, a circuit in which matter, information and energy are joined, is at the heart of all computers. The more capable the computer of integrating circuits, the greater its capacity and power.

Before long, circuits integrated into computers would be counted by the thousands, then by the millions, then by the billions. The human brain, which serves as a permanent model for researchers, has a capacity of 125 million billion recording circuits.

Considerable efforts were required to master the volume and

cost of machines that could integrate such an incredible number of transistors. From 1947 to 1959, scientists (for the most part Americans, and especially those of Texas Instruments and Fairchild Camera) succeeded in combining *several transistors* on a single wafer; they became integrated circuits that could be held in the palm of the hand, and they made it possible to reduce drastically the size of the computer. What would be called "the second generation" of computers was reached in the beginning of the 1960s, when a thousand transistors were put on the single wafer of an integrated circuit.

At that point we were still at the stage of a remarkable but not very revolutionary *aid* to work and decision-making. It was still not the decisive stage.

Another major jump occurred a few years later to create the "third generation" of miniaturization when it became possible to inscribe *ten thousand* transistors on one wafer. This was the stage of microcomputers and pocket calculators. These small, powerful computers of the third generation radically changed the capacity of all industrial machines, including robots, just as they increased the means of calculation and innovation at the disposal of the human brain. They were very quickly distributed and utilized. Nevertheless, we were still in the industrial economy.

Then the fourth generation arrived: the building of the "very-large-scale integration" (VLSI) chip on a scale capable of holding on one little wafer *one hundred thousand* transistors. Nor is that the end. In California's "Silicon Valley," and in Japanese laboratories, scientists are approaching the "fifth generation" which will put more than *one million* transistors on a "chip."

We are now experiencing the fourth-generation "computers-on-a-chip" which are spreading to all areas of production, to all activities. This stage of computer progress is crucial because it represents a dazzling breakthrough in computer equipment, or "hardware." *Hardware* simply has represented the most complex and most costly element in the creation of the computerized information world. *Software,* the "immaterial" part, the part that can be composed only by human brain, is the heart of the matter. It has been lagging far behind. It is in the realm of developing software, which commands computers and robots, that the whole future lies. Without waiting for their successors of the fifth generation, the present microprocessors are already establishing a computerized society. Under the guidance of human ideas, *which alone can nourish software* and, beyond that, the entire environment, the new social fabric is being built.

The microprocessor is quite simply a microplaque of compact sand on which a computer's entire chain of work is imprinted: calculating unit, memory, programming, output unit. The microprocessor can be programmed for any function, any task that one wants performed: controlling household appliances, radios, televisions, tape recorders, telephones, recorders; regulating automobile fuel injections; activating and controlling industrial processes; and so on. Thus, the tiny wafer contains powerful machines: complete microcomputer systems.

Computers will give people plenty of room for creative thought and progressively relieve them of dispensable tasks. Computerized systems will be capable of performing all nonhuman tasks on a planetary scale, and thus permitting, in fact demanding, the creative fulfillment of what is and always will be peculiar to man.

To give us an idea of the force and rapidity with which these advances in power and miniaturization have occurred, and of the speed with which the computerized society has developed, Christopher Evans proposes this illustration:

When the first big computers attracted the attention of the Press in the early '50s, they were given the not totally misleading name of "electronic brains." The human brain itself is made up of minute electronic binary switching units called neurones, and there are an awful lot of them—about ten thousand million in all. But even assuming that neurones and electronic switching units are functionally equivalent, it was ridiculous, scientists used to argue, to talk of computers as "brains" and even more ridiculous to imagine them doing brain-like things. Why, if you wanted to build a computer which contained the same number of functional elements as the brain, you would end up with something the size of New York City and using more power than the whole of the subway system.

This daunting example was generally used to silence the brain/computer parallelists in the all-tube days of the early '50s and it makes quaint reading when you come across it today. By the early '60s, with transistorization, the computer/brain had shrunk to the size of the Statue of Liberty, and a ten-kilowatt generator would have kept it ticking over nicely. By the early '70s, with integrated circuits, there had been a further compression: it was down to the size of a Greyhound bus, and you could run it off a mains plug. By the mid '70s, it was the size of a TV set, and at the time of writing is that of a typewriter. And such is the pace of development that, allowing a one-year lag between the time I write these words and the time you read them, the incredible shrinking brain will have continued to shrink—to what size? My guess is that it will be no bigger than a human brain, perhaps even smaller. And to power it, a portable radio battery will suffice.

At the same time we are seeing miniaturization that will make the computer one of the least expensive technological objects in the world, we are witnessing the dazzling development of the speed and the power of calculation and of data processing. In the 1970s we reached the millionth of a second for each operation. We are now at the billionth of a second. The latest IBM experiment on the passage of electrons (which indicate computer language) brought the speed of computation to the ultimate limits set by the laws of the physical environment: the speed of light.

A similar evolution in the reduction of the size of computers has followed the growth in its internal speed. Today the basic transistor, a "chip" cell, on which the microprocessor is based, measures 3 microns. The thickness of a strand of human hair is 100 microns. The transistor, the microprocessor's blood vessel, is thus thirty times finer than a strand of hair. As a result, the one-square-millimeter microprocessor is incredibly powerful, even though it is tiny and hardly more expensive than the sand of which it is composed.

Because of programming power and the multiplication of that power by the number of microprocessors that can be connected one to another, robots and all future artificial brains will be endowed with phenomenal capacity. We are entering the era of what is called the *exponential growth* of the power of computers. We are leaving "linear growth." Exponential growth is one last mathematical notion that must be understood for a firm grasp of the characteristics as a whole of the "technological revolution" which is destined to transform industry, the economy and society.

We borrow from Evans an excellent illustration of what this *exponential growth means for technology*—notably for our *microprocessors:*

In linear growth the increments of change remain constant, and as a result the future is easily predicted. In exponential growth the increments of change increase steadily, the simplest example being growth to the exponent 2, which is better known as a doubling effect. If plotted on a graph this gives a curve which starts off relatively flat but soon begins to accelerate upwards at an amazing rate. To give an example: take a sheet of paper of average thickness and fold it over on itself fifty times. Forget for a moment the physical difficulty involved and ask yourself how thick the paper will be when you have completed the operation. Remember that you are doubling the paper's thickness fifty times, so you should talk of its *height* and expect something pretty spectacular.

Most people who have not already heard the answer to this or a similar teaser talk about something a few inches thick. Others, realizing that a novel concept is involved, talk of a few feet, while bolder souls offer up Nelson's Column or even the Empire State Building. Once in a blue moon someone will produce Mount Everest in triumphal certainty that they have stretched their imagination far enough. But few realize that the stupendous block of paper will have pushed far above Everest, right out of the atmosphere, past the moon, beyond the orbit of the planet Mars and into the asteroid belt. Human beings just do not have a conceptual experience of the exponential. In our brief life-span we normally experience only linear change, and although the universe is full of exponential change, it is either irrelevant to us or so overwhelming when it occurs that there is nothing we can do about it. Most explosions, from hand grenades up through hydrogen bombs to supernovae, have a brief exponential component. Our inability to face up to such problems as impending global food shortages, atmospheric pollution and —most widely cited—population growth, are excellent examples of this weakness.

The point is important, for computer technology is embarking on a period of exponential growth, and social and economic changes will probably occur in its wake, for a brief period at any rate, at the same conceptually unmanageable pace. The first person to spell this out was Alvin Toffler, whose book *Future Shock,* published in 1970, warned that the world was moving into an era of change which would stretch existing institutions to their limits, and strain psychological concepts beyond breaking point. *Future Shock* was criticized for being sensationalist, but it is clear when one re-reads it ten years later that Toffler himself under-estimated the rate at which things were going to move. His book showed an astute awareness of impending technological developments, but it contains not one single reference to the most sensational instrument of change of all—the microprocessor—for the very good reason that when he wrote it *the microprocessor did not exist.*

The microprocessor revolution has already moved beyond the factory floor and is invading the office and the home. In the business world the "electronic office" will be equipped with automated copiers, self-correcting typewriters without a keyboard, programmable photocopying machines that can work out given texts according to the instructions they have received, computerized filing systems without any filing cabinets. All paper documents will be eliminated, and the telephone will be replaced by a single integrated apparatus with a few keys to send messages and a screen to receive them from anywhere around the world.

Almost all of the tasks performed every day in an office can be organized and programmed by a microcomputer, with a memory capable of storing much more information and documentation than is ever likely to be needed.

A good example of the speed with which microprocessors are being introduced into working situations is the White House center of information and decision making. In 1979, there were fifty-four computer terminals in the White House. By 1985, one thousand will have been installed. The President will then be in permanent communication with the entire government bureaucracy. And it will be the same for every office in the country and perhaps for every home. Already the "home computer" can perform many domestic household functions. Considered a toy when introduced just a few years ago, it is now recognized as a tool for managing everyday life, giving the ordinary family access to the miracles of information storage and automated functions.

The microprocessor revolution is also changing the entire nature of communications. By linking the computer to the telephone the development of *telecommunications* has now made *worldwide integration* possible. From the moment when telephones were able to adopt the same "code" as electronics, the binary code, "the digitalization" of communications, had begun. The incredible power of the computer was now behind the touch telephone.

From now on, the communication networks, the computers and the robots form a single universe. They make it possible to abolish distance in carrying out a whole series of tasks. The union of microprocessors and telecommunications increases the capacity of a doctor, for example, to examine, diagnose and care for his patients from a great distance. It also permits the doctor to delegate instructions given with the diagnosis to a specialized computer, which can then communicate directly with the patient.

The doctor himself no longer has to intervene except in unusual cases and his or her ability to handle a large number of patients is therefore sharply increased. At the same time, increasing specialization requires a *growing* number of specialists and medical experts. The computer thus solves a problem in health care and creates a need for more trained personnel.

In much the same way, energy now spent in transporting persons and goods can be replaced by the electronic transmission of information. Today, for example, in Tokyo, a meeting of officials or technicians does not necessarily mean their physical presence in the same room. A computerized meeting may be set up in one of the Imperial Hotel's rooms, facing the city's beautiful central park, where participants' images and voices are present, wherever they might be physically.

Based only on what is *already* being applied in industrial, urban and social life, the Mitsubishi Report concludes:

Of all human inventions since the beginning of mankind, the microprocessor is unique. It is destined to play a part in all areas of life, without exception—to increase our capacities, to facilitate or eliminate tasks, to replace physical effort, to increase the possibilities and areas of mental effort, to turn every human being into a creator, whose every idea can be applied, dissected, put together again, transmitted, changed.

And it adds:

> Now it is no longer a question of knowing the limits of the computerized society's capacities to produce and create according to the instructions and programs that men will provide. Physically, *there is no longer any limit*. The capacity to produce instructions and programs which is the realm of man himself has fallen far behind the information system's physical capacity to obey. The problem before us is that of the number of people available to make the system work—a number that must be increased constantly.

And that is the essential point. At the end of this long progression of human inventions—from Pascal's and Leibniz's "adding machines" to the hundred million microprocessors produced in 1980 alone, each one of which has a capacity for calculation equal to one billion times that of the machines of those early geniuses—what will become of man? What will be his work, his role, his function?

This is the only question that remains—but it is also the only one that counts. It would be possible to produce a science-fiction scenario in which robots produce, work, receive, transmit and multiply. It would be possible, in such a scenario, to do everything without human beings. Man would become useless. The robot would finally make people obsolete.

But this scenario, superficially possible as it seems, is absurd. It is the *very opposite* of the reality which we will experience and which is already unfolding. The larger the number of microprocessors, the greater the need for a vast human contribution. Each computerized function requires ten, one hundred, a thousand brains to compose, formulate, imagine and design the tasks of the programming environment, which can take root only in an increasingly developed and creative society. In this new world of "intelligent employment" and of nonmechanical tasks, we will no longer have to speak of transfer—of aid, of equality between the industrialized countries and the Third World, between the rich and the poor nations. Microprocessors will demand a different kind of human effort. All human beings, no matter which part of the world they come from, will progressively be called upon to perform tasks of the same type, for which they will have been trained in the same way.

Take two problems that are of extreme importance to the countries of the Third World: *overpopulation* and *illiteracy.* Overpopulation is the result of the fatalism felt by families in impoverished countries. They must have many children so that a few will survive and help support the family by working with their hands. This family "wealth" is a social catastrophe. Yet the phenomenon is closely linked to the usefulness, the value of physical work, of "manpower." As soon as this function disappears, births will decline because children no longer embody this physical value of exchange.

Illiteracy is perhaps as serious a problem as overpopulation. Yet here too the microprocessor offers us the opportunity of leaping beyond the conventional possibilities of education, which are too slow to help the illiterate millions of the Third World.

Seymour Papert of MIT has proven that the impact of the computer on illiteracy works in two dialectically related ways. (1) It allows access to the most modern forms of knowledge, communication and control by means other than the written word. (2) Papert shows that, far from increasing illiteracy, "since literacy might no longer be perceived as a necessity," the computer actually creates conditions for people to learn, read and write with greater ease and at lower cost than ever dreamed of before.

In a forthcoming work, *The Computer Manifesto*, he argues that to integrate the political impact of the computer, we must all, without exception, master this process.

Almost all computers today are combined through a keyboard whose use requires mastery of the alphabet. *But it need not be so.* In advanced laboratories, computers now *hear* commands given by voice, *see* gestures, *feel* the touch on a sensitive screen. They respond by synthetic voice, pictures and *actions* without necessitating the process of reading and writing. Thus, a person who cannot read and write, can learn to operate a computer and, through it, have access to all the power of the electronic age. He, or she, could obtain information from encyclopedias or any technical manuals. So he could also run a complex factory, or have access to the world of art and literature.

In projects conceived by Papert and his colleagues at MIT in collaboration with Texas Instrument, command of the computer has in fact been given to children who have not yet learned to read and write. And this is only a beginning. The methods are designed to be used universally to bring sophisticated forms of computer power to hundreds of millions of illiterate people. Thus, in one stroke, the distribution of knowledge in the world can be changed.

But the experiment also shows the way to even more remarkable results, for the technology and personal power that the computer brings also overcomes the barriers that made the conquest of illiteracy seem so difficult. In *Mindstorms*, Papert describes how the computer which might have made human knowledge seem a prerequisite, makes it, on the contrary, so easy for people to *acquire* this very knowledge, so that we can now anticipate a *renaissance* of learning—and most particularly in those countries and social classes where the need is presently greatest.

Henceforth, it is possible to conceive of what always seemed unattainable: a world in which standards of living will gradually become similar.

$\mathbf{T}$HE JAPANESE IMPERATIVE, developed and progressively applied from the 1920s to the 1980s, has a name: *deindustrialization*.

All the "plans for development" issued by government, industries and unions for the 1980s have embraced the "technological revolution." Traditional industrial development no longer represents progress but a regression, a waste of employment and investment. For the sake of production, *and of new employment opportunities*, men must come to terms with computerization.

It is above all a question of people, *the full employment* of people, not only in terms of a job for everyone, but also in the employment of each person's full faculties. And this cannot be achieved by an industrial system that systematically reduces manpower's numbers and uses only its *physical* labor.

The curve of industrial employment has dropped steadily. In the future it will dip even more rapidly. The goal agreed upon by the Japanese government, the Keidanren and the unions has been clearly stated:

It is urgently necessary to pass from the industrial society, which corresponded to the old methods of development, to a computerized society in the entire system of producing material goods. And to organize, at the same time, the development of the employment of human faculties. At the same time it is necessary to increase the quality of the machines' work through their programming, and to respond to the numerous social needs that arise as the computerized society progresses. We are short of men and we will continue to be short of men. The more we detach some of them from the mass of industrial workers, the more capable we will be of responding to the new society's needs in human capability, and to the growing efficiency of the new machines.

Henceforth, the urgent need to go from the industrial phase to the computer phase is valid everywhere, *regardless* of a particular society, population, or nation's wealth or level of development. The passage from the old method of production to the new *is valid everywhere and at the same time.*

It is certain that great public debates will be essential to understand, accept and develop these new ideas. Japanese leaders, who have put these directives in writing and who are applying them, realize that. They have also given a name to the apprehensions and anxieties that cannot fail to occur: *computer shock.* They dread it, but they have prepared for it. They have begun to lead their entire society along this new path, far beyond its present industrial and commercial successes, without drawing worldwide attention. Because of this reserve, ignorance of the progress of the "technological revolution" has overshadowed its consequences for the vast majority of other industrial societies—and for the Third World.

Perhaps one day the Japanese will be reproached for having shown discretion instead of explaining and spreading their knowledge of the nature and the spirit of their society's transformation. But we must reject the idea that the leaders of the Japanese economic and scientific system chose this position for Malthusian reasons. On the contrary, they feared that given the rate at which their society was being computerized, and the speed with which their products captured markets abroad, even in the most developed countries of America and Europe, they would confront hostile reactions. Lack of understanding of the phenomenon would heighten the reaction. And that is exactly what happened.

They also feared they would find themselves confronted with a shortage of outlets, because of the limited development of the only peoples numerous enough to absorb the new goods: the three billion people of the Third World.

From the very beginning of their computer takeoff, the Japanese had one obsessive worry: that their progress might isolate them and thus check or even interrupt their momentum. It was the discovery that the other countries "were not following" that led the Japanese representatives to participate so actively, so frequently, in the working sessions of the Paris Group.

They are not afraid that the others will imitate Japan and thus speed up their passage to the new world that everyone must inevitably enter. The Japanese want to *hasten* the movement. The information society's deployment and field of action can be effective only if it is worldwide.

Having mastered and analyzed the nature of the new technologies, they know that if deindustrialization does not become widespread, we run the risk of such imbalances, gaps and social tragedies that the storm will spare no one. Japan is no longer an island except geographically.

What is more, Japan has confronted the problem that haunts all industrial societies: employment. The special group of sixty experts, which the MITI formed in 1979 and baptized "The 60-Men Committee," was instructed to make a detailed assessment of the progress achieved and of the outlook for the 1980s. In its report, these lines are devoted to the question of unemployment:

> The generalized use of microprocessors does not have a negative effect on employment by diminishing the number of jobs. On the contrary, new needs and jobs are increasing more and more rapidly, thanks to the multiplying factor of microprocessors. The problem is a serious shortage of available men.

No one in America or in Europe, least of all in the Third World, can be convinced in advance of what may seem to be wishful thinking. When one observes the monthly increase in the number of men and women rejected or pushed to one side by industrial society, one is naturally inclined to blame, above all, automation.

Consequently, the leading advocates of the computerized society have carefully analyzed whether this new society would provide a job for each human being. One of the best known is a Frenchman, an engineer from the Ecole Polytechnique, a former director of Thomson, the leading French electronics firm, and later a director of the Institute of Computer Research. He is André Danzin, who, in 1976, was chosen by his European colleagues to head the European Committee of Research and Development. André Danzin sees in the information society the chance for a veritable renaissance. And he did not hesitate to use that as the title for his officially published study.

Danzin writes of a renaissance for Europe because that is his specific area of responsibility. But he insists that it is essential for every country to embark on this course, instead of trying to maintain the old structures, the old methods of production and consumption, the old machines and the old jobs—with no hope of succeeding, under the crushing weight of public and private deficits that inexorably accumulate.

First of all, there is the new potential of the electronic and computer industries themselves which, everybody now agrees, are going to form the "first sector of growth." Danzin writes:

New solutions that are extraordinarily economical and reliable are emerging for us today from the series of efforts, research, and inventions, the roots of which often go back to past centuries. Thus was born a whole range of new industries, the mere suggestion of which would have been inconceivable for our parents. The vocabulary itself was nonexistent. Except for the telephone, none of the inventions of today were conceivable. And though minds as concerned with imagining the future as Jules Verne or H. G. Wells were capable of dreaming of submarines, airplanes, and even the conquest of the moon, nothing in their writings predicted television or computers. There is a sort of extraordinary surprise, a veritable mutation for our humanity, especially when we look far back into the past. With electronics and computers was born a great, highly diversified industry to deal with a whole series of industrial productions. It has developed more rapidly than any other in the last twenty years. And its growth has not been stopped by the oil crisis, which caused so many slowdowns in other areas. On the contrary, there continues to be a shortage of men in the industry. But, compared with its effect on work, the creation of jobs in electronics and in the computer industry is by no means the most important phenomenon.

For computer technologies are powerful factors in the transformation of human societies. And their effects on the creation of jobs in other activities are even more important than the direct effects on work in their own domain.

These techniques are, in effect, tools in the service of the activities and concepts of a new society which needs, which continues to need, a growing number of men at work.

They are worth less in themselves than in their power of transformation: in agriculture, which they will lead toward a more rational exploitation of the land; in industry, whose capacities they increase considerably; in the services, the development and proliferation of which they accelerate.

Perhaps never before has such a leaven been put into the social and economic mix to transform it, and to direct men toward new functions and new destinies.

Situating the upheaval brought about by computers in its true historical perspective, André Danzin writes:

Until the last century civilization was essentially rural. Most of the active labor force was employed by agriculture. Then came industry. Its development proceeded at first without any appreciable modification in agricultural work. But soon competition obliged the farmers to mechanize in order to increase their productivity. The developed countries became urbanized. The proportion of men in industry increased markedly in relation to all other forms of activities. The complexity of industrial society developed rapidly. It demanded the creation of all types of services (administrative, commercial, financial, technical). It thus created new specialists, in a series of highly varied fields.

Then, in the last twenty years, following the unimaginable progress of electronics and computer science, a veritable "mutation" appeared in the nature of jobs. In the last decade, 1970–1980, we have seen the proportion of working men employed in computer activities surpass that in exclusively agricultural, industrial or service jobs.

It is therefore legitimate to say that circumstances, unless they are delayed by a deep crisis, lead us toward an economy in which the major portion of jobs and activity will be linked to information . . . This is a basic observation. For grasping, processing, and diffusing information consumes little energy and raw material, but demands a great number of men— trained, available men.

What Danzin and those who work with him are describing and trying to communicate to us is an important, forgotten notion: *that of social revolution which follows great technical changes.* Inevitably, the computerization of society will trigger an explosion of new needs, of exchanges, of communications, of knowledge which will open up other careers and give rise to other vocations.

The computer revolution marks the final passage of industrial society to a postindustrial world based on information. The microprocessor "computer on a chip" is replacing the assembly line, man's mind is replacing his labor as the means of production and the capacity for growth and change is accumulating at a stupendous rate.

The Japanese experience of the last seven years indicates that resistance to technological change occurs less frequently and is much weaker among workers or employees than among executives and directors. It is not the *mass* of the population that rejects computerization. If they are assured of finding a job, and a better job, workers do not cling to tedious and poorly paid work. But the leaders of industrial society—outside the realm of the computer industries—refuse to let the ferment of the new revolution penetrate their operations.

Two stories illustrate and confirm this observation: one from Kalmar in Sweden; the other from Chicago.

In 1979, at Göteborg, Volvo finished computerizing its most recent plant, which became the most highly automated plant in Europe. It used more robots than any other European operation. At that time, at the other end of Sweden, 250 kilometers south of Göteborg, the real jewel of the Volvo empire was at the Kalmar plant.

It was at Kalmar in the early 1970s that Volvo, encouraged and supported by Sweden's Socialist government, built and organized its largest factory according to very advanced social concepts. "Assembly-line work" was replaced by "autonomous groups" of workers performing their tasks according to programs and rates of production for which they themselves, together with their foremen and engineers, were responsible. At that time it was considered a bold and intelligent breakthrough, greeted as a decisive stage in the humanization of work and a step toward the greater efficiency of industrial society.

The plant at Kalmar continues to function on the original model. But today the model that was to herald the future has just played a decisive role in condemning the industrial past. Even though all the unions enthusiastically took part in setting up "Kalmar's pilot experiment" and spared no effort to make it a success, the results were disappointing. At the beginning, the productivity achieved at the more responsible, more human, better adapted Kalmar factory was appreciably better than that of Volvo's other plants. Then, year by year, the gap narrowed. Worker absenteeism there not only rose but even began to threaten the very survival of Volvo, whose output began to fall off. It averaged one fourth of the work force, severely damaging productivity.

More serious still, young people who seized every opportunity provided by an advanced code of a social-welfare system refused to work on the production line, despite the changes. Optimistic and proud when the plant was launched, the personnel director of the Kalmar complex now says, "The new generation clearly dislikes factory work. And let's be frank about it, we can't blame them." He added, "Actually, what I need to achieve regular attendance and satisfactory output is a worker of about thirty-five years old, no younger, who has several children to feed and educate, and who lives close enough to the plant to travel by bike. If I get enough of this type, I can function. If you know any, send them to me."

The Kalmar personnel director's judgment is confirmed by the more complete and conclusive study made by Volvo's directors during their attempt to change working conditions. In 1979 they announced seven thousand openings in their training schools, with the opportunity for skilled employment in the firm's factories at the end of the course. In spite of unemployment—as everywhere, highest in Sweden among young people—Volvo was unable to attract even half of the number needed. Only three thousand candidates applied.

"Last year," said the official in charge of Volvo's commercial services, "we had to refuse a substantial number of orders because of a lack of manpower. We can no longer supply."

That was the end. Volvo's directors had seen it coming. Four years earlier, after a long study trip to Japan, they had begun work on a computerization program for the day when it could be applied. The moment having arrived, they began with one of the group's largest plants, the one at Göteborg. Each one of the computerized plants, the one at Göteborg and those that followed, increased Volvo's productivity by a factor of four. Volvo's competitive position became less vulnerable. The labor unions, which sit on the board of directors and take part in its decisions, encouraged the change.

Joseph Kapronczay, one of the union leaders at the Torslada plant, where the most recent giant robots have come to take over the work, says plainly, "Our workers' councils have accepted the arrival of automation because no one wants to continue factory work. We know that if we do not side with Volvo's computerization, we will be unable to hold out for long against Japanese competition; then *all* the jobs will be threatened. In our negotiations with management, we got them to agree that as the computerization of Volvo proceeded, jobs outside the factory would be offered to workers leaving the production line." That is what was done.

All of the workers on Volvo's assembly lines have been trained for other tasks, tasks that utilize human abilities other than physical work.

In contrast to the Swedish example, a visit to one of the great banks of Chicago shows where the brakes on computerization are to be found. At the end of 1980 *The Wall Street Journal* published on its first page an article that dealt with the reactions of some American executives to computerization:

Alexander Pollock has seen the future, and so far he wants no part of it.

The glimpse was provided by the people who are automating the offices at Continental Illinois Bank & Trust Co., of Chicago, where Mr. Pollock is a vice president.

Sitting at his desk, he can push some buttons on the keyboard of a computer terminal, and staff memos will appear on a television-like screen.

He can respond with his own memos, which will instantly

materialize on the screens of colleagues overseas, or be stored for them to retrieve later if their terminals are busy or turned off.

And by pressing a few other buttons, he can view bank data stored in a computer down the street.

Mr. Pollock can do all that and more, but he doesn't. He detests this change.

He explains: "I think most managers, including me, are talkers. I would much rather talk than write."

As Mr. Pollock's resistance exemplifies, professionals and executives are being forced to make major psychological and behavioral adjustments as they begin their move into a paperless world. They must suddenly get used to infallible machines that remind them when their reports are due and when they should receive reports.

And the pressure does not ease, since the computerized desk can be carried as a portable computer terminal in a case which, in principle, should never be let out of one's sight. These resistances suggest that the move into the information society will be costly in human as well as financial terms. *For there has been no preparation for it.*

In spite of the human problems no one disputes, at least in theory, that computerization is inevitable, irreversible and desirable. That is the only way for a society, a factory or a bank to survive.

Specialists consider it vital, in the proper sense of the word, for executives to accept this change. They blame the serious slump in American productivity for the delay in achieving it. And they believe that any further delay will constitute an enormous risk. A great debate has finally opened.

In the *Wall Street Journal* article referred to above, the senior vice-president of Booz, Allen & Hamilton, a management consultant firm, says, "We figure that most managers and professionals spend 18% to 30% of their time doing what we term less productive tasks—seeking information, looking for people, scheduling."

Experts believe that it will be sufficient to design machines better suited to the use that executives will put them to. But the human adjustment that this change demands goes well beyond what might be considered the superficial fears and anxieties of Alexander Pollock and others like him. Joseph Ramellini, director of advanced office systems at CBS, is closer to the truth: "They say, 'I'm not going to use it,' but what they are really saying is, 'I'm scared that I'm not going to be able to use this right, and I'll look like a jerk.' "

The manager of public services of Continental Illinois has the following to say on the subject: "The ability to tote the office around is a workaholic's dream." But it can be a nightmare for those who are not workaholics. An executive at Continental says, "It's bad enough when the boss works twelve hours a day. But now he gets up at two or three in the morning and works. He inundates us. I feel like I have to bring the damn machine home just to keep up."

According to many specialists, among the first results of computerization is a reduction in meetings and the time devoted to them. But many of those who are concerned reply, "I like meetings. Why should I do things differently under the pretext that the machine says it is more efficient or more profitable? After all, the informal meetings, without any immediate goal, could be just as important as working meetings."

The conclusion is provided by Vincent Giuliano, an office technology consultant with Arthur D. Little, Inc.: "The technology is neutral." It is designed to free people from all the tasks that weigh them down. But we must realize that if men are not prepared for it, if the technology is improperly used, the consequences can be serious, even pathological. We should not reproach the men who resist and revolt. John Connell, director of the Office Technology Research Group in Pasadena, California, says, "Every time we design a system, we do it on the premise that people must adapt to the system. I think we have to adopt an ethic that says we adapt machinery to people."

No indictment could be more severe than the one drawn up by *The Wall Street Journal* against executives who should have understood and mastered the consequences of a computerized society. It should have been their task to provoke and answer questions to adapt management to the new possibilities, to explain the benefits of computerization instead of fearing its effects. That is what Japan has succeeded in doing.

If the executives want to find out the consequences of computerization in a society, there is no need for them to undertake a long inquiry or try to uncover secrets.

In one week in April 1981, the world press published these items:

—Plans are being made in Japan to launch a ten-year program of research and development to build a "thinking" fifth-generation computer whose functions will closely simulate those of the human brain. For that purpose, the MITI is building a new center for the nation's best scientists.

—In a move that augurs a major change in the way OPEC surpluses are being directed, the Saudi Arabian Monetary Agency decided, for the first time openly, to invest $1 billion in Japanese equities.

—The recession in West Germany raises troubling questions about whether the country can ever regain its role as Western Europe's financial leader. For the first time, Japanese makers of machine tools export more units to West Germany than the Germans send to Japan.

—U.S. bankruptcies in the first ten weeks of 1981 were at the highest level in thirty years.

—The Institute of National Economy in Tokyo, publishing the result of its forecasts for the next five years, announced an average growth of 5.5 percent a year for Japan—at the very moment when Europe is in the grip of zero growth for an indefinite period, and the American economy is shattered by "negative growth." The institute adds, "This forecast is made on the basis of oil prices expected to double to 60 dollars a barrel between now and 1985." It concludes that this rate of growth will permit Japanese industries to intensify the exportation of capital for investment in the only countries that offer new markets in rapid development—those of the Third World.

—Finally we learn, with a certain tact in the way it is expressed, that the Japanese National Union of Scientists and Engineers has agreed, with the Japanese Management Association and with the principal executives in charge of control systems at Matsushita Communications, to found an action group called the Organization for the Stimulation of the United States. The aim is to employ all useful means for the recovery of American productivity and for providing the American public with information on technological innovations in the hope of preventing the American slump from causing serious trouble in the world market as a whole.

These are some of the warning signals—for we are no longer facing a country or even a *culture* in Japan, but simply the vanguard of computerization, its revolutionary impact on all economic and social sectors. We must understand this—that Japan's leap into the future has to do with technology, not with being Japanese, and we must learn from the Japanese example if we are to master that technology in common, rather than having it *imposed* on us.

We must understand that computerization is to an exhausted industrial society what the latter was to agricultural society—a fundamental transformation, not only in methods of production and consumption, but in ways of living, in the organization of the social fabric, in the definition of needs. Some needs will disappear, while others we can hardly conceive of will emerge.

As is true of each major stage of social evolution, the tremendous difficulties of transition are due to the rigidity of our mental structure. At the same time, the knowledge that would facilitate this transition is confined for the most part to experts. Neither the general public nor the majority of businessmen and executives truly understand the "computer revolution" and its consequences.

But the truth is irresistible—and healthy. Once the first obstacles have been removed, the first demonstration given on the spot, once people have witnessed the progress that computerization entails, the human benefits are clear to them—and they themselves soon demand a faster pace, as has been the case in Japan.

In the years immediately ahead, computerization will spread more rapidly than electricity did at the beginning of the century. It will expand in the fields of creative activity as quickly as it does in daily work and leisure. Powerful, flexible and inexpensive microcomputers, adaptable to all functions, will become as indispensable, as omnipresent and as much a part of our lives as the air in which we live and breathe. Computerization will free every human being to make the maximum use of his or her faculties. The very nature of the computerized society rests on the full employment of every person's abilities. The more it is adapted toward *individuality,* the more it accelerates the process of new creativity, which in turn will demand greater human input and thought. Computerization is exponential. It is a vast, infinite tool at the service of man's imagination, ideas and dreams, a means of linking each person's individual work, whether routine or creative, to the whole.

W E HAVE ALREADY MENTIONED the two most important fields in which the computer can satisfy human needs—*health* and *education*. Together with *agriculture*, they are the most essential, the most universal concerns.

It is now believed that the computerization of health and education will drastically reduce our need for doctors and teachers. In Europe and America, we are actually seeing the organization of this reduction. It has been decided that during the 1980s the number of graduates in medicine and in teaching should be reduced, because we will simply need fewer of them.

This action not only misrepresents the true nature of the computer revolution, it is a serious miscalculation by the leaders of the United States and Europe.

Japan's plan for general computerization of its educational system indicates that, as a result of the computer program, the qualitative leap will involve the *multiplication* of teaching jobs and positions, not the shrinkage. The essential changes that computerization will make possible are:

1. The passage from collective to individualized education, from traditional classroom instruction to the minicomputer and to a regrouping around it that is flexible *and* adaptable to the learner's "flow of interest."
2. The transformation of passive education (recorder of knowledge) to active education (exchange and stimulation), with the creation of specialized teachers who will have learned to accompany and open up this "activism."

3. The replacement of our present compact block of "school years" by a flexible and indefinite distribution throughout life of time devoted to the accumulation of knowledge and the maximum development of one's faculties and capacities. Here again, specialized teachers will be needed to clarify at each stage the choice of new options based on individual desires and the progress achieved in the preceding stage.

4. The replacement of our traditional examinations and tests, given at predetermined times, by a permanent, individualized evaluation. It will no longer be a question of scores or marks, but of finding new areas to challenge each person's mind.

No one yet knows by what figure the number of teachers, assistants, specialists and generalists will have to be multiplied to open up these new paths of computerized education and provide every opportunity to train, exercise and utilize "individual creativity." Consequently, the Japanese have begun by computerizing *the teaching of teachers:* for it is there that the shortage of men and women will be felt most quickly. A shortage there could interrupt their development.

Several years ago, one of Japan's geniuses, Konosuke Matsushita, who in his nineties is still inventing, publishing and organizing, gave up his position at the head of Matsushita, the firm he founded, to assume leadership of those who devote themselves to the thorough study of education and who are concerned with the anticipated lack of teachers.

Matsushita is trying to ensure the future, to create the most modern, specialized school: the school of Thinkers of the XXI Century, which he finances with the portion of profit from his firms that is set aside for the Matsushita Foundation. He is building a "unified" system of education, training, supervision and organization, not just for Japan, but, in his words, for the "world into which Japan will one day be integrated."

His schedule leaves him very little free time. A quiet visit to him at home in his old villa in Kyoto usually finds him seated behind a low table covered with flowers, in a room paneled with strips of light-colored wood with little flags of the different countries in the world from which his visitors come. In spite of his age, his intellectual activity is intense, and his eyes examine or underline questions and answers with surprising vigor. This ninety-three-year-old man is interested only in the future. He asks to be excused for speaking into a small microphone "to avoid wasting energy by forcing his voice." He has a lot to do. He explains calmly that for the immediate future—the rest of the twentieth century—all of the solutions have been found. What remains is to apply them. He does not consider that his affair; his concern is with what follows.

Konosuke Matsushita is not a lone pioneer. The other leaders of Japan, each one in his respective field, are at work clearing vast new areas that the deployment of the computerized society is opening up to human activity.

Japanese plans for medicine are similar to those for the new education. The immediate goal is an integrated national network of medical care at all levels.

It is based on four approaches: *computerization of hospitals* on the basis of "rapid diagnosis," which can be done with computerized testing equipment; *remote* control or treatment for areas or districts without permanent doctors; *accelerated treatment of emergencies* through a warning system whose network covers the entire territory and is connected, everywhere, to a hospital center; finally, a general support apparatus for the *oldest segment of the population,* whose special problems must be treated with greater frequency and swiftness.

To fill all of the medical jobs that this will eventually entail, the program provides for an increase in the number of doctors and training for all types of assistants, called "health engineers," who will be less qualified than the doctors themselves. Already there are predictions that there will not be enough of them. Consequently, their tasks will have to be subdivided again and another group of medical assistants created.

To achieve this progress, the computerization of health will first demand a complete medical checkup *twice a year* so that all the means of *preventive medicine* can be deployed. If an entire population is to be treated twice a year, an even larger staff of medical personnel will be needed behind the computerized testing machines.

Finally, computerization, like electricity, will be placed at the permanent disposal of every citizen during the whole course of daily life. The home computer can be connected to provide work at home for persons who want to pursue their tasks outside the professional workplace; it will also bring into the home information, medical services, games, educational programs for children, all of it individualized according to need. This computerization of everyday life will develop human capacities in a natural and permanent way.

The true takeoff point will come with the final perfection of *oral communication* in the relationship between man and the machine, by means of the synthetic voice, without the need to be able to read or write to use the machine.

This new advance has already been perfected by several Japanese and American electronics firms on the basis of what is called "the fifth generation" of computers. These computers integrate the most rapid calculation on microprocessors with very large-scale integration—VLSI—the most advanced miniaturized chips, and the greatest speed of calculation, in such a way that the computer achieves the capacity to "recognize voices, and respond orally, and to read the texts, plans and diagrams presented to it."

This same system, based on the VLSI, will permit automatic translation from one language to another. The latest now provides simultaneous translation of six languages: English,

French, German, Italian, Spanish, Japanese. It will eventually be the mainspring of the internalization of communication systems.

This advance toward the new society *can be conceived only on a planetary scale.* The vast sums of capital required, the internal upheaval of social structures and acceptance of interdependence—all are linked to the new world equation. This equation supposes on the part of the rich but exhausted industrial nations, OPEC, whose wealth remains sterile, and the Third-World nations, who have everything to build, common dedication to the new revolutionary form of development, the worldwide application of computerized society. Time is running out.

"I HAVE JUST SPENT FOUR MONTHS in the United States. I was struck by the extraordinary loss of vitality, which seemed to me to be a serious and worrying phenomenon. At Harvard University I was completely lost. I suffered a cultural shock."

The man speaking is the French sociologist Michel Crozier, educated in both French and American universities and long an admirer of America's capacity for innovation. For ten years in the 1960s, during the time of the American challenge, Crozier explained America's innovativeness to Europe—to rouse and stimulate the old continent.

For those who know Michel Crozier and the restraint with which he expresses himself, these remarks are striking. He confirms what one knows, or fears—and he goes further:

> The phenomenon is due to a number of bad decisions that were taken when everything was going well. . . . There is no longer a place for the young. No more young people, no more renewal. The intellectual market is stagnating, people with influence have become protective of the system. . . . Since there is no longer enough work, people don't prepare themselves for it. There are no longer any good doctoral candidates, consequently there is no more good research. . . . Everyone is waiting, while continuing to act as they did in the past. The crisis that is now upon America goes beyond business, the university and the intellectual world. It is a moral problem. . . . The Americans now fear change, and

they are bewildered. There is no longer any enthusiasm for undertaking new things. America will, of course, recover. But we should not expect a spectacular recovery in the next four or five years.

There is no doubt that this diagnosis is colored by sentimental disappointment because of Crozier's fondness for America. Still, in more restrained language, the best-informed American minds share these views and do not hesitate to proclaim them in the legitimate hope that challenges from the outside will provoke a reawakening.

Thus a debate has begun around what some call the "reindustrialization" and others, more clear-sighted, call the "revitalization" of America. It is based on well-founded intuitions and objective analyses of the outside world, but also on ambiguous slogans and dogmatic quarrels. Neither its direction nor its effects can be predicted at the moment.

The most clearheaded are those who have mastered the recent scientific discoveries and the possibilities of the computerized society. Their teams and laboratories are still the first in the world in these technologies, and they themselves are the most passionate advocates of a leap toward the "intelligent society" for America. They struggle to prevent their country's political and social body from becoming involved in the chimera of "reindustrialization," which translates, in the European way, into demanding subsidies from the state to prolong the life of aging condemned industries. They back up the idea of "revitalization," which is the opposite: place all the available resources, which are now too scarce to be wasted, in the generalized computerization of production and training.

Robert Noyce, founder of Intel, one of America's most successful electronics firms and the envy of the Japanese, says that the only sector of the American economy that has a future is high technology, and whatever is connected with it. He believes that we should stop worrying about declining industries, industries of the past, and put our energies into telecommunications, semi-conductors, robots and training.

Texas Instruments, one of the leading American firms in this sector, proves its strength consistently. Fred Bucy, the firm's president, told his fellow citizens recently that the electronics and computer industries will be larger than the automobile and steel industries combined in less than ten years.

These men and many others are very well informed about what should be done without hesitation or delay. But their advice is disregarded or misunderstood—especially by their colleagues in the traditional industrial sectors. At the same time, politicians are naturally more attached to maintaining industrial employment than to basic change.

George Helmeir, an executive of Texas Instruments, has said that for the most part, American society is still living on the scientific and technological achievements of the sixties.

According to an executive from Intel, the first phase of the technological revolution poses a serious problem for employment. An entire new policy is required because new jobs will not be created automatically.

At the heart of the debate was, at an unfortunate moment, the "father of reindustrialization," the sociologist Amitai Etzioni, a professor at Columbia University and adviser to the Carter White House on industrial questions.

He prefaced his diagnosis and recommendations for recovery with this surprising statement:

As father of the campaign for "reindustrialization," I must wage it myself, so that everyone will know clearly and exactly what is at stake. . . .

If, in a world in full evolution, we define precisely what demands priority action on our part, we must begin with the energy problem, because of the dependency to which it condemns us; and the problem of national defense, because of the renewal of Soviet expansionism.

And to enable America to overcome what he considers to be these two major threats to its recovery, Etzioni does not hesitate to prescribe the remedy *least* likely to be adopted: "a very long period of austerity, and restrictions on public and private consumption that could last ten years."

There was nothing about electronics in his statement—the word was not even mentioned—nor about computerization.

Thus, in no small way, the "father of reindustrialization" had helped to cloud the issues. To American experts familiar with the necessity and the means of moving their country on to a computerized society—and its further worldwide application—such a nationalistic obsession seems extraordinarily out of date and wide of the mark. As far as the public is concerned, the idea that recovery must be preceded by ten years of austerity hardly arouses much enthusiasm.

The two errors go hand in hand. *The wrong target, remilitarization instead of computerization, will inevitably lead to weakness instead of the new creative power for which America, more than any other nation, has the adequate scientific potential and social resources.*

But the debate is alive, and perhaps that is the main thing. It should not be regretted that false prophets were the first to express themselves. They produced profound reactions that may spark the rebirth of American greatness, despite ten years of stagnation and decline.

Japanese society also approached the 1980s with a crisis of conscience that led to debate. In an exercise of self-criticism The 60-Men Committee summarized it in a huge study intended to "reform the direction and the nature of the country's efforts." It says:

1. Compared to previous years, we have entered a period of stagnation, as far as innovation is concerned.

2. We will need a better appreciation of the fact that technological progress has become more difficult. First of all because the new technologies demand more time and investment. Then, the assessment of the social problems raised by the technological breakthroughs must be more carefully studied.

3. Negative features of Japanese economic development have now appeared and must not be concealed: weakness of the system in stimulating creativity, weakening of the spirit of initiative due to the constant search for consensus, overestimation of the economic difficulties compared to the social benefits of the integration of a new technology.

4. These characteristics, which it would be dangerous to allow to develop, are due to a socioeducational system that has remained too conformist and which, by its very nature, inhibits truly strong, creative personalities.

5. It appears that if we expect to find the spirit needed for the eighties, we will have to change a certain number of our basic concepts and formulate an environment better adapted to creativity, to individual capacity, and to the tearing down of walls between university, industry and State.

6. If we want to control the next phase of worldwide application, we must have a more precise appreciation of the two basic transformations to be achieved:

The first is a revision of our ideas about the respective roles of the State and private industry. Up to now, private industry has been the principal source of innovation, but it can no longer develop, by its own means, the new technologies whose time limits are much more important and demand capital that surpasses its resources. Consequently, the State will have to intervene more in cooperation with the firms and laboratories of the private sector. New mixed forms of cooperation must be found.

The second is a change in the way we perceive the Third World and how we operate overseas in their countries.

More extensive and better suited preliminary studies will

be needed. We have not examined sufficiently the distinctive features, the specific needs, the social systems of the developing countries before extending our sphere of activities to them. This preparation is now indispensable. We must establish the bases of a genuine complementarity between computerized society as it is developing among us, and the basic, immediate, distinctive needs of still underdeveloped countries. We can succeed, but on the condition that we increase communication between them and us, through exchanges of people in both directions. Their coming to begin their training in our best institutions, and our learning to settle in new countries and adapt to their social patterns, is important so that solutions to problems of development can be fashioned on the spot.

The debate in Japan no longer centers on whether or not to move from an industrial society to a computerized society. The choice has been made. In the midst of passion and controversy, it began with these two problems, which were new for Japanese culture and difficult to apprehend: the change in the nature of the ties between the state and private interests, and the educational and social changes needed for genuine internationalization.

As with the American debate, and with the inevitable debates that are going to torment and transform all societies, there are no correct answers that can be obtained in advance.

The world seeks and will find the philosophical support for the transformations. *Finiteness, which oppressed us and imposed its law on us, is exploding.* Men are finally within reach of the only infinite resource—information, the growth of their minds.

PART-IV

TWENTY YEARS AGO, the two military superpowers backed the two largest underdeveloped nations in the race for development: the Soviet Union supported Mao's China, and the United States, Nehru's India.

Premier Khrushchev, an agriculture enthusiast, lent his best agronomists to the Chinese, whose absolute priority was to feed the country's exploding population—the opposite of Stalin-style forced industrialization.

President Kennedy appointed his friend and the man he considered the best American economist of his time, John Kenneth Galbraith, as ambassador to India. In Delhi, Galbraith was the link between the vast Indian subcontinent and American economic power. As an aid to winning "India's war against underdevelopment," the White House granted him the unusual privilege of a direct line to the President.

Neither of the two military giants was able to go the distance in this formidable race whose stake was the future of almost 1.5 billion men and women. The USSR lost China, and the United States lost India.

China broke away brutally from Moscow and its "model of development." It turned to Japan. Stimulated by Doko, his chosen successor, Inayama, the foremost expert on China, Kobayashi, the genius in world communications, and a few others, Tokyo lost no time in choosing the most rapid and the lightest technologies for China's modernization. The Japanese deliberately set out to develop the largest deposit of gray matter on the planet, while avoiding the costly waste of "industrialization." Thus, barring reversals, China is on the road to creative power. With India, neither Kennedy nor Galbraith truly had time to get down to work. And for the following administrations, with the rapid intensification of America's involvement in Vietnam and the acceleration of the arms race, India ceased to be a priority in America's global strategy. Forgotten by the West and abandoned to the mechanical forces of a market economy, India drifted toward a society characterized by inequality and disorder.

Today, in the vast Indian cities—Bombay, Delhi, Calcutta, Madras—a population of scientists, engineers, academics, executives, agronomists, skilled workers of the highest caliber, numbering seventy million Indians, lives alongside hundreds of millions of illiterates, often on the edge of starvation, deprived of medical care, education and prospects for the future.

One famous winter evening the directors of the vigorous JRD Tata, India's leading industrial empire, gathered in Bombay House, that splendid legacy from British colonialism, to await with mixed feelings the results of the most uncertain election in the history of the world's largest democracy.

Their conversation centered on the improbable but not impossible victory of Indira Gandhi, Nehru's daughter. Before defeat, abandonment and imprisonment, "Madam," as she is often called in India, had held power for ten years, following her father. Businessmen generally considered her an enemy. She was seen as a slave to the Soviet Union.

At the moment that India's future hung on tens of thousands of sacks filled with ballots, Indira Gandhi was being discussed in Bombay as though she came from outer space. No leading businessman had communicated with her, no one had met her, the worst was thought of her entourage and she herself was alleged to have dark ulterior motives.

Yet, the men waiting for the outcome, sharing their fears, had placed their bets on Indira, a standard paradox for this unusual country. None of the great private interests, neither the Tata nor the Birla, had failed to answer the call. Although Nehru's daughter had run up against formidable problems—the entire state machinery was against her, as was the party created by her father, along with the police force; her chief colleagues and allies were in exile; her sons were persecuted; her communications were sabotaged—she had had no financial problems. Indians of means feared this woman, but they detested even more the chaos, incompetence and corruption that had accompanied her successors between 1977 and 1979. A phone call from Bombay to Delhi is next to impossible, airplane schedules are uncertain, a journey by train is an expedition of almost twenty hours, and a hotel reservation is out of the question. Between Bombay, a great industrial center and a vast port open to the world, and Delhi, the center of political decisions, there is an immense logistical gulf—a minor but significant aspect of the underdevelopment that makes India nearly ungovernable.

So these men believed the firm hand of the devil was preferable to her incompetent predecessors. Emotionally, they opposed her, but rationally her victory was needed desperately.

Also, there was always the possibility that this woman, of legendary energy, had learned something in her political exile and had changed.

Near the steep bend of Wellington Crescent Street in a modest section of New Delhi where few automobiles come, the usual crowd of people, but slightly larger and noisier, has gathered in long, surging streams around the small unguarded garden that surrounds the low-roofed, five-room house where the woman most often simply referred to as Gandhi lives and works.

Beyond the entrance there is a small passage which opens on the room she uses as her office. Visitors are constantly coming and going. She likes that. She is not disturbed by it. From time to time she speaks to someone, but nobody approaches her unless she indicates that he or she may. She always knows the whereabouts of the clever Yashpal Kapoor, the assistant her father left to protect and help her. When she wants to telephone someone or speak to a visitor alone, she informs Kapoor, who clears the room. Then, uninterrupted, she turns her thoughts to India.

Her extreme fatigue at the end of the campaign, during which she got little sleep for twenty-eight days, gives her a special charm, an austere beauty. It intensifies her inner flame, her forcefulness of expression and her willingness to discuss, without delay, building the future. She has come back from the south, from the edge of the ocean and from Madras. She has come back from the eastern border, the Burmese border and from Calcutta. She has come back from Bengal and the mouth of the Ganges. She has come back from Punjab at the foot of the Himalayas. Night after night she had gone to the villages, lighting her face with an electric light, so that peasants standing in front of their cob houses could see that she had come to them. She has returned from the depths of India. What no one knew then was that she had won. India had been entrusted to her; she would be in power before the end of the week. As Prime Minister, as she was in prison, she would be alone. Now in her office she ponders the future.

How, where, should one begin to develop India, to bring it out of its misery and despair? She does not pretend to know. She has nothing but innumerable, constant, precise questions. Where should one begin?

What she finds most overwhelming is the enormous number of young people who have never received an education.

No one, not even she, could say exactly how many there are: "There must be, I think, about two hundred million young people under fifteen who have not yet learned to read and write. . . . So where does one begin?"

She was surprised to read in *The New York Times* a story

saying she didn't have a chance to succeed. According to the story, it was unlikely that she would be able to guide India through the uncontrollable inflation, the crushing unemployment, and the free fall of productivity that bar the country's path to development.

It might indeed be so. There is a brief flash in her calm eyes after reading the story and a moment of silent anger:

"America always betrayed my father. They always looked down on me. They abandoned India. They think only of themselves and don't understand the rest of the world. How is it possible? What disdain. So everywhere they say that I am pro-Soviet. What nonsense. . . . Was my father lenient toward the Communists? Am I? I am neither for America nor for Russia. Both look upon India as an object and a stake. I am for India and its people, for whatever can aid India, from whatever source, by whatever means. But where should one begin?"

So far, India cannot break the bonds of its poverty. Its per capita income remains at the miserable threshold of $200 per year and has little chance of reaching in the normal pattern of "industrialization," $300 by the year 2000. The economic situation has deteriorated even more in these past years.

From 1978 to 1980 the national budget not only stopped growing at the weak previous rate of 2 percent to 3 percent, but it fell by more than 3 percent. There are now three hundred million Indians "in a state of absolute poverty." Counting only those who once had a regular job, have lost it and have succeeded in registering somewhere, there are fifteen million Indians officially unemployed. The others are not recognized as such, since they have never had worker's status anywhere.

The twenty-year program of massive industrialization which was based on heavy industry, following the Soviet model, has only resulted in failure. The enormous, uncontrollable bureaucracy that employs two, three, four bureaucrats instead of one for each job has only made India more barren. The bureaucracy was incapable of building roads or increasing the number of schools, or making land fertile or expanding health services. It was only able to control, verify and say no.

What is impressive and seductive about Indira—beyond courage, detachment and intelligence—is her modesty. She knows that she is capable of understanding, but she says that she knows almost nothing. She knows how to communicate with her people, how to restore hope when they lose it, how to find them in places where no one ever goes, how to make them feel, sometimes without a word, that she knows their pain and is thinking only of them. She knows how to tell them that she loves them. But that is all she knows.

She has heard about "technology," a mysterious realm which she says she hardly distinguishes from industry. Now, India must have industries at all costs, many industries.

Tens upon tens of thousands of hands must be given work. All those willing to help India industrialize may enter the country. They will be well received. If technology means more industries, then India needs a lot of technology. She believes OPEC is right to declare that it is going to use its power to get this "transfer of technology" from the West. Moreover, she is on good terms with the Gulf "because the Moslems know that with me they are protected in India. The OPEC countries know it. They should be for the Third World, and they are Moslems, so they will help India to obtain many transfers of industries or, if you wish, technology, to meets its tremendous needs."

She wants to know more about this little wafer that she looks at for the first time. She can just make out fine, hardly visible grooves on it. It is a microprocessor.

American or Japanese? she asks.

What does it matter? They are all the same. The machines that are the source of the new revolution have no homeland, know no borders. They are all made from sand ("From sand, really, how do you mean from sand?" she asks), and they work wherever they are installed, wherever it is understood that they not only replace industrial manpower, but free men themselves from the most onerous tasks.

Indira, who always listens well, interrupts: what she wants is the opposite. Or rather her people want the opposite. They want work. It doesn't matter what sort of factories are established as long as they employ people. There can never be too many factories.

Indira also needs many schools, and roads to travel to them, and housing, and many teachers and schools to train these teachers, and trained personnel so that the huge labor force will learn to work better, to increase its output in the factories.

But is Indira right?

Today, India's per capita income is $200 a year, against $10,000 for the United States, Europe or Japan. Is there reason to believe that even with a tremendous industrialization effort Indira can reach 50 percent of the industrialized world's standard of living between now and the beginning of the century?

The answer is no. If the annual growth of Third World countries remains at the rate of 5 percent a year, and the average rate of the developed world at 2.5 percent *it will take 150 years for the income of Third World peoples to equal that of peoples of the industrial countries*. It is doubtful that the Indians will have the patience to wait 150 years.

"Mind the Third World's despair, world chaos can come out of it," exclaimed Kurt Waldheim, at the inauguration of the last session of the UN's Economic and Social Council. "Between the two populations of the planet, that of the developed part and that of the undeveloped part, there is a seismic rift so deep that it can produce terrible splits causing everything to explode," repeated Robert McNamara, then head of the World Bank, in drawing up the distressing balance sheet of two decades of development. And Willy Brandt, after two years at the head of a commission of capable international officials who devoted themselves to development, wrote at the beginning of his report: "Our commission was unanimous in considering a fundamental revision of relations between the two parts of the world an urgent imperative. The system established at the end of the war has now resulted in a situation that puts the Third World at such a serious disadvantage that it demands correction in depth. That is what the widely spread and accepted demand for a new international economic order expresses. It is truly a question of a historical reckoning."

That reckoning is at hand, and the only way to come to terms with it is for a massive transfer of technology to the Third World that will make the *training and development of human resources* the priority of all priorities.

In March 1975 the political leaders of OPEC who gathered in Algeria demanded "the acceleration of the process of development through an appropriate transfer of modern technology." This was the first time such a demand was made and it was announced in the name of the Third World.

The West resented the call for change as an attack and preferred to ignore it, hoping it would quietly disappear. But the opposite happened. First energy, *then investment,* became weapons in OPEC's hands. There was no longer any hope of emerging from the crisis on any long-term basis *without espousing the transformation* between the two worlds.

In the years 1978–1981 the development of the microprocessor and telecommunications equipment has laid the groundwork for providing the means of speeding up a process of development that would make it possible to equalize the North and the South, *not in 150 years but within a generation.* Yet a considerable part of the problem still has to be grasped: how can this "transfer of modern technology" be carried out?

On this point, the Saudi Arabian economic monthly *Saudi Business* expressed what everyone was thinking: "The transfer of technology is like motherhood. Everyone is for it, no one really knows its nature. But we know that it is the matrix of all progress and all development."

One thing is certain, however. As the industrial West transforms itself into a computerized, information-based society, the

Third World must get the same chance. If the Western world adopts this new course, more productive as far as the performances of machines are concerned, and more human in regard to employment of men's capacities, how can we imagine that the Third World would continue to supply "cheap labor" to outmoded factories whose products would no longer find any outlets? To do so would be the height of absurdity.

So the Third World must enter this new era without going through the preliminary stages of heavy industrialization that would further aggravate its underdevelopment. Computerization will be applied and adapted to the needs of the Third World. Robots will be available for work everywhere at the same price. By definition, all information, data and knowledge will be instantly and universally accessible. The only transfer that counts, the one that all development will depend on, is each person's move from the stage where the means of learning are lacking to the stage where he or she can develop his or her own faculties, abilities and creativity. For learning how to learn is the essence of the "computer revolution."

What is needed to begin such a transfer to huge, impoverished countries? Nothing that dislodges outdated machines. Nothing that resembles the huge steel and concrete equipment characteristic of classical industrialization. What is needed is simply the extension of the soft infrastructure of computerized society: the means that link every workplace, in every location, to a worldwide network of knowledge; the means that make it possible to combine all essential information with human work, the means that disseminate the elements necessary for on-the-spot training of people according to their needs.

Communication and education, then, are the first of these soft infrastructures that can be extended all around the planet. There will be no magic wand—everything will become feasible in stages as soon as the essentials are in place: the opening up of minds and the ability to understand. It is the race "between education and catastrophe" predicted by Toynbee.

Everyone who has devoted himself to Third World problems over the past thirty years, often using India as an example, has come to the same conclusion: the strategy was all wrong. In attempting to industrialize Third World countries without delay, we have, with rare exceptions, aggravated their problems. We have uprooted men from their land, and they have then crowded into sprawling cities. With no reasonable expectations, and based on the hope of a high growth rate that has proved to be deceptive, we have followed the most antinatural path: abandon the land, which can provide nourishment, and congest the cities, which no longer provide work. What should have been done was to *decentralize* jobs and build up the villages with the aid of computerization.

Among the men who have continually drawn attention to the needs of the Third World (make the land fruitful, check rural exodus, fight against urbanization, decentralize at all costs) is Maurice Guernier. He worked with Jean Monnet immediately after World War II, as a member of the commission for French reconstruction, and was entrusted with "overseas questions" —the Third World. He has been at it ever since. Today a colleague of Aurelio Peccei's at the Club of Rome, he is in charge of the same problems. In 1968 he published a cry of alarm: *The Third World's Last Chance.* That chance has not been seized. He was not listened to then or since. Rural areas continue to be abandoned, and, with ten, fifteen, twenty million inhabitants, the great cities of these countries are becoming the ghettos of the planet.

Today, seeing new means for true decentralization, he describes how these could be integrated into each human environment:

We have always thought that development was solely economic. But it is mainly sociological and human. I have found levels of true development higher in certain Asian and African towns than in certain sections of New York or Chicago.

. . . The development of the Third World can emerge only from the complete flowering of men. Above all, it is most urgent that we stop the rural exodus, the hideous development of the huge shantytowns of Caracas, Lagos, Calcutta and hundreds of other megalopolises.

The state is incapable of guiding and supervising farmers. Nowhere has it succeeded in doing so. All decisions must be decentralized toward rural villages. Only there is true country life to be found. The village must be transformed into a veritable development enterprise, a decision and management center.

Microcomputers are now the very tools of this vision and provide the means which have escaped us for thirty years. By their very nature, they can work the miracle of true Third World decentralization. A village committee, for example, can help its people if it is connected to data banks and telecommunications networks that provide information, knowledge, education and medicine. The village, however, must exploit computerization by making use of a very small number of intermediaries who will make it possible to link the larger computerized society to the local community. Guernier describes it in detail:

It is a question of introducing into each small, regional community, of not more than 50,000 to 100,000 inhabitants, a small, light administration composed of an agronomist, a doctor and an educator. They would be the village's "progress advisers."

By their presence, these three technicians would inspire in each village the natural selection of three to six young people who would act as "message transmitters." In a way, these young men and women would be barefoot doctors, barefoot agronomists, barefoot educators. They would not take any courses, they would have no diplomas. But they would be capable of transmitting the adviser's message to the village. For example:

When your eyes ache, put three drops of the prescribed medicine into them. Put Mercurochrome on sores. . . . Here is the fertilizer for the next cotton field. We have been told when the monsoon will arrive. Here is the seed that has been chosen. . . . The pictures that you see on the poster will help you to read. There will be new ones every week. . . ."

Using Third World life as an example, Maurice Guernier has attempted to imagine and describe the nature of the human training that would be capable of exploiting and disseminating, on the spot, the contributions of world computerization.

The most recent president of the Forum of the Third World, the Egyptian Ismail-Sabri Abdalla, confirms the golden rule of decentralization as the only realistic road to development and specifies the basic human environment that will enable computerization to fertilize the Third World:

Development strategy should begin with autonomous rural evolution. No ministerial or administrative approach will be equal to this task: modernization, in the full sense, of the village community. The farmers themselves must be put into a position to take destiny in their hands. External technological contributions are indispensable. The dialogue between farmers and "technical advisers" must be mutually educational, with the power of decision remaining in the hands of the farmers. For the farmer's own development is what matters most. It can only be achieved and maintained by using technological means to increase local democracy by restoring the peasant's rights as a man and a citizen.

Comparing his experience and proposals with those of the Egyptian, Guernier concludes: "On the whole there is a complete identity of views between the notion presented by Sabri Abdalla and ours. I give it absolute priority without hesitation. It directly affects the lot of two billion human beings."

These village committees, progress advisers, message transmitters to whom Third World specialists assign a developmental role will be fully effective with the dissemination, the decentralization of information that the new technology will make accessible.

The few intermediaries of the kind just described will have to implant the computer system progressively; it will be present entirely in the form of a simple, local antenna—*the terminal.* The microcomputer will no longer be costly and will be capable of being utilized after a few weeks or months of training.

But how will this solve the essential problem of hunger in the world? How can microprocessors feed the millions of human beings who die of starvation each year?

Hunger, and its corollary sickness, are the invariable characteristics of poverty. "The majority of the poor live in poor countries," states McNamara's last message. This simple reminder indicates that development reduces poverty (although it may not reduce inequality and injustice). It provides increasingly larger segments of the population with the financial means to buy food. At the world level, there is no food shortage, only the agonizing question of purchasing power, and the Third World purchasing power can no longer come from classical industries, whose prospects are now limited by the technological superiority of the North.

The industrialization model that has been fashionable for so long has often been pursued at the expense of traditional agriculture, with the result that harvests and products that once fed local populations are no longer available to them.

The technology of information is based on people. It enables them to work in their own areas, their own villages, and thus helps stem the rural exodus. It makes the choice of crops to be planted, the preparation of the soil, and so forth more intelligent and helps gauge the interplay of supply and demand in a more rational way. Information technology is more effective in dealing with problems of distribution.

Information technology also helps to make formerly barren areas fertile. For example, in the deserts, in Israel's Negev as well as in the Arabian Gulf, it is now possible to farm in sandy and rocky soil. Under huge plastic covers that prevent evaporation, crops are irrigated drop by drop by networks of specially designed pipes. Water, ofter salt water, is rationed to each plant, to each blade of grass, to each tomato plant. A computer governs the entire system, calculates pressure, regulates salt content, monitors temperature, and measures growth under the most economical conditions imaginable of water consumption. From this we can see how the use of intelligent, computerized information will enable us to achieve vastly more rational irrigation and fertilization of the soil in the future.

TEN YEARS BEFORE OPEC WON its first success, thirteen years before the first microprocessor appeared, twenty years before Taif, a young man from the Third World had a vision of the future based on technology transfer. Karl Schiller saw him at work in the 1970s, and said without hesitation, "He is a young genius."

Schiller suggested that this young man participate in the work of the small group from Europe, Japan and the Gulf countries who had come together seeking paths for the future. Even though this Kuwaiti was the head of the most powerful international investment fund and was, at the time, his country's permanent representative on the Brandt Commission, he accepted.

At every stage he demonstrated the easily forgotten fact that truly to understand the conditions of the Third World's development, to direct actions that can be effective, *one must be part of the Third World oneself.* He is Abdulatif al-Hamad.

At the age of twenty-two, Abdulatif al-Hamad already knew what he wanted when he declined a career in his country's ministry of foreign affairs and chose instead the very small Kuwait Fund for Arab Development. He was not interested in the international circles, the speeches, the diplomatic games, the fashionable dinners. He wanted to emphasize development.

In 1962, believing that his country's oil would one day earn it considerable income, he decided to become an international investor. He asked the World Bank to send one of its foremost experts to spend two years teaching him financial mechanisms and helping him to evaluate projects. A man of the Third World, he also realized how much of what he learned would have to be adapted to be applicable to his world.

An agricultural development project, in Tunisia, provided Abdulatif al-Hamad with his first opportunity. The project had been presented to the World Bank, which had refused to finance it because it required a long-term loan. The project couldn't offer the minimum economic return required by the international organization.

Abdulatif presented the same project to his board and to his country's government, declaring in his report: "Beyond the uncertain return that can be expected in economic terms, we should measure the *social effects* of this investment, which, by its very implementation, is destined to modify local methods of working, cultural habits and the ability to grasp conditions of growth."

The Kuwait Fund adopted the project, financed and managed it. Implemented exclusively by local Tunisian teams, its success far surpassed expectations. A new criterion, "social return," was established, and in the name of efficiency it took precedence over financial return.

In a few years the Kuwait Fund proved, by means of many other projects, that by concentrating on accelerating the development of men's training and aptitudes, capital outlay could be recovered several times over.

Fifteen years later, in recounting the experience of what has now become a leading worldwide investment fund, controlled, staffed and managed by men of the Third World, the British economist Robert Stephens wrote concerning the future:

According to OECD's estimates OPEC's available investment capital could reach almost $250 billion by the early 1980s. That is to say almost 6 percent of all of the combined national product of the twenty leading industrial powers in the world. The manner, the principles, the criteria for the utilization of OPEC's investment capacity will be of vital importance, not only to the Arab world, but to the entire Third World and, consequently, to the new balance in the world economy. . . . At that point, the basic example that the Kuwait Fund represents, its pioneer work in placing human progress at the top of the list of investment priorities, will be recognized.

If the wealth derived from oil revenues is to be used for efficient development, a serious, inventive, and incorruptible human framework is essential. Proof that these rare, but essential qualities can be found and proof of their decisive effectiveness on the duration will have been furnished by the Kuwait Fund's vital contribution to new modes of development.

After twenty years of work in fifty Third World countries, Schiller's "young genius" no longer feels young, but there is no letup in his work. He himself draws a simple, rigorous lesson from this experience:

The first factor of all economic development is the development of man himself. Development is first of all a mental process. It begins with a mental attitude. A development activity's success is measured very precisely by the level of consciousness and responsibility to which it raises the people to whom it is addressed.

He concludes:

It is according to this rule, and in setting this goal, that the alliance between *OPEC's financial capacity* and the *technological capacity* of the *developed countries* to transform the conditions for starting up the economies of the *Third World* can be considered. This alliance could give rise to worldwide conditions of development which would be more rapid, and even more spectacular, than what we dare hope for at present.

Referring to Taif and OPEC's demand for technology transfer he says: *"In sowing oil, we must reap development."*

Abdulatif al-Hamad's theories have grown out of real-life experiences, of projects in full development, in areas that expand, year by year, farther west from the Arabian Gulf, toward the Sudan, Algeria, Niger, Cameroon, and east of the Gulf toward Iran, Pakistan, India, Burma. He has had the same success everywhere, by implementing the same priorities: *food* (self-sufficient agricultural techniques), *health* (flying teams, linked to modern centers), *education* (now aided by computerized methods).

Abdulatif isn't trying to impress the Westerners who are the decision makers in all the large institutions. When he expresses himself, it is without compromise, because his country's wealth has not shaken his conviction that the Gulf countries are part of the Third World. In March of 1980, the *Middle East Economic Survey* asked him the following question: "What is your message for the Arabs? What is the role of a nation such as yours, which has oil resources, which is part of the Third World, and which must establish close relations with the industrial world?" He replied:

> We are absolutely a nation of the Third World, of the South. We are not, and we will never agree to be an integral part of the industrial world, of the North. For we must not let the present appearances of wealth delude us, nor must we yield to the temptation to believe that we are members of the Club of developed nations. The truth is that we are only privileged members of the Club of underdeveloped nations. Therefore our solidarity with the South is total. Interdependence between the Arab world and other countries of the Third World is much greater and economically more essential than our ties with the North.

Was this a declaration of hostility? No, simply a statement of identity. If Abdulatif al-Hamad is in the forefront of the architects of the "new international order," it is as much because of his deep sense of belonging to the world of the South as it is of his personal values.

In the head office of the London bank that is one of his subsidiaries; in a seminar in Brussels on the follow-up to the Brandt Report; in Paris in his hotel lounge, where he has taken over a corner to receive visitors, one might take him for an ascetic British professor with the keen expression of an intellectual. He doesn't look like a son of the desert—until one sees him at home, dressed in his country's customary long white robe and round hood, happy and relaxed with the team of men whom he trained and with whom he works. There, on the large terrace overlooking the courtyard of a building put up by the Kuwait Fund, he is in his milieu.

A small electronic transmitter-receiver links him to his city and from there to the rest of the world. He doesn't eat lunch. Work lasts until two, then everybody goes home. He himself dines at home, where he is always in control of the network of his development projects, each of which he knows individually and has visited many times.

When he has the time, he goes for a long walk in the dunes, working out new ideas for the future—a future that he looks forward to more than he fears. He believes in the unlimited superiority of human resources. *

In the spring of 1980, in Paris, Abdulatif al-Hamad participated in one of the meetings of the Paris Group to discuss with the members why the Brandt Commission's basic work had reached only an audience of specialists. It was during this discussion that the need was expressed for a public statement of the new facts of the world. The idea led to the present work.

*In March 1981 Abdulatif was promoted to Minister of Finance *and* Planning for his powerful country.

The Paris meeting lasted two days and was made up of Abdulatif al-Hamad; two Japanese representatives—Doko's, this time his successor as the head of Ishikawajima-Harima, Shinto;* and the young Vice-Minister of Finance, Matsukawa, who had given up his only week of vacation with his family—Minister Karl Schiller, who, between trips to Saudi Arabia or Pakistan, had come once again from Hamburg; Professor Herbert Giersh, the president of the Kiel Institute; the international lawyer and author, Samuel Pisar,† unruffled in his difficult and determined crusade to create constructive economic ties between hostile societies, between East and West, and North and South, with a thesis which has come to be widely known as "Weapons of Peace"; and finally, a fascinating Swiss, Peter Huggler.

Giersh, better informed than most about the worsening global economic situation and especially worried about Germany itself, asked his colleague from the Gulf how they could help create the "salutary shock" necessary to create an awareness of the nature and scope of the problem.

Al-Hamad replied that as long as they were content to address specialists and officials with studies and documents, there would be no mobilization. Something else would have to be done.

The new problems—energy crises, computer revolution—are considered, by the ones who know, too complex for the average citizen, or so they think. The fear aroused by a statement of the facts could very well be premature as long as there are no precise solutions to propose.

The president of the Kiel Institute refuted this position: only a public from whom one hides nothing of the truth will be capable of gathering the courage and the will to act to pave the way *for the renaissance of a unified world.*

---

*Now president of the large public company Nippon Telephone and Telegraph, the equivalent of AT&T.

†Whose latest book, *Of Blood and Hope,* has since become an international best-seller.

Abdulatif al-Hamad declared:

I am from a region of the world, the Arabian Gulf, that all of you think about, but whose true realities the West has never wanted to know. Our oil is known, but no one tries to find out who *we* are. It is true for us, it is true for the rest of the Third World. But the definite innovation of this era is the total interdependence between the two worlds. Energy, food, production, markets, inflation, unemployment, nothing, absolutely nothing, can be approached any longer by persisting in the belief that some of us can come out of it without the others. All our worlds make up only one: a "global village." We must begin to knit the ties that will give this village—this planet—a new life. There is very little time.

You Europeans, you Japanese, must keep in mind the condition of your countries in the days following the war. You were in very dire straits. But vision and generosity came to restore you to life and launch you on the path of new development: it was the Marshall Plan. Today the entire Third World is in a situation even worse than the one in which you found yourselves. It is on this scale and in accordance with the conditions of our times that we need such vision and determination again. There is no doubt that we must address ourselves to the collective conscience by knowing how to move and enlighten it. My experience in so many different countries inspires me with confidence. But we must know how to have confidence.

At the end of the second day of work, it was decided to organize the work of both Europeans and Japanese around a team in Paris to develop a common vision before the end of the year. The Japanese were not easily convinced that it was advisable to publish, under any form at all. They were not empowered to commit themselves. But the Swiss, Peter Huggler, accustomed to the difficulties and misunderstandings that arise because of cultural differences, undertook "to speak to Doko about it."

Peter Huggler is a remarkable person. He was born in Zurich

into a great German-Swiss Protestant family, and became a very unusual link between the two worlds of the North and the South. His father was a sculptor, a friend of Giacometti, a student of Bourdelle; his mother was a psychiatrist, student of Freud at the school of Vienna. As far back as childhood, he spoke German, English and French. At the end of his studies in 1955, he decided to leave Switzerland—the world of his friends and fellow students who were going off to Harvard, London, the Sorbonne.

Among the offers Huggler received, he chose one from a mining firm which gave him the opportunity to work in India, Ceylon and Burma. Without hesitating, he took off for the Third World. After six years in and around India, he pushed on farther to an even more distant world: Japan.

At the end of the 1950s, Japan was still hanging on unsteadily to America, grabbing everything that came its way from the country that had crushed it and then opened it to the world.

Huggler found Japan simmering with excitement. Far from being the anthill of indistinguishable workers that he had so often heard described, the Japan of 1960 appeared to Peter Huggler to be a breeding ground where everyone was determined to create, learn, invent, do better than others and better than yesterday. That was what he was looking for: the yeast that would make the heavy dough of the Third World rise. In love with the Third World, he married Japan—and a Japanese woman.

Making his home in Tokyo, Huggler now zeroed in on what was always his objective—the masses of Asia. These abandoned people with whom he identifies are his dream and his obsession.

For a long time he preached in the wilderness. Neither Tokyo nor Zurich cared about the Third World. Then he created the instrument for his struggle: a half-Swiss, half-Japanese bank. But he himself would be the very heart of his plan of action, the first soft infrastructure that would be effective in uniting the two worlds with a thin living thread.

His plan was simple: he would live in both Tokyo and Zurich, working one month in Japan, one month in Europe, making the round trip every month, living, as he put it, "the life of a suburbanite of the world," with nothing but an overnight case, no other baggage.

For Europeans he became a Japanese specialist, and for the Japanese, a European representative. On both sides, those interested in the other got into the habit of coming to see him. And he has talked to them tirelessly for twenty years now about the Third World.

The Paris spring meeting followed one held in his office in Zurich where, months earlier, Europeans and Japanese met initially to form the little group. It was there, with all the difficulties of a first contact of this type, and the slow translation of each contribution, that it all began. The first Arab officials were invited to the next meeting in order to round out the Paris Group by uniting the three worlds—the European Community, the Arabian Gulf and Japan. The meeting had become, in short, a cell of Abdulatif al-Hamad's "global village."

The urgent request for a new Marshall vision that Abdulatif presented to the Northerners in 1980 is now at the core of the current North–South discussion. What America represented to devastated Europe and Japan at the end of World War II, the developed world as a whole now represents to the Third World.

George C. Marshall's vision was one of enlightened self-interest. Following the war, it would have been tempting for America to entrench itself in its dominant position and make use of its economic superiority to extend its "empire." Such a policy would have been disastrous. Surrounded by a world in ruins, the United States would not have been able to develop its full productive capacity. With Europe insolvent, its industry gutted, America would have become an island in an ocean of poverty and misery. Few overseas export markets would have existed, and continued "welfare" payments to Europe and Japan could have been costly. Marshall's team understood what was in the greatest interest of the United States: *help others to help themselves.*

Today a similar vision, on a global scale, commands the attention of the developed world in regard to the less developed countries. But the conditions for applying this vision must be very different. They will have to be adapted to another era, to other economies, to other peoples.

The Marshall Plan consisted of financial aid to countries that retained under the rubble of war all the infrastructures necessary to rebuild their societies. Cities, roads, factories, qualified workers, laboratories, educational systems, everything was there ready to be restored. The Marshall Plan provided the means to do that. Gradually, America saw the countries that had once been victims of war regain their strength and become active partners again.

The West then entered an era of unprecedented growth and expansion that lasted thirty years. The resultant prosperity repaid the original Marshall aid to America a hundredfold. A superior international system was established whereby everybody benefited. Each country, as it recovered, helped and accelerated the recovery of the others. It was a new type of economic cycle of a higher nature which was profitable to *all*. To all, that is, within a closed circle. The rest of the world did not exist, was ignored or was simply exploited.

But now the West *needs* the Third World as an equal *partner* in its own revitalization, just as America, forty years ago, needed Europe and Japan. The West will fail to rediscover its own path of economic growth, it will suffocate and will see its social order fall apart, unless it is rejuvenated by a true burst of development in Third World countries. Interdependence now involves the entire planet—this is the *new dimension* of the problem.

The *nature* of the problem is also new. Another Marshall Plan consisting simply of financial aid would not work. What the Third World needs is a complete network of infrastructures that will establish the foundation of development. In an era of automation and computerization, old infrastructures based on heavy industry are no longer productive. What is now needed is a more subtle, more powerful, infrastructure that will enable any part of the Third World to become its own source of creation.

One of the leading Westerners who pays most attention to this, a man who for years has seen the need for this plan because of his regular discussions with Arab officials, is Bruno Kreisky, Chancellor of Austria. From Vienna, home of OPEC, Kreisky has become a permanent link between industrial Europe, the Gulf and the Third World.

At the beginning of 1981, he spoke at an international meeting, organized by the United Nations, to discuss the next decade of development. He began by paying homage to the memory of Pandit Nehru:

Nehru was one of the great strategic thinkers of our times. He showed all new generations the way to the future: to an integrated world development. The admiration that I felt for him in my youth inspires me today in all of my thoughts about our common duty in regard to this development. Nehru's vision has become an even more urgent imperative for us. The time has come to translate it into a concrete reality, without delay and without further negotiation. We have already lost considerable time and wasted many opportunities.

The starting point for all consistent effort, I will never stop repeating, is for the developed countries to assign themselves the task of allowing the Third World access to the network of modern infrastructures, a network which would place each underdeveloped country in a position to exploit its *own* resources and find its own path of development. If we can equip a country this way it will be able to develop according to its own culture, its own creativity, its own capacities for invention.

Everything begins with these infrastructures. It is the necessary and, from now on, the sufficient condition for all development. People will thus have the means of converting into production the major resource at their disposal, the only one they will need, thanks to new technologies: their own intelligence.

What networks of railroads, highways, and canals were, in another age, networks of telecommunications, information and computerization, education and training according to the most modern technologies are today. It is the absolute *right* of the people who want to develop to have these tools at their disposal without any transition. It is our duty and in our interest that they have and make use of them. It is, indeed, a question of a new Marshall vision, but adapted to our times and to the new nature of the economy.

Computerized infrastructures for the Third World could make it possible for whole stages of development to be bypassed. From the abacus to the multiplication table, to the logarithmic rule, to adding machines, to the first computers, to transistors took centuries. And from this long progress and series of inventions emerged the microprocessor—a wonderful device from which the three basic elements of all wealth converge: *information, matter, energy.*

The peoples of Asia, Africa and Latin America should not have to repeat this process. Telecommunications, microprocessors and their tendency to converge in the new creative process should be placed freely and completely at the disposal of Third-World peoples—*so that they can become creators themselves.*

Education is the foremost example. Computerization will transform its fundamentals. It will accelerate the educational process by applying it on a worldwide scale. As early as 1975, Jan Tinbergen, the Dutch Nobel Laureate in economics and author of *The Rebirth of an International Order*, saw the importance of the technological revolution for the Third World. He wrote that this revolution will make it possible to conceive of a unique network of education, which, while respecting local and cultural differences, will be based on common structures.

Three years later, the Englishman Christopher Evans, studying areas in which computerization would transform the conditions of progress for underdeveloped countries, also placed education at the head of the list. In *The Mighty Micro* he wrote:

The third factor promoting the rise of the underdeveloped world concerns the way in which computer power may be brought directly to bear on its problems. The areas most likely to benefit are medical science, meteorology, climate control, crop control, agricultural science and long- and short-term economic planning. Machine intelligence may not be applied to these areas until the last decade of the century, but when it is, the effects on society will be felt immediately. Most important of all, however, will be its application to education.

Of all the barriers that divide the world, making one segment of mankind wealthy and putting the other in the direst poverty, the biggest and most intractable is ignorance. Education and knowledge have enriched men's lives from the beginning of time and affluence has only sprung up where ignorance has been conquered. The cycle is self-perpetuating, for the more affluent the society, the better it educates its members, and so, in turn, its affluence increases. At the other end of the scale ignorance results in despair, indifference, waste and needless over-population.

There is no instant cure for these ills, but it is clear that the problems of the underdeveloped world will remain intractable until a massive educational program is got under way. Until recently this would have been unthinkable because of prohibitive costs, but with virtually free computer power about to be unleashed and with commercial organizations turning their eyes to the enormous markets for teaching computers, the scene will be changed. The first moves in this direction will probably occur in the next decade. . . .

The rebirth of Marshall's vision for the eighties of a computer revolution as a collective, creative response to the demands of countries that have for so long ignored or exploited one another, can provide the foundation for a new worldwide prosperity. Science's latest achievements have occurred at the right moment, if we have the wisdom and the will to seize the chance, for science has brought us the decisive discovery of the fundamental relationship among matter, energy and information, Mastery of this relationship is to the technological revolution what Einstein's equation was to the nuclear age. The computer explosion, transforming the learning process, can be to the crisis in the world economy what the nuclear bomb was to World War II.

It is the source of new life which has been delivered to us, with the discoveries that can now create resources and riches —beyond those provided by nature. Computerized society offers us the means of turning every individual into a creator.

The silicon chip is becoming the resource of resources. Inexhaustible and available to all, this silicon is the only resource the new technology will ever need. With oxygen, it is the most widespread resource in the universe. It is found on every beach and in every desert. Half of the earth's crust is made of it. The limits nature normally places on her raw materials no longer apply.

THE INFORMATION SOCIETY is already emerging as a transition toward a new approach to the secret of life—and of creation itself. Among those who predict this is the Frenchman Jacques Maisonrouge, head of IBM's operation in Paris and one of the experts of the computer revolution: "We already know that biology is the science in the best position to take over from electronics and create new activities. It will have impact on fields as diverse and essential as food, health and energy."

The editorial writer of an American scientific publication goes further and calls genetic engineering the most promising development since the development of the transistor.

And the Japanese report that described the passage from the microprocessor to a computerized society delivers a similar message for bioengineering *based on several years of laboratory experiment*. It describes the means which places at man's disposal new resources based on the "programmable work" of basic living organisms: microbes, bacteria, viruses.

Up to now, the potential of science and technology has been discovered and exploited only in terms of the advances in microelectronics. Now we are at the next stage: the exploitation of the wealth of data in the information transmitted through the genetic chain itself. This information is carried by DNA— deoxyribonucleic acid—a sort of genetic "chip." By combining the information of various genetic circuits, through engineering that is more delicate than anything in electronics, we can now move to the actual "work" of creation. The power such knowledge will unleash will make microprocessors look puny.

The first applications of this scientific breakthrough already exist in agriculture and drugs. We are now "programming" organic cells to produce all sorts of new food from old vegetation. Plants that will adapt to tropical conditions, that will make deserts yield food, are already being developed by genetic engineering.

This new engineering makes it possible to "program" bacteria to produce many other products. It has long been recognized that enzymes are capable of transforming grapes into wine, or milk into cheese. Now, organized by "genetic programming," bacteria are being put to work in the laboratory to synthesize petrochemical products and to create hydrocarbons themselves —energy.

The creativity of science thus traces, in less than a generation, a stupendous trajectory: the discovery and exploitation of the atom; the revelation of electronics and the implementation of microprocessors, the technological revolution and computerized society; biological and genetic engineering with tremendous potential—food, drugs and energy itself.

The explosion of scientific discoveries and the ability to exploit them more and more rapidly combine to give the resources placed at man's disposal for the 1980s much more productive potential. These discoveries will soon be joined by man's mastery of the two forms of energy themselves. First, advances in solar energy will tap the *sun,* from which we receive ten thousand times more energy than the whole of humanity consumes. Later in the century, we will harness nuclear *fusion*—the mechanism by which energy is produced inside the sun.

It would be a suicidal illusion to live through the present turmoil dreaming of outpourings to come. If one chooses to wait, this future will never arrive. If it is true that everything is possible, including unlimited development, it is also true that *the next two or three years will be those of the greatest dangers.*

The imbalances, the risks of confrontation between East and West, the social fissures of the North and the South, the breakdown of communications between peoples, passion and ignorance make the next few years a frightening period.

We know the concrete reality of the hope for tomorrow. But this new future depends on our intelligence. We now have the means to meet the world challenge. But will the human race take the first step—now?

This book is aimed at informing the general public of a few truths which are changing the horizon but have not yet penetrated our minds. If we do not change man's view of the world and its future, we cannot hope to change reality.

At the beginning of the 1970s, the President of France opened his first news conference on the international situation with these words: "The world is unhappy. It is unhappy because it does not know where it is going. And because it suspects that if it did know, it would only be to learn that it is headed for disaster."

These words are still echoing. At the time he spoke, neither I nor anyone else had the means or the foreknowledge to thwart the inevitable slide to disaster. These means did not then exist. Now we know that it is reasonable to bet on the power of truth to invent a new society which can overcome the forces of unhappiness. The bet can be won.

The fact is that at the moment it is not yet won.

If the world and humanity were unhappy all during the 1970s —and even more so in the early 1980s—it is because our minds were possessed by a special fear. The era of continuous growth that followed World War II was coming to an end. Suddenly, all of nature seemed to put barriers in the paths of the industrial nations. If nature's resources were indeed limited, such a social emergency would demand the imposition of a plan of sharing, which could only mean a sharing of scarcity. In a closed world, the battle for an advantage is a battle against everyone else. That is what is happening.

In the 1970s, the developed world used its technical superiority only to undermine its competitors, to devalue the price of energy, to keep the Third World at a distance. OPEC, aware of its limitations and weaknesses within an international monetary and industrial system controlled by the West, withdrew into itself. The Third World festered in poverty and turmoil.

Thus, out of poverty were born fear and distrust. Meetings for "negotiations" between North and South were held, but, one after another, they failed. And each failure aggravated the bitter powerlessness felt by the Third World. Negotiation became the "pursuit of war by other means."

The symptoms and traces of this embittered heritage of the seventies are everywhere. Representatives of the Third World have never been more disillusioned. For them the era that has just ended was one of despair. The great majority of the Third World rallied in the 1970s to the hope of a new "international economic order." Its principles and foundations were clearly set forth by several thinkers of the South: Manuel Pérez Guerrero of Venezuela, Muhbul Ul-Haq of Pakistan and Raúl Prebish of Argentina. They were supported by the diplomatic efforts of other leaders of the South: Carlos Andrés Pérez of Venezuela and Julius Nyerere of Tanzania.

Their objective was greater equity in the distribution of the international system's wealth and income. They wanted it, not only for moral and ideological reasons, but also to ensure a new burst of high economic growth for the world.

The concept of a new international economic order quickly died as the global economy was hit with oil crises. The negotiating process was baptized the North–South dialogue and was integrated into the bureaucratic machinery of the United Nations, where it eroded through an uninterrupted series of conferences and meetings. In 1977, the North–South dialogue was visibly dead.

In its first report of this decade, the organ of the International Monetary Fund gave the following diagnosis: "The '70s came to a close with evidence that production facilities, ways of life, concepts of growth would all have to be transformed and restructured in the '80s. The international system has collapsed."

But at the very moment of the collapse, materials and tools are being assembled to make it possible to build a new intelligent society where nature no longer puts any limits on man and where the politics of scarcity would disappear. This is the passing chance to be seized.

Chancellor Helmut Schmidt, a European leader who came to power at the height of the storm and who felt that the nature of the world problem had begun to change without anyone noticing, expressed his intuition as follows: "And what if, in the final analysis, our society's future suffers less from the lack of raw materials than from a universal lack of historical consciousness, from the inability of nations to relate to one another as partners?"

Relations between Paris and Bonn have grown increasingly closer. Between 1977 and 1981, efforts at rapprochement, and other initiatives, have often come from the Europe created by this atmosphere. Also, at last, the European Community has chosen as its president a political leader whose independence and authority have long been recognized, Gaston Thorn of Luxembourg. Even before he assumed office, he was at work in the Middle East and in New York on behalf of the Third World.

What counts now is the European use of the word *partner*. One wonders whether this word that never took on meaning during the seventies will at last do so in the eighties.

Relations can only be conflicting in a "negotiation" aimed at finding formulas for dividing up a fixed but already declining mass of resources and wealth. No one can be sure of his share, except at the expense of others. In negotiations of this nature, in a closed, finite world, there are no "partners," only antagonists.

Partnership is linked to a universe that is totally *different* from a world of scarcity. It is associated with expansion and creativity, precisely the characteristics of the kind of world that the most recent innovations, examined in this book, hold in store for us.

Men from various countries have spoken about the technological revolution, but their message has been blurred by the passions of the day. We are passing from an industrial society, one which consumes natural resources, to a *computerized society,* one which creates material goods and develops human faculties. We are passing from commercial wars over limited markets to a worldwide system of production and communication. We are moving from one historical era to another. How should we negotiate it?

By not returning to any "negotiating table." It is now obvious what the world needs, and time is too short for lengthy meetings. Each group of nations already knows its responsibilities.

Jean Monnet wrote prophetically:

> I have seen from experience that people who think that they have understood me fail to apply the consequences of their understanding to their behavior. Negotiation is natural to them and seems to be an end in itself. I believe that we are here not to negotiate benefits for ourselves but to seek our benefit in the common good. Only by eliminating all attitudes of specialness will we find a solution. Our outlook will change, gradually, to the extent to which we succeed in changing our methods. *Consequently, I ask that the very word "negotiation" be abandoned.*

The West cannot recover from its economic crisis unless it equips and develops the Third World with the most advanced technology. That is what the Arabian Gulf demands in the spirit of Taif. The West must realize that the development of the

Third World is in its own urgent interests. And this identity of interests avoids the necessity of negotiating.

The oil producers' response to the needs of the West does not have to be negotiated, either: it has been given. They will invest the revenues from oil if the industrial nations lead a massive, worldwide technology transfer. More importantly, they will at last have a valuable outlet for massive investments, for the transformation of oil revenues into development: worldwide computerization and training of human resources.

Finally, the Third World has nothing to negotiate. It is asking to be transformed in order to live and create. What the Third World asks is that the computerized infrastructures it seeks be utilized as efficiently as possible, so that it can enrich itself and become the vast market for the rest of the world. Revitalization of international economic growth depends on this transformation.

Triggering the new dynamic among the nations of the West, OPEC and the Third World is a matter not of negotiation but of something else: a common recognition by different partners of the same path to the future.

Recognition is the key word—recognition of the new world economy, of the information society, of the future that is common to all. And, at the same time, recognition of each other as partners in a general movement.

This recognition, in turn, is *not negotiable*. It either will or will not occur. There is no negotiating the obvious. It is up to everyone to look, to reflect, to decide. This awareness alone will determine the chances for our future.

At the end of the last century, the great Socialist leader Jean Jaurès, the conscious herald of this postindustrial society, wrote:

> We are still only in prehistory. Human history will not truly begin until man, escaping the tyranny of unconscious forces, controls production itself through reason and will.

It will be the bursting forth of humanity's free and passionate life that will take over the world through science, action, and dreams.

An optimistic vision then, now becoming clearer. Its echo is found in a report by Sylvia Crossman, *Le Monde*'s correspondent in California:

About 150 kilometers north of Los Angeles, just after Santa Barbara, you take Paradise Road on the right and plunge down a bumpy road into an endless golden valley. The name of the road suggests a vacation camp. Near the gate, someone has put up a canary-yellow sign: COMPUTER CAMP.

In the cottage where the residents study, eat and sleep, the child with the sweet little face covered with freckles pushed aside the keyboard of his Apple-II computer. He smiled, showing the braces on his teeth. "You want to know something? I use the computer at home to intimidate my parents' friends. I get them in my room, I tap the keyboard furiously and I make three-dimensional figures appear on the screen . . . It terrifies them."

His smile has broadened. He has put his baseball cap on again. He excuses himself. Before noon, he must put finishing touches on an electronic game, with unknown planets, flying saucers, and invaders. He is twelve years old. "Thirteen in April 1981," he says with precision. . . .

From the other corner of the dining room comes metallic music with a familiar melody: Neil Diamond's "Song Sung Blue." John, an eleven-year-old, light-haired boy with a passion for music, has programmed his Texas Instruments 99/4 to reproduce his favorite tune. John is thrilled. Not a single false note. He shows off a bit. "It's complicated, but actually it didn't take me more than three hours!"

"David swiped my computer!" This whining voice is actually a relief. "There are eleven computers for twelve children," says George. "It's not fair. I had just finished learning Pascal and Michele had promised to show me what you can do with Fortran.'' These children of the future speak Basic, an elementary language for conversing with the computer, but also Pascal, a more complex linguistic code.

The three monitors of the Computer Camp always know where to find the children: in front of the computers. They enjoy themselves wildly: they repeat the morning's exercises, they raise the top of the keyboard, they fiddle with the silicon chips, disconnect and connect the electronic circuit's wires, insert in their machines a code packed with ''chips,'' to improve their capabilities. When they pack their bags, after a four-week stay, the computer has hardly any mysteries for them anymore.

The first week the novices learned basic and the workings of the machine. Those students who had learned by themselves or were already initiated perfected their knowledge. The second week, each child started translating his hobby into electronic language: games, music, design, science fiction, mathematics, composition.

The computer is a tool, like the book after Gutenberg. Like books, it is a springboard for creative persons. Faced with the electronic revolution, there is only one alternative, according to camp director Denis Bollay: learn to control technology or be controlled by it. In order to form children healthy in body as well as in mind, he installed his computers under the foliage of 120 hectares of forests.

It is true that at close range the residents of the Computer Camp are muscular, affectionate and sociable. And they soon drop their swaggering masks. When you ask them, they will make a place for you beside them, guide your fingers on the keyboard and find excuses for you when you make a mistake. In the swimming pool, they splash each other and yell, like children all over the world; but then they hurry back to the computer to build for their parents, when they go home, a new age.

These children from ten to fifteen years old have come to Santa Barbara from the four corners of the United States but also from Tokyo and Provence, France. Arabian Gulf parents have announced that theirs will be coming next summer.

Gregory, the only little genius, is plump and dimpled like a baby. He has succeeded in decoding a program conceived by technicians and protected by its inventors against possible reproduction. Then he reformulated the code. At the moment he is working on perfecting an electronic game that Mr. Bollay hopes to patent soon.

The teacher points to George with his finger: "These are our leaders of tomorrow. We're interested in getting them on the side of the good guys. It's important for the future."

Beyond the flames, the passions, indeed the human sufferings of today, who would abandon the hope that we shall emerge from prehistory?

BIBLIOGRAPHY

Part One

BOOKS

Abdel Malek, Anouar. *La pensée politique arabe contemporaine*. Paris: Seuil.

Adelman, Morris. *The World Petroleum Market*. Baltimore: Johns Hopkins University Press.

Al Chalabi, Fadhil. *OPEC and the International Oil Industry: A Changing Structure*. New York: Oxford University Press.

Aujac, Henri and Rouville, J. de. *La France sans pétrole*. Paris: Calmann-Lévy.

Benoist-Mechin, Jacques. *Ibn Séoud*. Paris: Albin Michel.

——. *Fayçal*. Paris: Albin Michel.

Blair, John M. *The Control of Oil*. New York: Pantheon.

Brown, Lester; Flavin, Christopher and Norman, Colin. *Running on Empty: Future of the Automobile in an Oil Short World*. New York: Norton.

Club of Rome. *The Limits to Growth*. Edited by Denis L. Meadows and Donella H. Meadows. Cambridge, Mass.: Wright-Allen Press.

Commoner, Barry. *The Politics of Energy*. New York: Knopf.

Derogy, Jacques and Gurgand, Jean-Noël. *Israël, la mort en face*. Paris: Flammarion.

Ford Foundation. *A Time to Choose: America's Energy Future*. Cambridge, Mass.: Ballinger Publishing Co.

Fulbright, J. William. *The Arrogance of Power*. New York: Random House.

Hayes, Denis. *Rays of Hope*. New York: Norton.

Hubbert, Marion King. *Nuclear Energy and Fossil Fuels*. Washington, D.C.: American Petroleum Institute.

Jacoby, Neil H. *Multinational Oil*. New York: Collier Macmillan.

Kiernan, Thomas. *The Arabs*. Boston: Little Brown.

Kissinger, Henry A. *Le chemin de la paix*. Paris: Denoël.

———. *White House Years*. Boston: Houghton, Mifflin.

Lawrence, T. E. *Seven Pillars of Wisdom: A Triumph*. Garden City, N.Y.: Garden City Publishing Company.

Mabro, Robert. *World Energy: Issues and Policies*. New York: Oxford University Press.

Montbrial, Thierry de. *Energy, the Countdown: A Report to the Club of Rome*. New York: Pergamon.

Mosley, Leonard. *Power Play: Oil in the Middle East*. New York: Random House.

Odell, Peter R. *Oil and World Power*. New York: Taplinger.

Patai, Raphael. *The Arab Mind*. New York: Charles Scribner's Sons.

Rodinson, Maxime. *Les Arabes*. Paris: PUF.

Sampson, Anthony. *The Seven Sisters*. New York: Viking.

Sid-Ahmed, Abdel Kader. *L'OPEP, passé, présent et perspectives*. Paris: Economica.

Sohlberg, Carl. *Oil Power*. New York: New American Library.

Stobaugh, Robert and Yergin, Daniel. *Energy Future*. New York: Random House.

Thesiger, Wilfred. *Arabian Sand: Desert, Marsh and Mountain*. London: Collins.

Yergin, Daniel. *Shattered Peace*. Boston: Houghton, Mifflin.

ARTICLES

Abu-Khadra, Dr. Rajaï M., *The spot oil market: genesis, qualitative configuration and perspectives*, Opec Review, vol. III/4 1979.

Al-Ani, Dr. Awni S., *Opec oil for western Europe*, Opec Review, vol. III/4 79/80.

Al-Chalabi, Fadhil, *Opec and the international oil industry: a changing structure*, Oxford University Press; *Past and present patterns of the oil industry in the producing countries*, Opec Review, vol. III/4 79/80.

Akins, James, *The oil crisis: this time the wolf is here*, Foreign Affairs, April 1973.

Economist (The), London, *The phony oil crisis*, 7/7/73.

Express (L'), *Vivre demain, numéro spécial*, n° 1221 de décembre 1974.

BIBLIOGRAPHY

International Herald Tribune, *Special Issue on Saudi Arabia*, February 1980.

Levy, Walter, *A series of future emergencies centering around oil will set back world progress for many, many years*, Foreign Affairs, June 1980.

Mansur Saad, Dr. Jafar, *Conservation: towards a comprehensive strategy*, Opec Review, vol. III/4 1979.

New York Times, *Saudi push on petrochemicals*, March 8, 1980.

Ortiz, René, *Oil upstreams: opportunities, limitations, policies*, Opec Bulletin, 1979.

Petroleum Weekly, *The future of Saudi Arabia oil production*, Staff report to the subcommittee of Foreign Affairs, 23/4/80.

Richburg, Keith, *Soviet will be importing oil within 3 years, CIA reports say*, Washington Post, 30/6/79.

Stauffer, Thomas, *Arguments for Arab oil cuts*, International Herald Tribune, 23/3/80.

Wall Street Journal, *Russia's know-how. Technology of finding and producing oil is weak point for Soviets*. 1980.

Yamani, Ahmed Zaki, *The new era in the oil industry*, Middle East Economic Survey, 20/12/74; *Oil Fact. From illusion to reality.* Speech to Dumbarton Oaks energy conference reprinted by the US Congressional Record, 6/11/79.

Part Two

BOOKS

Bairoch, Paul. *Le Tiers-Monde dans l'impasse*. Paris: Gallimard.

Banque Mondiale. *Rapport annuel sur le développement dans le monde*, 1980.

Berthelot, Yves and Tardy, Gérard. *Le Défi économique du Tiers-Monde*. Paris: Documentation française.

Bessis, Sophie. *L'Arme alimentaire*. Paris: Maspero.

Castro, Josué de. *Géographie de la faim*. Paris: Seuil.

Chaliand, Gérard. *L'Enjeu africain*. Paris: Seuil.

Combret, François de. *Les Trois Brésils*. Paris: Denoël.

Daniel, Jean. *L'Ere des ruptures*. Paris: Grasset.

Derogy, Jacques and Carmel, Hesi. *Histoire secrète d'Israël*. Paris: Olivier Orban.

Djilas, Milovan. *Tito,* Molden.

Dumont, René. *L'Afrique noire est mal partie*. Paris: Seuil.

———. *L'Utopie ou la mort*. Paris: Seuil.

Fanon, Frantz. *Les Damnés de la terre*. Paris: Maspero.

Fontaine, André. *Histoire de la guerre froide*. Paris: Fayard.

Galbraith, J. K. *The Nature of Mass Poverty*. Cambridge, Mass.: Harvard University Press.

Georges, Susan. *Comment meurt l'autre moitié du monde*. Paris: Laffont.

Guernier, Maurice. *Tiers-Monde, les trois quarts du monde*. Paris: Dunod.

Harrisson, Paul. *Inside the Third World*.

Heykal, Mohamed. *Le Sphinx et le Commissaire*. Editions Jeune Afrique.

Lacouture, Jean. *Nasser,* in *Quatre Hommes et leur peuple*. Paris: Seuil.

Laurent, Eric. *Un Monde à refaire*. Paris: Mengès.

Linhart, Robert. *Le Sucre et la faim*. Paris: Editions de Minuit.

Meir, Golda. *Ma Vie*. Paris: Laffont.

Mende, Tibor. *De l'aide à la recolonisation*. Paris: Seuil.

Mendès-France, Pierre. *Dialogue avec l'Asie*. Paris: Gallimard.

Morgan, Dan. *Les Géants du grain*. Paris: Fayard.

Moussa, Pierre. *Les Etats et les nations prolétaires*. Paris: Seuil.

Myrdal, Gunnar. *Challenge of World Poverty*. New York: Pantheon.

Naipaul, V. S. *India, A Wounded Civilization*. New York: Knopf.

Nasser, Gamal Abdel. "Philosophie d'une révolution," *L'Express, 3/8/56*.

Roy, Jules. *La Bataille de Dien Bien Phu*. Paris: Julliard.

Sadat, Anouar. *A la recherche d'une identité*. Paris: Fayard.

Saifail, Amin. *The Rise and Fall of the Shah*. Princeton University Press.

Sampson, Anthony. *La Foire aux armes*. Paris: Laffont.

Tevoedjere, Albert. *La Pauvreté, richesse des peuples*. Paris: Editions ouvrières.

Van Tien Dung (Général). *Et nous prîmes Saïgon*. Sycomore.

Ward, Barbara. *Program for a Small Planet*. New York: Norton.

Warnecke, Steven J., *Stockpiling of Critical Raw Materials*. London: Royal Institute of Foreign Affairs.

Part Three

BOOKS

Agama. *Yamamoto, the reluctant admiral*. Tokyo: Kodansha.

Arnaud, J. F. *Le Siècle de la communication*. Paris: Albin Michel.

Attali, Jacques. *La Parole et l'outil*. Paris: PUF.

Bell, Daniel. *The Coming of Post-Industrial Society*. New York: Basic Books.

Chamoux, Jean-Pierre. *L'Information sans frontière*. Paris: Informatisation et société.

Clark, Ronald. *Einstein: The Life and Times*. New York: World Publishing.

Crozier, Michel. *Le Mal américain*. Paris: Fayard.

Danzin, André. *Science et Renaissance de l'Europe*. Paris: Chotard.

Evans, Christopher. *Micro Millennium*. New York: Viking Press.

Giarini, O. and Louberge, H. *La Civilisation technicienne à la dérive*. Paris: Dunod.

Grapin, Jacqueline. *Radioscopie des Etats-Unis*. Paris: Calmann-Lévy.

Honda, Soichiro. *Honda*. Paris: Stock.

Ibuka. *Kindergarten Is Too Late*. New York: Simon and Schuster.

Lattès, Robert. *Mille Milliards de dollars*. Paris: Ed. Publications premières.

Lord, Walter, *Pearl Harbour*. Paris: Laffont.

Lorenzi, J. M. and Le Boucher. *Mémoires volés*. Paris: Ramsay.

Luria, A. R. *The Working Brain*. New York: Basic Books.

Manchester, William. *The Glory and the Dream: A Narrative History of America, 1932–1972*. Boston: Little, Brown.

Nora, S. and Minc, A. *L'Informatisation de la société*. Paris: Documentation française.

Passy (Colonel). *Souvenirs 2ᵉ Bureau Londres*. Paris: Solar.

Pisar, Samuel. *Le Sang de l'espoir*. Paris: Laffont.

Restack, Richard M. *The Brain: The Last Frontier*. New York: Doubleday.

Rodgers, William. *L'Empire IBM*. Paris: Laffont.

Ruffié, Jacques. *De la Biologie à la culture*. Paris: Flammarion.

Schlesinger, Arthur M., Jr. *The Age of Roosevelt*. Boston: Houghton, Mifflin.

———. *Thousand Days*. New York: Fawcett.
Toffler, Alvin. *Future Shock*. New York: Bantam.
———. *The Third Wave*. New York: William Morrow.
Vogel, Ezra. *Japan As Number One*. Cambridge, Mass.: Harvard University Press.
Wessel, Milton. *Freedom's Edge: The Computer Threat*. Reading, Mass.: Addison-Wesley.
Wittrock, M. C. *The Human Brain*. Englewood Cliffs, N.J.; Prentice-Hall.

ARTICLES (ENGLISH)

Business Week, *The US decline; Microprocessors: a revolution for growth*, special report of March 13, 1979; *Robots join the labor force*, special report of June 9, 1980.
Economist (The), *All that is electronic does not glitter*, March 1, 1980.
Far Eastern Review (Hong Kong), December 14, 1979, *Electronics Revolution: success in innovation is the main problem ahead*.
International Herald Tribune, Kandell, Jonathan, *Robots answer Volvo's blue collar blues*, March 31, 1980; Schuyten, Peter, *Technology paves US industrial path*, August 22, 1980; Etzioni, Amitai, *Father of the re-industrialization thesis renews call for new US growth base*, June 30, 1980.
Jacudi (Japan Computer Development Institute), *The Plan for Information Society: A national goal forward year 2000*, May 1972.
Articles from Japan Economic Journal (The), weekly edition in English of the Nihon Kezai.
Newsweek, *And man created the chip*, cover story of June 30, 1980.
New York Times, Sullivan, Walter, *Japan ushers in new era of production*, January 11, 1980.
Time, *The Year of Dr. Einstein*, cover story of February 19, 1979.
Wall Street Journal, Rout, Laurence, *Many managers resist "paperless" technology*, June 24, 1980.

ARTICLES (FRENCH)

Boston Consulting Group, *Les Mécanismes fondamentaux de la productivité*, Hommes et techniques 80.

BIBLIOGRAPHY

Cepii (Centre d'Etudes Prospectives Industrielles et Internationales), *Etats-Unis, croissance, crise et changement technique*, juillet 1980.

Commission des Communautés Européennes, *La société européenne face aux nouvelles technologies de l'information: une réponse communautaire*, juillet 1980.

Documentation Française 80 (La), *Actes du colloque international informatique et société* (5 volumes).

Echos (Les), *L'Europe pourrait faire les frais du choc industriel nippon-américain*, 4 janvier 1980.

Expansion (L'), Spécial Informatique: *Où en est l'informatication de la société française? La course au microprocesseur*, 19/9/80.

Monde (Le), Drouin, Pierre, *L'essoufflement du progrès technique: Prométhée au creux de la vague*, 29/6/79; *La fin du laisser-faire technologique*, 9/1/80; *L'attente du Tiers-Monde*, 11/7/80; *Avenirs possibles 2000 et des poussières*, 20/4/80.

Monde (Le), Grapin, Jacqueline, *La bataille de la technologie*, 29-30/10/77; *Investissement dans les nouvelles technologies*, 3/10/78.

Monde (Le), Interview d'Etienne Davignon par Ambroise Rendu, *Il faut former les jeunes aux technologies nouvelles*, 4/3/80.

Monde (Le), Maisonrouge, Jacques, *Reconnaître les industries de l'avenir*, 16/11/79.

Nouvel Observateur (Le), Alia, Josette, *Ordinateurs: la révolution chez vous*, 19/5/80.

Organisation des Nations unies pour le développement et l'industrialisation, *Industrie 2000: perspectives*, United Nations 1979.

Quatre Vérités (Les), Crozier, Michel, *La Vitalité et la morale perdue*, juin 1980.

ARTICLES (GERMAN)

Der Spiegel, *L'électronique, pétrole de notre époque*, n° 33, août 1980.

Part Four

Books

Armand, Louis and Drancourt, Michel. *Le Pari européen*. Paris: Fayard.

Bonnot, Gérard. *La vie c'est autre chose*. Paris: Belfond.

————. *Les Hommes malades de la science*. Paris: Belfond.

Closets, François de. *Le Bonheur en plus*. Paris: Denoël.

Cotta, Alain. *La France et l'Impératif mondial*. Paris: PUF.

Fabra, Paul. *L'Anticapitalisme*. Paris: Flammarion.

Gandhi, Indira. *Ma Vérité*. Paris: Stock.

Garaudy, Roger. *L'Appel aux vivants*. Paris: Seuil.

Grosser, Alfred. *Les Occidentaux*. Paris: Fayard.

Guernier, Maurice. *La Dernière Chance du Tiers-Monde*. Paris: Laffont.

Jouvenel, Bertrand de. *Un voyageur dans le siècle*. Paris: Laffont.

Julien, Claude. *Le Suicide des démocraties*. Paris: Grasset.

Kaldor, Mary. *The Disintegrating West*. New York: Hill and Wang.

Lattès, Robert. *Pour une autre croissance*. Paris: Seuil.

Mansholi, Sicco. *La Crise*. Paris: Stock.

Megrelis, Christian. *Danger protectionnisme*. Paris: Calmann-Lévy.

Melman, Seymour. *The Permanent War Economy*. New York: Simon and Schuster.

Monnet, Jean. *Mémoires*. Paris: Fayard.

Muller, Ronald. *Revitalizing America*. New York: Simon and Schuster.

Paléologue, Eustache. *Les nouvelles relations économiques internationales*. Paris: PUF.

Palme, Olaf. *Le Rendez-vous suédois*. Paris: Stock.

Peccei, Aurelio. *La Qualité humaine*. Paris: Stock.

Phillips, John Aristotle. *Mushroom*. New York: William Morrow.

Pisani, Edgard. *Défi du monde, campagne d'Europe*. Paris: Ramsay.

Pisar, Samuel. *Transactions entre l'Est et l'Ouest*. Paris: Dunod.

————. *Les Armes de la paix*. Paris: Denoël.

Revel, Jean-François. *Ni Marx, ni Jésus*. Paris: Laffont.

————. *Les Idées de notre temps*. Paris: Laffont.

BIBLIOGRAPHY

Rougemont, Denis de. *L'Avenir est notre affaire*. Paris: Stock.
Sauvy, Alfred. *La Machine et le Chômage*. Paris: Dunod.
Schmidt, Helmut. *La Volonté de paix*. Paris: Fayard.
Stephens, Robert. *The Arab New Frontier*. London: Temple Smith.
Stoffaes, Christian. *La grande menace industrielle*. Paris: Calmann-Lévy.

ARTICLES

Brandt Report, *North-south: A program for survival*. London: Pan Brooks.
Club of Rome (Botkin, Elmandjra, Malitza), *No limits to learning*. New York: Pergamon.
Far Eastern Review, *Opec's helping hand for the third world*, 1/8/80.
Gros, Jacob, Royer, *Sciences de la vie et Société*, La Documentation française.
Hamad, Abdulatif Al, Interview in the Middle East Economic Survey, March 1980.
Leontieff, Wassily, *The future of the world economy*, United Nations study 1977.
McNamara, Robert, Speech at the University of Chicago, 22/5/79.
Monde (Le), Crossman, Sylvie, *Les futurs maîtres des robots*, 7/9/80.
Ocde, Lesourne Jacques, *Rapport Interfuturs*, 1979.
Tinbergen, Jan, *Nord-Sud: Du défi au dialogue*, 3° rapport au Club de Rome, SNED/Dunod.
Unesco-Moraze, Charles, *La Science et les Facteurs de l'inégalité*.
Washington Post, Oberdorfer, Don, *The global economies*, March 23, 1980.

INDEX